SG24-5139-00

IBM

International Technical Support Organization

IBM Certification Study Guide AIX V4.3 System Support

February 1999

Take Note!

Before using this information and the product it supports, be sure to read the general information in Appendix A, “Special Notices” on page 359.

First Edition (February 1999)

This edition applies to AIX Version 4.3 (5754-C34) and subsequent releases running on an RS/6000 server.

Comments may be addressed to:
IBM Corporation, International Technical Support Organization
Dept. JN9B Building 003 Internal Zip 2834
11400 Burnet Road
Austin, Texas 78758-3493

When you send information to IBM, you grant IBM a non-exclusive right to use or distribute the information in any way it believes appropriate without incurring any obligation to you.

Contents

Figures

Tables

Preface

The AIX & RS/6000 Certifications offered through the Professional Certification Program from IBM, are designed to validate the skills required of technical professionals who work in the powerful and often complex environments of AIX and RS/6000. A complete set of professional certifications are available. They include:

- IBM Certified AIX User
- IBM Certified Specialist - RS/6000 Solution Sales
- IBM Certified Specialist - AIX V4.3 System Administration
- IBM Certified Specialist - AIX V4.3 System Support
- IBM Certified Specialist - RS/6000 SP
- IBM Certified Specialist - AIX HACMP
- IBM Certified Specialist - Domino for RS/6000
- IBM Certified Specialist - Web Server for RS/6000
- IBM Certified Specialist - Business Intelligence for RS/6000
- IBM Certified Advanced Technical Expert - RS/6000 AIX

Each certification is developed by following a thorough and rigorous process to ensure the exam is applicable to the job role, and is a meaningful and appropriate assessment of skill. Subject Matter Experts who successfully perform the job, participate throughout the entire development process. These job incumbents bring a wealth of experience into the development process. Thus making the exams much more meaningful than the typical test which only captures classroom knowledge. These experienced Subject Matter Experts ensure the exams are relevant to the *real world* and that the test content is both useful and valid. The result is a certification of value, which appropriately measures the skill required to perform the job role.

This redbook is designed as a study guide for professionals wishing to prepare for the certification exam to achieve: IBM Certified Specialist - AIX V4.3 System Support.

The support specialist certification validates a broad scope of AIX problem determination and resolution skills and the ability to perform general AIX software system maintenance. The certification is applicable to support professionals who conduct the AIX problem determination and resolution activities needed to successfully support system administrators, customers, and/or clients in an AIX environment, in order to maintain system reliability.

This redbook helps AIX support professionals seeking a comprehensive and task-oriented guide for developing the knowledge and skills required for the certification. It is designed to provide a combination of theory and practical experience needed for a general understanding of the subject matter. It also provides sample questions that will help in the evaluation of personal progress and provide familiarity with the types of questions that will be encounter in the exam.

This book will not replace the practical experience you should have, but is an effective tool which when combined with education activities and experience, should prove to be a very useful preparation guide for the exam. Due to the practical nature of the certification content, this publication can also be used as a desk side reference. So, whether you are planning to take the support exam, or if you just want to validate your AIX system support skills, this book is for you.

For additional information about certification and instructions on *How to Register* for an exam call IBM at 1-800-426-8322, or visit our Web site at: http://www.ibm.com/certify

The Team That Wrote This Redbook

This redbook was produced by a team of specialists from around the world working at the International Technical Support Organization (ITSO), Austin Center.

Aamir Chaudry is an Assistant IT Specialist in IBM Pakistan. He has four years of experience in the IT field. He holds a Masters degree in computer science, from International Islamic University, Islamabad, Pakistan. His areas of expertise include RS/6000 and AS/400. He has written extensively on AIX and OS/400. He teaches AIX and AS/400 courses at IBM education centers, covering all areas of the operating systems.

André de Klerk is the IBM Global Services South Africa UNIX Team Leader in the Enterprise System Department. He has been working for IBM since May 1996. He started his career as a field technician in a small company and has worked on various platforms, but eventually ended up working on the UNIX platform.

Yun-Wai Kong is a Software Engineer in IBM Global Services Australia. He has been working for IBM since July 1989.

Elaine Reid is an IT Availability Specialist at IBM Jamaica. She has three years experience in the IT industry. She holds a Bachelor of Sciences degree in computer science and management studies from the University of the West Indies. Her area of expertise includes AIX, Lotus Domino (Administration and Development), and OS/2 Warp. She has written extensively on AIX.

Narinder Pal Singh is a Technical Manager (Product Support Services) at IBM, India. He is a graduate electronics and telecommunications engineer with twelve years of experience in the IT industry.

The project that produced this publication was managed by:

Scott Vetter	IBM Austin

Thanks to:

Rebecca Gonzalez	Program Manager, AIX & RS/6000 Certification

and special thanks to the following reviewers for their invaluable contribution to this project:

Kyle Cline	Techical Specialist - AIX Support
Kevin McInerney	Techical Specialist - AIX Support

Comments Welcome

Your comments are important to us!

We want our redbooks to be as helpful as possible. Please send us your comments about this or other redbooks in one of the following ways:

- Fax the evaluation form found in "ITSO Redbook Evaluation" on page 387 to the fax number shown on the form.
- Use the electronic evaluation form found on the Redbooks Web sites:

For Internet users	`http://www.redbooks.ibm.com`
For IBM Intranet users	`http://w3.itso.ibm.com`

- Send us a note at the following address:

  `redbook@us.ibm.com`

Chapter 1. Certification Overview

This chapter provides an overview of the skill requirements for obtaining an IBM AIX Specialist certification. The chapters following are designed to provide a comprehensive review of specific topics that are essential for obtaining the certification.

1.1 IBM Certified Specialist - AIX V4.3 System Support

This certification validates a broad scope of AIX problem determination and resolution skills and the ability perform general AIX software system maintenance. The certification is applicable to support professionals who conduct the AIX problem determination and resolution activities needed to maintain system reliability and successfully support system administrators, customers, and clients in an AIX environment.

Certification Requirement (1 Test):
To attain the IBM Certified Specialist - AIX V4.3 System Support certification, candidates must pass one exam: *Test 189: AIX V4.3 System Support*

Recommended Prerequisites:

- Minimum of six months Experience providing AIX Support in Version 4 environments. Note: The exam contains AIX V4 content up to and including AIX V4.3.
- One to two years general AIX or UNIX experience.
- Training in system administration and advanced system administration, or equivalent experience.
- Training in TCP/IP and AIX Performance Tuning, or equivalent experience.

Registration for the Certification Exam:
For information about *How to Register* for the certification exam, please visit the following Web site:

`http://www.ibm.com/certify`

1.2 Certification Exam Objectives

The following objectives were used as a basis when the certification exam was developed. Some of these topics have been regrouped to provide better organization when discussed in this publication.

Section 1 - System Recovery

- Use LED output to isolate boot failure problems, such as 223-229 and 551
- Access rootvg in maintenance mode using boot media to repair or restore file system (`fsck`, missing files)
- Determine whether hang is resource versus OS hang
- Use crash LEDs to determine if crash is likely to be due to hardware or software
- Examine errlog entries

Section 2 - Disk Management

- Answer questions from clients on how to create or remove drives
- Answer questions from clients on how to create/extend or remove paging space
- Answer questions from clients on how to migrate data from one PV to another
- Perform storage management activities (disk stripping, multiple JFS log devices, and the like)
- Troubleshoot file system errors (identify missing file space, check order of mounting, `fsck`, and so on)
- Troubleshoot disk error (after improper removal, identify missing physical volume, `synchlvodm`, and other tasks)

Section 3 - Devices

- Answer questions from clients on how to add, delete and/or modify devices
- Answer questions from clients on how to configure network devices (SSA loops, SCSI devices, modems, PPP communications, ttys, Async Controllers, and so on)
- Troubleshoot problems related to configuring network devices
- Troubleshoot X-Windows error: unable to open display
- Troubleshoot print problems

Section 4 - Performance

- Troubleshoot performance problems based on system configuration
- Use `vmstat` command to identify CPU, RAM and paging bottlenecks
- Use `iostat` command to identify I/O bottlenecks
- Use `netstat` command to identify network bottlenecks

- Correct CPU, RAM, and paging shortages
- Correct network bottlenecks
- Optimize disk resources

Section 5 - Networking

- Troubleshoot when there is a problem communicating to other machines on the network
- Troubleshoot hostname problems (for example not expected value)
- Troubleshoot when system is not forwarding packets
- Setup default route and routing strategy when network traffic is not reaching destination
- Troubleshoot when interface has proper IP address but cannot ping another host
- Check/set TCP tuning values for improved network performance
- Troubleshoot inability to Telnet or rlogin to machine
- Use different network troubleshooting commands to determine why client cannot Telnet beyond default gateway
- Debug problems when trying to ping/telnet/rsh to other systems
- Add and remove interface (`ifconfig`, `detach`, `rmdev`, and so forth)

Section 6 - System Configuration & Management

- Analyze simple scripts to determine output
- Check critical system scripts and what they start/control (for example, `/etc/rc`, `/etc/rc.net`, and `importvg`)
- Check for possible exposure in system access files (for example, hosts.equiv, .rhosts, netrc, and forward)
- Check for suspect activity on system
- Add entries to crontab to run at specific times
- Check existence of cron and at job files
- Use flags for listing, editing and deleting crontabs (crontabl -1, crontab -e, to name two)
- Set/change environment variables
- Use common vi manipulation subcommands to edit ksh script
- Use commands for viewing different file types (`ascii = cat`, `view`, `more pg:` `binary=strings`, and so forth)

Section 7 - Backup & Restore

- Explain usage and limitation of various backup methods to the customer (for example, `backup`, `mksysb`, `tar`, `CPIO`, and `remote backup`)
- Verify backup is successful
- Troubleshoot backup failures
- Instruct customer on how to restore

Section 8 - Install & NIM

- Answer questions from clients regarding when to use migrate and when to preserve install
- Locate and analyze installp log files
- Navigate through smit menus to perform different installs
- Check and verify system installation integrity (`lppchk`, `lslpp`, `oslevel`, and so forth)
- Check client definition and use debug tools (for example, `boots` and `iptrace`)
- Initiate and capture nimboot debug (for example, createdevig boot image)

1.3 Certification Education Courses

Courses and publications are offered to help you prepare for the certification tests. These courses are recommended, but not required, before taking a certification test. At the printing of this guide, the following courses are available. For a current list, please visit the following Web site:

`http://www.ibm.com/certify`

AIX Support Certification Test Preparation Workshop	
Course Number	Q1825 (USA)
Course Duration	Two days
Course Abstract	This two-day workshop will provide a knowledgeable AIX professional with a review of AIX concepts necessary for the AIX Support Certification exam. A pretest is used to help identify student's readiness and assist in areas of selected study. The lecture and discussion-oriented workshop will cover a variety of topics to help the student refresh their knowledge and improve understanding of concepts to increase their confidence for the exam. Students will also be given an out-of-class reading assignment. The classroom will contain lab equipment for those students who desire hands-on activities. The AIX Support Certification exam will be available at the end of the second day.
Course Content	•System Initialization and Boot •Hardware Installation and Device Configuration •Problem Determination •System Installation and Maintenance •Printers •Storage Management and LVM •Networking •Paging Space •System Resource Controller •System Performance •System Backup and Restore •Cron Daemon

AIX Version 4 System Administration	
Course Number	Q1114 (USA); AU14 (Worldwide)
Course Duration	Five days
Course Abstract	Learn the basic system administration skills to support AIX RS/6000 running the AIX Version 4 operating system. Build your skills in configuring and monitoring a single CPU environment. Administrators who manage systems in a networked environment should attend additional LAN courses.
Course Content	•Install the AIX Version 4 operating system, software bundles, and filesets •Perform a system startup and shutdown •Understand and use AIX system management tools •Configure ASCII terminals and printer devices •Manage physical and logical volumes •Perform file systems management •Create and manage user and group accounts •Use backup and restore commands •Use administrative subsystems, including cron, to schedule system tasks, and security to implement customized access of files and directories

AIX Version 4.3 Advanced System Administration	
Course Number	Q1116 (USA); AU16 (Worldwide)
Course Duration	Five Days
Course Abstract	Learn how to identify possible sources of problems on stand-alone configurations of the RS/6000 and perform advanced system administration tasks

AIX Version 4.3 Advanced System Administration	
Course Content	•Identify the different RS/6000 models and architects •Explain the ODM purpose for device configuration •Interpret system initialization and problems during the boot process •Customize authentication and set up ACLs •Identify the TCB components, commands, and their use •Obtain a system dump and define saved data •Identify the error logging facility components and reports •List ways to invoke diagnostic programs •Customize a logical volume for optimal performance and availability •Manage a disk and the data under any circumstance •Use the standard AIX commands to identify potential I/O, disk, CPU, or other bottlenecks on the system •Customize SMIT menus and define how SMIT interacts with the ODM •Define the virtual printer database and potential problems •List the terminal attributes and create new terminfo entries •Define the NIM installation procedure

AIX Version 4 Configuring TCP/IP and Accessing the Internet	
Course Number	Q1107 (USA); AU07 or AU05 (Worldwide)
Course Duration	Five days
Course Abstract	•Learn how to perform TCP/IP network configuration and administration on AIX Version 4 RS/6000 systems •Learn the skills necessary to begin implementing and using NFS, NIS, DNS, network printing, static and dynamic routing, SLIP and SLIPLOGIN, Xstations, and the Internet
Course Contents	•Describe the basic concepts of TCP/IP protocols and addressing •Explain TCP/IP broadcasting and multicasting •Configure, implement, and support TCP/IP on an IBM RS/6000 system •Use networking commands for remote logon, remote execution, and file transfer •Configure SLIP and SLIPLOGIN •Use SMIT to configure network printing •Connect multiple TCP/IP networks using static and dynamic routing •Implement DNS, NFS, and NIS •Perform basic troubleshooting of network problems •Configure an Xstation in the AIX environment •Explain how to access Internet services •Understand and support TCP/IP •Plan implementation of NFS •Support LAN-attached printers •Support AIX networking •Determine network problems •Implement network file system

1.4 Education on CD: IBM AIX Essentials

The new IBM AIX Essentials series offers a dynamic training experience for those who need convenient and cost-effective AIX education. The series consists of five new, content rich, computer-based multimedia training courses based on highly acclaimed, instructor-led AIX classes that have been successfully taught by IBM Education and Training for years.

To Order, and for more information and answers to your questions:

- In the U.S., call 800-IBM-TEACH (426-8322), or use the online form at the following URL: `http://www-3.ibm.com/services/learning/aix/#order`
- Outside the U.S., Contact your IBM Sales Representative, or
- Contact an IBM Business Partner

Chapter 2. System Installation and Maintenance

One of the most primary of support roles is the installation of a new software image or updating an existing one. In this chapter, the most common ways of performing these tasks are discussed.

There are three types of installation methods:

- New and Complete Overwrite

  Use this method if you have a new machine or if you want to completely overwrite an existing version of the Base Operating System (BOS) that is installed on your system. The New and Complete Overwrite installation overwrites all data on the selected destination disk.

- Migration Install

  Use this installation method to upgrade AIX between versions and releases, while preserving the existing root volume group. This method preserves all file systems except /tmp, as well as the root volume group, logical volumes and system configuration files.

- Preservation Install

  Use this installation method when a version of BOS is installed on your system and you want to preserve the user data in the root volume group. However, this method overwrites the /usr, /tmp, /var, and / (root) file systems by default, so any user data in these directories is lost. These file systems are removed and recreated, so any other LPPs or filesets that you installed on the system will also be lost.

To upgrade AIX modification levels, use the SMIT fastpath `smit update_all`.

The following sections describe the installation methods in more detail.

2.1 New and Complete Overwrite Installation

The only times to use the New and Complete Overwrite installation method are:

- You have a new machine. In this case, the hard disk or disks on which you are installing BOS are empty.
- Your root volume group has become corrupted and you do not have a backup to restore it. So, you want to install onto a hard disk that contains an existing root volume group that you wish to completely overwrite.
- You want to reassign your hard disks to make your rootvg smaller.

The New and Complete Overwrite installation overwrites all data on the selected destination disk. This means that after the installation is complete, you will have to manually configure your system using the Configuration Assistant application, SMIT, or the command line.

2.2 Migration Installation

Use the Migration Installation method to upgrade AIX to a different version or release to while preserving the existing root volume group.

The following can be said about a migration installation:

- During a Migration installation, the installation process determines which optional software products must be installed on AIX Version 4.3. AIX Version 3.2, AIX Version 4.1, or AIX Version 4.2 software that exists on the system and has been replaced by new software in AIX Version 4.3 is installed at the AIX Version 4.3 level.
- This method preserves all file systems except /tmp, as well as the root volume group, logical volumes, and system configuration files. In most cases, user configuration files from the previous version of a product are saved.
- Non-software products remain on the system.
- When migrating from Version 3.2, all files in /usr/lib/drivers, /usr/lib/microcode, /usr/lib/methods, and /dev are removed from the system, so software support for non-IBM device drivers must be reinstalled.

2.3 Preservation Installation

Use the Preservation Installation method when a version of BOS is installed on your system and you want to preserve the user data in the root volume group.

The following can be said about a preservation installation:

- The /etc/preserve.list file contains a list of system files to be copied and saved during a preservation BOS installation. The /etc/filesystems file is listed by default. Add the full path names of any additional files that you want to save during the Preservation Installation to the preserve.list file. You must create the /etc/preserve.list file on an AIX Version 3.1 machine. On an AIX Version 4.1 or later system, edit the file that exists on your system.

- Ensure that you have sufficient disk space in the /tmp file system to store the files listed in the /etc/preserve.list file.
- This method overwrites the /usr, /tmp, /var, and / (root) file systems by default, so any user data in these directories is lost. These file systems are removed and recreated, so any other LPPs or filesets that you installed on the system will also be lost. Think of a preservation install as an overwrite installation for these flle systems. System configuration must be done after doing a Preservation Installation.

2.4 The lppchk Command, Verifying Installed Software

The `lppchk` command verifies that files for an installable software product (fileset) match the Software Vital Product Data (SWVPD) database information for file sizes, checksum values, or symbolic links.

The available flags are briefly described:

-c Performs a checksum operation on the input FileList items and verifies that the checksum and the file size are consistent with the SWVPD database.

-f Checks that the FileList items are present and that the file size matches the SWVPD database.

-l Verifies symbolic links for files as specified in the SWVPD database.

-m Displays three levels of information.

-O Verifies the specified parts of the program. This flag is not needed with standalone systems because without this option all parts are verified by default.

-u Updates the SWVPD with new checksum or size information from the system when the system information does not match the SWVPD database. This flag sets symbolic links that are found to be missing. This flag is valid with only the -c or -l flag.

-v Verifies that the / (root), /usr, and /usr/share parts of the system are valid with each other. In other words, this flag verifies that all software products installed on the / (root) file system are also installed on the /usr file system and, conversely, all the software products installed in the /usr file system are also installed on the / (root) file system. You cannot specify FileList items with this flag. This flag also verifies requisites.

Note

Only one of the -c, -f, -l, and -v flags can be specified with each use of the `lppchk` command.

The installation of the bos.dosutil fileset is interrupted in the following example. An example of the `lppchk -v` command is shown in Figure 1 before and after the inconsistency is cleaned up:

```
# lppchk -v
lppchk:  The following filesets need to be installed or corrected to bring
         the system to a consistent state:

  bos.dosutil 4.3.0.0                     (APPLYING)

# installp -C

installp:  Cleaning up software for:
        bos.dosutil 4.3.0.0


Installation Summary
--------------------
Name                        Level           Part        Event       Result
-------------------------------------------------------------------------------
bos.dosutil                 4.3.0.0         USR         CLEANUP     SUCCESS
# lppchk -v
# 
```

Figure 1. Sample lppchk -v Command

2.5 The smit.log File as the installp Command Output Log

By default, the output of the `installp` command goes to stdout and stderr, unless SMIT or VSM is used, in which case the output goes to the smit.log file. When SMIT is used and the installation of a PTF fails, the error messages are recorded in the smit.log file. Part of the smit.log file is shown in Figure 2 on page 15. This example shows the installation of a PTF that has failed during pre-installation verification:

```
+----------------------------------------------------------------------------+
                    Pre-installation Verification...
+----------------------------------------------------------------------------+
Verifying selections...done
Verifying requisites...done
Results...

FAILURES
--------
  Filesets listed in this section failed pre-installation verification
  and will not be installed.

  Requisite Failures
  ------------------
  SELECTED FILESETS:  The following is a list of filesets that you asked to
  install.  They cannot be installed until all of their requisite filesets
  are also installed.  See subsequent lists for details of requisites.

    bos.up 4.3.1.4                          # Base Operating System Unipro...

  MISSING REQUISITES:  The following filesets are required by one or more
  of the selected filesets listed above.  They are not currently installed
  and could not be found on the installation media.

    bos.up 4.3.1.0                          # Base Level Fileset

  << End of Failure Section >>

FILESET STATISTICS
------------------
    1  Selected to be installed, of which:
        1  FAILED pre-installation verification
  ----
    0  Total to be installed
smit.log (99%)
```

Figure 2. Error Messages from the installp Command Recorded in the smit.log File

2.6 Determining Maintenance Levels

The `oslevel` command reports the level of the operating system using a subset of all filesets installed on your system. The `oslevel` command also prints information about maintenance levels, including which filesets are not at a specified maintenance level. The optional flags for this commands are:

-l Level Lists filesets at levels earlier than the maintenance level specified by the Level parameter.

-g Lists filesets at levels later than the current maintenance level.

-q Lists names of known maintenance levels that can be specified using the `-l` flag.

The sample output in Figure 3 shows that the operating system level is at 4.3.0.0, only 4.3.0.0 can be specified in the `-l` flag, there is no fileset at levels later than 4.3.0.0, and the filesets are at levels earlier than 4.3.0.0:

```
# oslevel
4.3.0.0
# oslevel -q
Known Maintenance Levels
------------------------
4.3.0.0
# oslevel -g
# oslevel -l 4.3.0.0
Fileset                                    Actual Level        Maintenance Level
-----------------------------------------------------------------------------
X11.msg.en_US.Dt.helpmin                   4.2.0.0             4.3.0.0
X11.msg.en_US.Dt.rte                       4.2.0.0             4.3.0.0
X11.msg.en_US.apps.aixterm                 4.2.0.0             4.3.0.0
X11.msg.en_US.apps.clients                 4.2.0.0             4.3.0.0
X11.msg.en_US.apps.custom                  4.2.0.0             4.3.0.0
X11.msg.en_US.apps.pm                      4.2.0.0             4.3.0.0
X11.msg.en_US.apps.rte                     4.2.0.0             4.3.0.0
X11.msg.en_US.base.common                  4.2.0.0             4.3.0.0
X11.msg.en_US.base.rte                     4.2.0.0             4.3.0.0
X11.msg.en_US.motif.lib                    4.2.0.0             4.3.0.0
X11.msg.en_US.motif.mwm                    4.2.0.0             4.3.0.0
X11.msg.en_US.vsm.rte                      4.2.0.0             4.3.0.0
printers.msg.en_US.rte                     4.2.0.0             4.3.0.0
#
```

Figure 3. Sample oslevel Command Output

2.7 Modification Update Using update_all from SMIT

You can use the SMIT fastpath `smit update_all` to update currently installed software to a modification level or apply all updates to currently installed software. You can either use the installation CDs or download the maintenance-level fixes using the FixDist package.

2.7.1 Downloading Maintenance Levels Using FixDist

The following describes a procedure to download the AIX 4.3.1 base maintenance level using the FixDist package:

1. Double-click to select **Base Maintenance Levels** in FixDist as shown in Figure 4 on page 17:

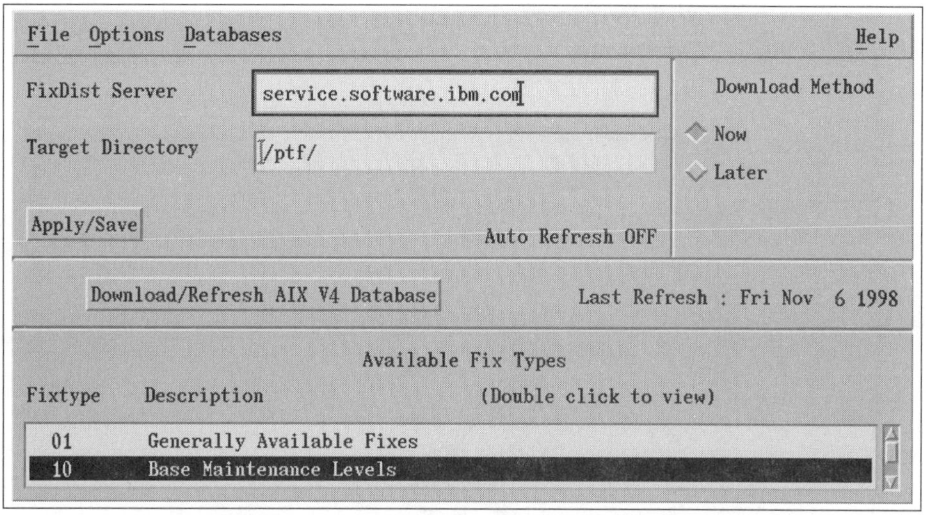

Figure 4. Select Base Maintenance Levels in FixDist

2. Select **AIX 431 Maintenance Level**, then select **OK** as in Figure 5:

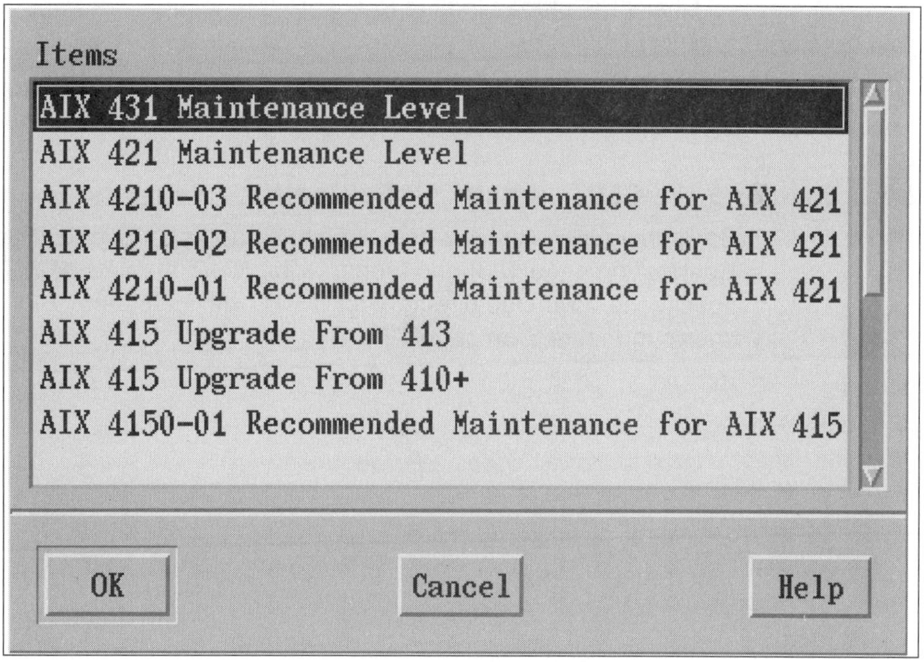

Figure 5. Select AIX 431 Maintenance Level in FixDist

3. Ensure that you have sufficient disk space to store the files to be downloaded as indicated by FixDist shown in Figure 6 and select **Start Download**:

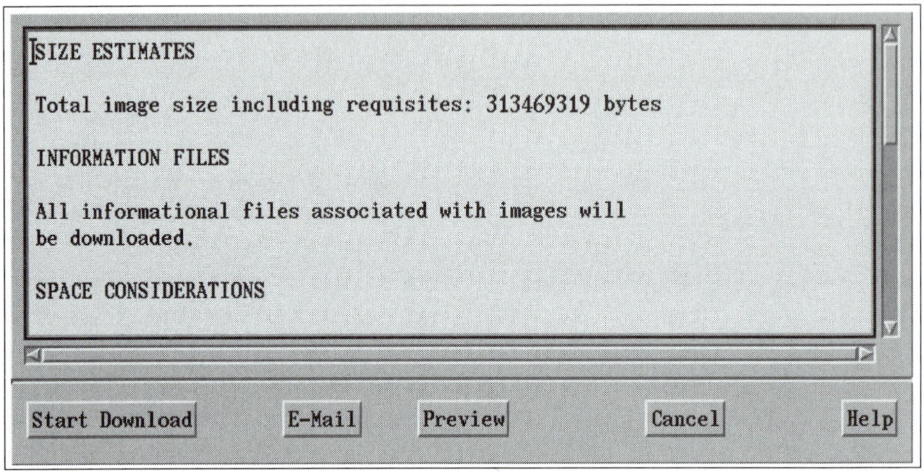

Figure 6. Estimated Size of Files To Be Downloaded

4. Check the ptfload.log file to ensure that all files are transferred successfully.
5. The stacklist file will show you what fixes have been downloaded. You should see all the backup format files (BFF) with the fix level 4.3.1.0.

2.7.2 Invoking the SMIT update_all Fastpath

Back up your system (as described in Chapter 8, "System Backup and Restore" on page 183) and then use the SMIT fastpath `smit update_all` and specify the download directory for INPUT device/directory for software as shown in Figure 7 on page 19:

```
              Update Installed Software to Latest Level (Update All)

Type or select values in entry fields.
Press Enter AFTER making all desired changes.

                                                        [Entry Fields]
* INPUT device / directory for software               /ftp
* SOFTWARE to update                                  _update_all
  PREVIEW only? (update operation will NOT occur)     no                     +
  COMMIT software updates?                            yes                    +
  SAVE replaced files?                                no                     +
  AUTOMATICALLY install requisite software?           yes                    +
  EXTEND file systems if space needed?                yes                    +
  VERIFY install and check file sizes?                no                     +
  DETAILED output?                                    no                     +
  Process multiple volumes?                           yes                    +




F1=Help             F2=Refresh          F3=Cancel           F4=List
F5=Reset            F6=Command          F7=Edit             F8=Image
F9=Shell            F10=Exit            Enter=Do
```

Figure 7. Using SMIT update_all to Upgrade Modification Level

If you are using the AIX 4.3 installation CDs, enter `/dev/cd0` for the `INPUT device / directory for software` field. You may need to replace Volume 1 of the AIX 4.3 installation CDs with Volume 2 and then switch back to Volume 1 again depending on what filesets you have installed on the 4.3.0.0 system. The swapping of CDs is normal.

2.8 Finding a Fileset That Contains a Given Command

It is a common task to upgrade a single component, but it is difficult to determine what fileset requires the update. This section describes a process to accomplish this.

Suppose a user suspects that there is a problem with the nfsd program. The system administration wants to download the latest fix level of the fileset. The following steps are planned:

1. Find out the full path of the nfsd program using the `whence` command.
2. Find out which fileset the nfsd program belongs to using the `lslpp -w` command.
3. Find out the maintenance level of the fileset installed on the system using the `lslpp -l` command to ensure that a fileset with a higher fix level is to be downloaded.

The following is an example using nfsd:

```
# whence nfsd
/usr/sbin/nfsd
# lslpp -w /usr/sbin/nfsd
  File                                        Fileset               Type
  ----------------------------------------------------------------------------
  /usr/sbin/nfsd                              bos.net.nfs.client    File
# lslpp -l bos.net.nfs.client
  Fileset                      Level  State      Description
  ----------------------------------------------------------------------------
Path: /usr/lib/objrepos
  bos.net.nfs.client         4.3.2.0  COMMITTED  Network File System Client

Path: /etc/objrepos
  bos.net.nfs.client         4.3.2.0  COMMITTED  Network File System Client
#
```

2.9 References

The following publications contain more information about system installation and maintenance:

- *AIX Version 4.3 Installation Guide*, SC23-4112
- *AIX Version 4.3 Commands Reference, Volume 3*, SC23-4117
- *AIX Version 4.3 Commands Reference, Volume 4*, SC23-4118

2.10 Quiz

1. A technical specialist working on an RS/6000 Model 397 running AIX 4.3.1 determines that the system needs to be reinstalled with the same version of the operating system. What is the best method to perform the reinstallation without erasing /home and /data, a filesystem used to store project data?

   A. Reinstall bos.rte from the installation media

   B. Perform a preservation installation from a mksysb

   C. Perform a migration installation from the installation media

   D. Perform a preservation installation from the installation media

2. The support specialist is installing the latest fixes for the bos.rte.tty fileset using SMIT. There is an error during the installation of the APAR. Where is the installation log file located?

   A. $HOME/smit.log

   B. /intallp.log

   C. /tmp/bos/bosinst.log

D. /var/adm/ras/install.log

3. The marketing department has requested that their RS/6000 server be upgraded from 4.2.0 to 4.2.1. Using the 4.2.1 installation CD-ROM, which of the following commands would the system administrator use to accomplish this task?

   A. `smit update_all`

   B. `smit easy_install`

   C. `smit update_latest`

   D. `smit maintain_software`

4. Which of the following commands can be run to find the release of the operating system on an RS/6000?

   A. `oslevel`

   B. `oslevel -release`

   C. `lslpp -ah bos.obj`

   D. `lslpp -l bos.obj`

2.10.1 Answers

1. D
2. A
3. A
4. A

2.11 Exercises

1. On a test system that does not affect any users, perform a new and complete overwrite installation.
2. On a test system that does not affect any users, perform a migration install to upgrade AIX to the next release level. Note what data is saved and what data is removed.
3. On a test system that does not affect any users, perform a `smit update_all` to upgrade AIX to the next modification level.
4. On a test system that does not affect any users, perform a preservation install to reinstall the same version, release, and modification level of the operating system. Note what data is saved and what data is removed.

5. Use the various flags of the `lppchk` command to verify the checksum, the file sizes, the symbolic links, and the requisites of the software products installed.
6. Check the $HOME/smit.log for the `installp` command output log.
7. Use the various flags of the `oslevel` command to show the level of the operating system, the known maintenance levels of the operating system installed on the system, the lists at levels earlier than the specified level parameter, and the filesets at levels later than the current maintenance level.
8. Use the `lslpp` command to find out which fileset is used to package a given command.

Chapter 3. System Initialization and Boot

A support specialist must understand the system initialization process, common startup errors, and how to customize the startup of software. This chapter introduces the concepts needed to better understand this process.

During system startup, after the root file system has been mounted in the pre-initialization process, the following sequence of events occurs:

1. The `init` command is run as the last step of the startup process.
2. The `init` command attempts to read the /etc/inittab file.
3. If the /etc/inittab file exists, the `init` command attempts to locate an initdefault entry in the /etc/inittab file.
    a. If the initdefault entry exists, the `init` command uses the specified run level as the initial system run level.
    b. If the initdefault entry does not exist, the `init` command requests that the user enter a run level from the system console (/dev/console).
    c. If the user enters an S, s, M or m run level, the `init` command enters maintenance run level. These are the only run levels that do not require a properly formatted /etc/inittab file.
4. If the /etc/inittab file does not exist, the `init` command places the system in the maintenance run level by default.
5. The `init` command rereads the /etc/inittab file every 60 seconds. If the /etc/inittab file has changed since the last time the `init` command read it, the new commands in the /etc/inittab file are executed.

3.1 The /etc/inittab File

The /etc/inittab file controls the initialization process.

The /etc/inittab file supplies the script to the `init` command's role as a general process dispatcher. The process that constitutes the majority of the `init` command's process dispatching activities is the /etc/getty line process, which initiates individual terminal lines. Other processes typically dispatched by the `init` command are daemons and the shell.

The /etc/inittab file is composed of entries that are position-dependent and have the following format:

```
Identifier:RunLevel:Action:Command
```

Each entry is delimited by a newline character. A backslash (\) preceding a newline character indicates the continuation of an entry. There are no limits (other than maximum entry size) on the number of entries in the /etc/inittab file. The maximum entry size is 1024 characters. The entry fields are:

Identifier A one or two character field that uniquely identifies an object.

RunLevel The run level at which this entry can be processed.

The run level has the following attributes:

- Run levels effectively correspond to a configuration of processes in the system.
- Each process started by the `init` command is assigned one or more run levels in which it can exist.
- Run levels are represented by the numbers 0 through 9. For example, if the system is in run level 1, only those entries with a 1 in the runlevel field are started.
- When you request the `init` command to change run levels, all processes without a matching entry in the runlevel field for the target run level receive a warning signal (SIGTERM). There is a 20-second grace period before processes are forcibly terminated by the kill signal (SIGKILL).
- The runlevel field can define multiple run levels for a process by selecting more than one run level in any combination from 0 through 9. If no run level is specified, the process is assumed to be valid at all run levels.
- There are three other values that appear in the runlevel field, even though they are not true run levels: a, b, and c. Entries that have these characters in the run level field are processed only when the `telinit` command requests them to be run (regardless of the current run level of the system). They differ from run levels in that the `init` command can never enter run level a, b, or c. Also, a request for the execution of any of these processes does not change the current run level. Furthermore, a process started by an a, b, or c command is not killed when the `init` command changes levels. They are only killed if their line in the /etc/inittab file is marked off in the action field, their line is deleted entirely from /etc/inittab, or the `init` command goes into single-user mode.

Action Tells the `init` command how to treat the process specified in the process field. The following actions are recognized by the `init` command:

respawn If the process does not exist, start the process. Do not wait for its termination (continue scanning the /etc/inittab file). Restart the process when it dies. If the process exists, do nothing and continue scanning the /etc/inittab file.

wait When the `init` command enters the run level that matches the entry's run level, start the process and wait for its termination. All subsequent reads of the /etc/inittab file, while the `init` command is in the same run level, will cause the `init` command to ignore this entry.

once When the `init` command enters a run level that matches the entry's run level, start the process, and do not wait for termination. When it dies, do not restart the process. When the system enters a new run level, and the process is still running from a previous run level change, the program will not be restarted.

boot Process the entry only during system boot, which is when the `init` command reads the /etc/inittab file during system startup. Start the process, do not wait for its termination, and when it dies, do not restart the process. In order for the instruction to be meaningful, the run level should be the default or it must match the `init` command's run level at boot time. This action is useful for an initialization function following a hardware reboot of the system.

bootwait Process the entry the first time that the `init` command goes from single-user to multi-user state after the system is booted. Start the process, wait for its termination, and when it dies, do not restart the process. If the initdefault is 2, run the process right after boot.

powerfail Execute the process associated with this entry only when the `init` command receives a power fail signal (SIGPWR).

powerwait Execute the process associated with this entry only when the `init` command receives a power fail signal (SIGPWR), and wait until it terminates before continuing to process the /etc/inittab file.

off If the process associated with this entry is currently running, send the warning signal (SIGTERM), and wait 20 seconds before terminating the process with the kill signal (SIGKILL). If the process is not running, ignore this entry.

ondemand Functionally identical to respawn, except this action applies to the a, b, or c values, not to run levels.

initdefault An entry with this action is only scanned when the `init` command is initially invoked. The `init` command uses this entry, if it exists, to determine which run level to enter initially. It does this by taking the highest run level specified in the runlevel field and using that as its initial state. If the run level field is empty, this is interpreted as 0123456789: therefore, the `init` command enters run level 9. Additionally, if the `init` command does not find an initdefault entry in the /etc/inittab file, it requests an initial run level from the user at boot time.

sysinit Entries of this type are executed before the `init` command tries to access the console before login. It is expected that this entry will only be used to initialize devices on which the `init` command might try to ask the run level question. These entries are executed and waited for before continuing.

Command A shell command to execute. The entire command field is prefixed with exec and passed to a forked sh as `sh -c exec` command. Any legal sh syntax can appear in this field. Comments can be inserted with the # comment syntax.

The `getty` command writes over the output of any commands that appear before it in the /etc/inittab file. To record the output of these commands to the boot log, pipe their output to the `alog -tboot` command.

The stdin, stdout, and stdferr file descriptors may not be available while init is processing inittab entries. Any entries writing to stdout or stderr may not work predictably unless they redirect their output to a file or to /dev/console.

The following commands are the only supported method for modifying the records in the /etc/inittab file:

chitab Changes records in the /etc/inittab file.

lsitab Lists records in the /etc/inittab file.

mkitab Adds records to the /etc/inittab file.

rmitab Removes records from the /etc/inittab file.

An example of /etc/inittab entries is shown in Figure 8 on page 27.

```
:
: Note - initdefault and sysinit should be the first and second entry.
:
init:2:initdefault:
brc::sysinit:/sbin/rc.boot 3 >/dev/console 2>&1 # Phase 3 of system boot
powerfail::powerfail:/etc/rc.powerfail 2>&1 | alog -tboot > /dev/console # Power
 Failure Detection
rc:2:wait:/etc/rc 2>&1 | alog -tboot > /dev/console # Multi-User checks
fbcheck:2:wait:/usr/sbin/fbcheck 2>&1 | alog -tboot > /dev/console # run /etc/fi
rstboot
srcmstr:2:respawn:/usr/sbin/srcmstr # System Resource Controller
rctcpip:2:wait:/etc/rc.tcpip > /dev/console 2>&1 # Start TCP/IP daemons
rcdce:2:wait:/etc/rc.dce all >/dev/console 2>&1 #Start DFS deamons
rccm:2:wait:/usr/bin/cm setsetuid /usr/prod/bin/* -state on >/dev/console 2>&1
dceupdt:2:wait:/etc/rc.dce_update >/dev/console 2>&1 #Start DCE update script
lafs:2:once:/usr/vice/etc/lafs
rcnfs:2:wait:/etc/rc.nfs > /dev/console 2>&1 # Start NFS Daemons
cron:2:respawn:/usr/sbin/cron
piobe:2:wait:/usr/lib/lpd/pio/etc/pioinit >/dev/null 2>&1  # pb cleanup
qdaemon:2:wait:/usr/bin/startsrc -sqdaemon
writesrv:2:wait:/usr/bin/startsrc -swritesrv
uprintfd:2:respawn:/usr/sbin/uprintfd
logsymp:2:once:/usr/lib/ras/logsymptom # for system dumps
pmd:2:wait:/usr/bin/pmd > /dev/console 2>&1 # Start PM daemon
dt:2:wait:/etc/rc.dt
cons:0123456789:respawn:/usr/sbin/getty /dev/console
imnss:2:once:/usr/IMNSearch/bin/imnss -start imnhelp >/dev/console 2>&1
httpdlite:2:once:/usr/IMNSearch/httpdlite/httpdlite -r /etc/IMNSearch/httpdlite/
httpdlite.conf >/dev/console 2>&1
i4ls:2:wait:/etc/i4ls.rc > /dev/null 2>&1 # Start i4ls
#
```

Figure 8. Entries in /etc/inittab

3.1.0.1 Order of /etc/inittab Entries

The base process entries in the /etc/initab file is ordered as follows:

- 1 - initdefault
- 2 - sysinit
- 3 - Powerfailure Detection (powerfail)
- 4 - Multiuser check (rc)
- 5 - /etc/firstboot (fbcheck)
- 6 - System Resource Controller (srcmstr)
- 7 - Start TCP/IP daemons (rctcpip)
- 8 - Start NFS daemons (rcnfs)
- 9 - cron
- 10 - pb cleanup (piobe)
- 11 - getty for the console (cons)

The System Resource Controller (SRC) has to be started near the beginning of the etc/inittab file since the SRC daemon is needed to start other processes. Since NFS requires TCP/IP daemons to run correctly, TCP/IP daemons are started ahead of the NFS daemons. The entries in the /etc/inittab file are ordered according to dependencies, meaning that if a process (process1) requires that another process (process2) be present for it to operate normally, then an entry for process2 comes before an entry for process1 in the /etc/inittab file.

3.2 Initialization Customization and Problem Determination

Generally, if you encounter a problem in the booting process, you receive a three-digit LED error code. In this section, several software problems are discussed along with their possible solutions.

3.2.1 Using the bootlist Command

You can change the way your system looks up devices to find its boot code. The `bootlist` command displays and alters the list of boot devices available to the system. The general syntax of the command is as follows:

```
bootlist [ { -m Mode } [ -r ] [  -o  ] [ [ -i ] | [ [ -f File ] [ Device [
Attr=Value ... ] ... ] ] ]
```

The most common flags used with `bootlist` command are given in Table 1.

Table 1. bootlist Command Flags

Flag	Description
-m mode	Specifies which boot list to display or alter. Possible values for the mode variable are normal, service, both, or prevboot.
-f File	Indicates that the device information is to be read from the specified file name.
-i	Indicates that the device list specified by the -m flag should be invalidated.
-o	Displays bootlist with -m flag. Applies only to AIX Version 4.2 or later.
-r	Indicates to display the specified bootlist after any specified alteration is performed.

The `bootlist` command allows the user to display and alter the list of possible boot devices from which the system may be booted. When the system is booted, it will scan the devices in the list and attempt to boot from the first device it finds containing a boot image. This command supports the updating of the following:

Normal boot list The normal list designates possible boot devices for when the system is booted in normal mode.

Service boot list The service list designates possible boot devices for when the system is booted in service mode.

Previous boot device This entry designates the last device from which the system booted. Some hardware platforms may attempt to boot from the previous boot device before looking for a boot device in one of the other lists.

Support of these boot lists varies from platform to platform, and some platforms do not have boot lists. When searching for a boot device, the system selects the first device in the list and determines if it is bootable, if no boot file system is detected on the first device, the system moves on to the next device in the list. As a result, the ordering of devices in the device list is extremely important.

In order to display a boot list (Version 4.2 or later) use the command:

```
# bootlist -m normal -o
fd0
cd0
hdisk0
```

If you want to make changes to your normal boot list use the command:

```
bootlist -m normal fd0 hdisk0 cd0
```

This will change the normal bootlist to indicate that when the system is booted, it will first attempt to boot from the floppy disk, if it cannot find a boot image in fd0, it will then look for hdisk0 to find the boot code, then it will search the CD-ROM. Otherwise, it will give an LED code and wait for user intervention.

3.2.2 Accessing a System That Will Not Boot

If you are unable to boot your system, the first step is to access the system and see what is the probable cause of the failure. This procedure enables you to get a system prompt so that you may attempt to recover data from the system or perform corrective action that will enable the system to boot from the hard disk.

In order to access the system:

1. Turn the system key (if present) to the Service position or alternatively press **F5** on PCI based system to boot from the tape/CD-ROM drive (during step 4).

2. Turn on all attached external devices, such as terminals, CD-ROM drives, tape drives, monitors, and external disk drives before turning on the system unit. Turn on the system unit to allow the installation media to be loaded.

3. Insert Volume 1 of the installation media into the tape or CD-ROM drive, and power the system unit off.

4. Turn the system unit power switch to the On position. When booting from alternate media, a screen will appear (before the following figure) asking you to press a function key (such as F1) to select the proper display as the system console. Each display on the system will receive a function key number in order to identify it as the system console. The system begins booting from the installation media. After several minutes, c31 is displayed in the LED (if your system has an LED, otherwise a screen similar to the one in Figure 9 is shown).

```
               Welcome to Base Operating System
                 Installation and Maintenance

Type the number of your choice and press Enter.

>>> 1 Start Installation Now with Default Settings

    2 Change/Show Installation Settings and Install

    3 Start Maintenance Mode for System Recovery



 88 Help ?
 99 Previous Menu

 Choice [1]:
```

Figure 9. BOS Installation and Maintenance Screen

5. Select option 3 **Start Maintenance Mode for System Recovery** and press **Enter=DO.** A screen similar to the one in Figure 10 is shown.

```
                          Maintenance

Type the number of your choice and press Enter.
>>> 1 Access a Root Volume Group
    2 Copy a System Dump to Removable Media
    3 Access Advanced Maintenance Functions
    4 Install from a System Backup



    88 Help ?
    99 Previous Menu
>>> Choice [1]:
```

Figure 10. Maintenance Menu

6. Enter 1, **Access a Root Volume Group**. A screen similar to the one in Figure 11 is shown.

```
        Warning
  If you choose to access a root volume group, you will not be able to return
  to the Base Operating System Installation menus without rebooting.

  Type the number of your choice and press Enter

            0 Continue


      88 Help ?
  >>> 99 Previous Menu
  >>> Choice [99]:
```

Figure 11. Warning Message Window

7. Enter a 0 and press **Enter=DO**, a screen similar to Figure 12 is shown.

```
                    Access a Root Volume Group
Type the number for a volume group to display logical volume
information and press Enter.

1)      Volume Group 00615147b27f2b40 contains these disks:
          hdisk0 958 04-B0-00-2,0
2)      Volume Group 00615247b27c2b41 contains these disks:
          hdisk1 2063 04-B0-00-6,0



Choice:
```

Figure 12. Accessing a Volume Group

8. Select the volume group whose logical volume information you want to display. This is important since rootvg will have hd5 that is the boot logical volume. Enter the number of the volume group and press **Enter=DO**. A screen similar to Figure 13 is shown.

```
                        Volume Group Information
------------------------------------------------------------------------
Volume Group ID 00615147b27f2b40 includes following logical volumes:
   hd5       hd6        hd8        hd4        hd2         hd9var

   hd3       hd1        lv00       lv01
------------------------------------------------------------------------
Type the number of your choice and press Enter.
   1) Access this Volume Group and start a shell
   2) Access this Volume Group and start a shell before mounting file systems


  99) Previous Menu
     Choice [99]:
```

Figure 13. Volume Group Information

9. Select one of the options from the Volume Group Information screen and press **Enter**. Each option does the following:

Choice 1 Selecting this choice imports and activates the volume group and mounts the file systems for this root volume group before providing you with a shell and a system prompt.

Choice 2 Selecting this choice imports and activates the volume group and provides you with a shell and system prompt before mounting the file systems for this root volume group.

Choice 99 Entering 99 returns you to the **Access a Root Volume Group** screen.

After either choice 1 or 2 is selected and processed, a shell and system prompt are displayed.

10. Take appropriate measures to recover data or take action (such as using the `bosboot` command) to enable the system to boot normally.

3.2.3 Common Boot Time LEDs and Their Solution

The most common boot problems and how to get around to getting your system up and running again are given in Table 2.

Table 2. Common Startup LEDs and Solutions

LED 201 - Damaged Boot Image
1. Access your rootvg following the procedure described in 3.2.2, "Accessing a System That Will Not Boot" on page 29.
2. Check / and /tmp filesystems. If they are almost full create more space.
3. Determine the boot disk by using the command `lslv -m hd5`
4. Re-create boot image using `bosboot -a -d /dev/hdiskn`
5. Check for CHECKSTOP errors in the error log. If such errors are found, it is probably failing hardware.
6. Shutdown and restart the system.

LED 223-229 - Invalid Boot List

1. Set the key mode switch to service (F5 for systems without keylock) and power up the machine.
2. If display continues normally, change the key mode switch to Normal and continue with step 3. If you do not get the prompt, go to step 4.
3. When you get the login prompt, login and follow the procedure described in 3.2.1, “Using the bootlist Command” on page 28 to change your bootlist. Continue with step 7.
4. Follow the procedure in 3.2.2, “Accessing a System That Will Not Boot” on page 29 to access your rootvg and continue with step 5.
5. Determine the boot disk by using the command `lslv -m hd5`.
6. Change the bootlist following the procedure given in 3.2.1, “Using the bootlist Command” on page 28.
7. Shutdown and restart your system.

LED 551, 555, and 557 - Corrupted File System, Corrupted JFS log, and so on.

1. Follow the procedure described in 3.2.2, “Accessing a System That Will Not Boot” on page 29. To access the rootvg before mounting any file systems (Option 2 on the Maintenance screen).
2. Verify and correct the file systems as follows:

```
fsck -y /dev/hd1
fsck -y /dev/hd2
fsck -y /dev/hd3
fsck -y /dev/hd4
fsck -y /dev/hd9var
```

3. Format the JFS log again by using the command:

```
/usr/sbin/logform /dev/hd8
```

4. Use `lslv -m hd5` to find out the boot disk.
5. Recreate boot image by using the command:

```
bosboot -a -d /dev/hdiskn
```

Where n is the disk number of the disk containing boot logical volume.

LED 552, 554, and 556 - Super Block Corrupted or Corrupted Customized ODM Database

1. Repeat steps 1 through 2 for LEDs 551, 555, and 557.
2. If fsck indicates that block 8 is corrupted, the super block for the file system is corrupted and needs to be repaired. Enter the command:

```
dd count=1 bs=4k skip=31 seek=1 if=/dev/hdn of=/dev/hdn
```

   where `n` is the number of the file system.
3. Rebuild your JFS log by using the command:

```
/usr/sbin/logform /dev/hd8
```

4. If this solves the problem, stop here otherwise continue with step 5.
5. Your ODM database is corrupted. Restart your system and follow the procedure given in 3.2.2, "Accessing a System That Will Not Boot" on page 29 to access rootvg with Choice 2.
6. Mount the root and usr file system as follows:

```
mount /dev/hd4 /mnt
mount /usr
```

7. Copy system configuration to a back up directory:

```
mkdir /mnt/etc/objrepors/backup
cp /mnt/etc/objrepors/Cu* /mnt/etc/objrepos
```

8. Copy configuration from RAM file system as follows:

```
cp /etc/objrepos/Cu* /mnt/etc/objrepos
```

9. Unmount all file systems by using the `umount all` command.
10. Determine bootdisk by using the `lslv -m hd5` command.
11. Save the clean ODM to the boot logical volume by using the command:

```
savebase -d/dev/hdiskn
```

12. Reboot, if system does not come up, reinstall BOS.

LED 553 - Corrupted /etc/inittab file

1. Access the rootvg with all file systems mounted by following the procedure described in 3.2.2, "Accessing a System That Will Not Boot" on page 29.
2. Check for free space in /, /var and /tmp by using `df` command.
3. Check the /etc/inittab file and correct the inittab problems if there is one empty inittab file, missing inittab file or wrong entry in inittab file.
4. Check problems with:

```
/etc/environment file
/bin/sh
/bin/bsh
/etc/fsck
/etc/profile
/.profile
```

5. Shutdown the system and reboot.

3.2.3.1 lslv -m hd5 Example Output

The following is an example of the `lslv -m hd5` command used when locating the boot device in single user mode.

```
# lslv -m hd5
hd5:N/A
LP    PP1  PV1               PP2  PV2               PP3  PV3
0001  0001 hdisk0
#
```

3.3 References

See the following publication for more information.

- *AIX Version 4.3 System Management Guide: Operating System and Devices*, SC23-4126

3.4 Quiz

Figure 14 on page 37 is an exhibit pertaining to question 1.

```
init:2:initdefault:
brc::sysinit:/sbin/rc.boot 3 >/dev/console 2>&1 # Phase 3 of system
boot
powerfail::powerfail:/etc/rc.powerfail 2>&1 | alog -tboot >
/dev/console # Power Failure Detection
rc:2:wait:/etc/rc 2>&1 | alog -tboot > /dev/console # Multi-User checks
fbcheck:2:wait:/usr/sbin/fbcheck 2>&1 | alog -tboot > /dev/console #
run /etc/firstboot
srcmstr:2:respawn:/usr/sbin/srcmstr # System Resource Controller
rctcpip:2:wait:/etc/rc,tcpip > /dev/console 2>&1 # Start TCP/IP daemons
rcnfs:2:wait:/etc/rc.nfs > /dev/console 2>&1 # Start NFS Daemons
cron:2:respawn:/usr/sbin/cron
piobe:2:wait:/usr/lib/lpd/pio/etc/pioinit >/dev/null 2>&1  # pb cleanup
qdaemon:2:wait:/usr/bin/startsrc -sqdaemon
writesrv:2:wait:/usr/bin/startsrc -swritesrv
uprintfd:2:respawn:/usr/sbin/uprintfd
logsymp:2:once:/usr/lib/ras/logsymptom # for system dumps
pmd:2:wait:/usr/bin/pmd > /dev/console 2>&1 # Start PM daemon
diagd:2:once:/usr/lpp/diagnostics/bin/diagd >/dev/console 2>&1
dt:2:wait:/etc/rc.dt
cons:0123456789:respawn:/usr/sbin/getty /dev/console
cfgmceh:2:once:/usr/lib/methods/cfgmceh >/dev/null 2>&1 # Configure
Machine Check Error Handler
infod:2:once:startsrc -s infod
browser:2:respawn:/usr/lpp/xlC/browser/pdnsd
```

Figure 14. Exhibit for Question 1

1. After booting, NFS is not available. Based on the exhibit, what can be concluded?

   A. /etc/rc.nfs is corrupted.

   B. The /var filesystem is corrupted.

   C. The TCP/IP initialization is incorrect.

   D. The start NFS call should read "rcnfs:1:wait:/etc/rc.nfs > /dev/console 2>&1.

2. During bootup, the system administrator notices that the system is hung at LED 553. This most commonly indicates:

   A. A corrupted /etc/inittab.

   B. The system could not complete a network boot.

   C. The system could not vary on the root volume group.

D. The configuration manager could not locate a valid boot device.

3. After a power failure, the system attempts to reboot but hangs on 557. This indicates file system corruption. Which of the following actions should be taken to recover?

   A. Restore /etc/filesystems from mksysb.

   B. Execute chfs -a size=+1 against all filesystems in rootvg.

   C. From a maintenance shell, run `lppchk -v` against all filesets installed.

   D. From a maintenance shell, run `fsck -y` against all filesystems in rootvg.

3.4.1 Answers

1. C
2. A
3. D

3.5 Exercises

1. Locate the boot devices on your systems.
2. Comment out tasks started in /etc/inittab and experience the error messages caused by errors generated like this.

Chapter 4. Hardware Installation and Configuration Management

Configuration management involves adding new devices to the system, their configuration, troubleshooting, and problems that result. RS/6000 systems include support for several buses, such as the Peripheral Component Interconnect (PCI) and Industry Standard Architecture (ISA), as well as new devices that are different from the ones that are supported on the microchannel-based RS/6000 systems.

AIX system configuration architecture and methodology uses information stored in the Object Data Manager (ODM) database to configure devices. The configuration of devices which do not support automatic configuration, for example non-native ISA devices, must be performed manually. This chapter includes step-by-step procedures on how to configure devices on the PCI-based RS/6000 servers.

4.1 Finding Out about Your System

RS/6000 servers are available in a variety of models. An RS/6000 system can be single processor or multiprocessor. Currently, models comply to a number of architecture specifications such as Micro Channel, PowerPC Reference Platform (PREP), Common Hardware Reference Platform (CHRP), and RS/6000 Platform Architecture (RPA).

The hardware platform type is an abstraction that allows machines to be grouped according to fundamental configuration characteristics such as the number of processors and/or I/O bus structure. Machines with different hardware platform types will have basic differences in the way their devices are dynamically configured at boot time. Currently available hardware platforms, which are able to be differentiated by software, in RS/6000 family are:

rs6k Micro Channel-based uni-processor models

rs6ksmp Micro Channel-based symmetric multiprocessor models

rspc ISA-bus models

chrp PCI-bus models

In order to determine the hardware platform type on your machine, enter the following command:

```
bootinfo -p
```

This will return rs6k, rs6ksmp, rspc, or chrp as output.

You can also use the `lscfg` command to determine the type of hardware platform you have. The `lscfg` command provides output similar to Figure 15:

```
INSTALLED RESOURCE LIST

The following resources are installed on the machine.
+/- = Added or deleted from Resource List.
*   = Diagnostic support not available.

  Model Architecture: chrp
  Model Implementation: Multiple Processor, PCI bus

+ sysplanar0          00-00               System Planar
+ mem0                00-00               Memory
+ proc0               00-00               Processor
+ L2cache0            00-00               L2 Cache
* pmc0                00-00               Power Management Controller
+ proc1               00-01               Processor
+ proc2               00-02               Processor
+ proc3               00-03               Processor
* pci0                00-f8400000         PCI Bus
* isa0                10-78               ISA Bus
+ fda0                01-D1               Standard I/O Diskette Adapter
+ fd0                 01-D1-00-00         Diskette Drive
* siokma0             01-K1               Keyboard/Mouse Adapter
+ sioka0              01-K1-00            Keyboard Adapter
:
```

Figure 15. Finding Out the Hardware Platform Type

It is important to know what kind of system you have and what its capabilities are if you decide to use your system for special purposes, such as a Web server, a CATIA workstation, or for running heavy database applications.

Web servers require fast networking connections, CATIA workstations require a powerful graphics adapter, and database applications require large responsive disk drives.

You can determine a specific subset of the configuration by using `grep`, or additional command flags. For example, in order to find out the number of processors you have, enter either of the following commands:

- `lscfg | grep proc | wc -l`
- `lsdev -Cc processor | wc -l`

4.2 Adapter and Device Configuration

PCI-based RS/6000 servers support attachment of devices using the following bus types:

- SCSI

- PCI
- ISA

Devices on PCI-based RS/6000 systems might be of two types: native devices, such as the integrated SCSI controller and the serial controller or attached (non-native) devices, such as the supported PCI or ISA adapters.

The device information required to configure the integrated devices is contained in the firmware and is passed to the operating system through the residual data written to NVRAM. Thus, integrated devices are configured automatically to AIX after system reboot. Attached PCI devices and adapters are configured automatically at system start-up, provided required device drivers are installed on the system. However, ISA adapters have to be configured manually.

4.3 Displaying Installed Devices

In order to display devices that are either supported or defined on your system, you can either use the `lsdev` command or use the SMIT fastpath as follows:

1. `smitty lsattr`

   A screen similar to the one shown in Figure 16 will be shown:

```
                                List Devices

Move cursor to desired item and press Enter.

  List All Supported Devices
  List All Defined Devices
  Show Characteristics of a Supported Device
  Show Characteristics of a Defined Device












F1=Help              F2=Refresh           F3=Cancel            F8=Image
F9=Shell             F10=Exit             Enter=Do
```

Figure 16. List Devices SMIT Panel

2. Select **List All Defined Devices**. (`lsdev -C` command is run in the background)
3. Press **Enter**.

A list of all the devices that are either in the Defined or in the Available state are listed. An output similar to Figure 17 on page 42 is shown:

```
                              COMMAND STATUS

Command: OK            stdout: yes           stderr: no

Before command completion, additional instructions may appear below.

[TOP]
aio0       Defined                  Asynchronous I/O
bus0       Available 00-00          PCI Bus
bus1       Available 04-A0          ISA Bus
cd0        Available 04-B0-00-3,0 SCSI Multimedia CD-ROM Drive
copied     Defined                  Logical volume
en0        Available                Standard Ethernet Network Interface
ent0       Available 04-D0          IBM PCI Ethernet Adapter (22100020)
et0        Defined                  IEEE 802.3 Ethernet Network Interface
fd0        Available 01-C0-00-00   Diskette Drive
fda0       Available 01-C0          Standard I/O Diskette Adapter
fslv00     Defined                  Logical volume
gxme0      Available                Graphics Data Transfer Assist Subsystem
[MORE...59]

F1=Help            F2=Refresh          F3=Cancel           F6=Command
F8=Image           F9=Shell            F10=Exit            /=Find
n=Find Next
```

Figure 17. lsdev -C Command Output

Note

The predefined ODM database contains default characteristics for devices. These devices may not exist on the system, but have device support loaded. For example, if a tape drive was detected at the installation time, there will be a number of types of tape drives in the list, but if, on the other hand, no multiprotocol adapter was found, no such support will be added to the predefined database. Use `lsdev -P` command to see a list of supported devices.

4.4 Configuring New Devices

Depending on the kind of device you plan to configure, you will go through a different sequence of configuration steps. PCI device configuration and ISA device configuration differs considerably. The following sections discuss the various configuration approaches.

4.4.1 PCI Device Configuration

If you add a new PCI or SCSI device to your system, the system will automatically configure the device (provided no conflict is found in case of SCSI devices, for example the same SCSI ID for two different SCSI devices) at system restart or by using the `cfgmgr` command provided the required device drivers are installed.

When using PCI adapters, the slot number is as important as it is in microchannel devices. If you change the adapter from slot A to slot B, the original adapter information for slot A will be kept in defined state and a new definition will be created for slot B and a new device will be configured.

4.4.2 ISA Device Configuration

Devices like PCI or Micro Channel integrated devices such as SCSI controllers, integrated ISA devices like keyboard, mouse, and audio are self configuring. However non-integrated ISA devices such as adapters plugged into ISA slots, should be configured manually.

In the case of ISA devices, five resources should be managed before your system can run smoothly. These five resources are:

- Bus I/O ranges
- Bus memory address ranges
- System interrupts (IRQ)
- Direct Memory Access (DMA) channels
- Bus memory DMA address ranges

These settings must be different for all ISA adapters to avoid conflicts otherwise you will not be able to use the adapter. If these resources cannot be dynamically set, they must be set by adjusting switches or jumpers on the adapter. In case the adapter does not have switches, you may need a System Management Services (SMS) disk to configure the adapter.

The first step is to install the device drivers for ISA adapters if you have not already done so. In order to check whether device support for ISA has been installed, use the `lsdev` command as shown in Figure 18 on page 44:

```
# lsdev -Pc adapter -s isa
adapter tokenring   isa IBM 16/4 PowerPC Token-Ring Adapter (isa)
adapter portmaster isa Multiport Model 2 Adapter
adapter ethernet    isa IBM ISA Ethernet Adapter
adapter articmpx    isa X.25 CoProcessor/1 Adapter
adapter pcxr        isa IBM 8-Port Async, EIA-232 (ISA)
adapter pc8s        isa IBM 8-Port EIA-232/RS-422A (ISA) Adapter
adapter cxia        isa IBM 128-Port Async, EIA-232 (ISA)
```

Figure 18. Checking ISA Device Support

This provides you with a list of all the adapters that have been defined in the predefined ODM database. If you see a blank display when you run this command you need to install the support for ISA adapters.

4.4.2.1 Installing Device Drivers for ISA Devices

In order to install device support for ISA devices follow the SMIT fastpath:

1. `smitty devinst_isa`
2. Select the devices.isa fileset. By default it is already entered in the field.
3. The device support for ISA devices will be installed once the command finishes execution.

4.4.2.2 Recording Settings of Already Configured ISA Adapters

ISA devices may not work properly if there are clashes in their settings suxh as IRQ or bus I/O ranges. It is best to note all the settings of any ISA devices already present in your system. In order to do that, issue the following command:

```
lsdev -Cc adapter -s isa
```

This command will show you all the ISA devices that are already configured with your system. The output of this command will be similar to:

```
# lsdev -Cc adapter -s isa
cxia0 Available 01-01 IBM 128-Port Async, EIA-232 (ISA)
apm0  Available 01-02 4-Port Selectable Multiport Model 2 Adapter
# 
```

Figure 19. Finding Out Currently Defined Devices

Once you have the names of the ISA devices that are configured on your system use either the `lsresource` command or the `lsattr` command to get the current settings of your ISA devices. The `lsresource` command writes a list of assigned bus resources to standard out, or determines if the bus resources for devices resolve. On the command line enter:

```
lsresource -l apm0
```

An output similar to Figure 20 will be shown:

```
# lsresource -l apm0
TYPE DEVICE ATTRIBUTE     S G CURRENT
B     apm0   bus_mem_addr       0x000e2000 - 0x000e3fff
O     apm0   bus_io_addr        0x000006a0 - 0x000006a6
N     apm0   bus_intr_lvl                7     (A0)
# █
```

Figure 20. Finding Out Current Resource Settings Using lsresource

Use `lsattr` command to find out the current settings of all of your ISA devices. The `lsattr` command displays information about the attributes of a given device or kind of device. Use the `lsattr` command as shown in Figure 21.

```
# lsattr -l apm0 -E -H
attribute      value    description user_settable

bus_intr_lvl  7                    True
bus_io_addr   0x6A0                True
bus_mem_addr  0xE2000              True
window_size   0x2000  Window Size False
intr_priority 2                    False
# █
```

Figure 21. Finding Out Current Resource Settings Using lsattr

Once you have the current values for the installed devices, refer to your device documentation and select the recommended values for the device to work properly. Next configure the adapter using the SMIT fastpath:

1. `smitty isa`

A screen similar to Figure 22 on page 46 will be shown:

```
                                ISA Adapters

Move cursor to desired item and press Enter.

  Install ISA Adapter Software
  Add an ISA Adapter
  Change / Show Characteristics of an ISA Adapter
  Remove an ISA Adapter
  List all Defined ISA Adapters
  List all Supported ISA Adapters
  Configure a Defined ISA Adapter













F1=Help             F2=Refresh          F3=Cancel           F8=Image
F9=Shell            F10=Exit            Enter=Do
```

Figure 22. SMIT ISA Adapter Options

2. Select **Add an ISA Adapter** and press **Enter**. A screen similar to Figure 23 will be shown:

```
                                ISA Adapters

Move cursor to desired item and press Enter.

  Install ISA Adapter Software
  Add an ISA Adapter
  Change / Show Characteristics of an ISA Adapter
  +--------------------------------------------------------------------+
  |                         Add an ISA Adapter                         |
  |                                                                    |
  | Move cursor to desired item and press Enter.                       |
  |                                                                    |
  |   tokenring  isa IBM 16/4 PowerPC Token-Ring Adapter (isa)         |
  |   portmaster isa Multiport Model 2 Adapter                         |
  |   ethernet   isa IBM ISA Ethernet Adapter                          |
  |   articmpx   isa X.25 CoProcessor/1 Adapter                        |
  |   pcxr       isa IBM 8-Port Async, EIA-232 (ISA)                   |
  |   pc8s       isa IBM 8-Port EIA-232/RS-422A (ISA) Adapter          |
  |   cxia       isa IBM 128-Port Async, EIA-232 (ISA)                 |
  |                                                                    |
  | F1=Help                 F2=Refresh              F3=Cancel          |
  | F8=Image                F10=Exit                Enter=Do           |
F1| /=Find                  n=Find Next                                |
F9+--------------------------------------------------------------------+
```

Figure 23. Adding an ISA Adapter - Step 1

Note

You can try to configure the adapter without actually installing it since some adapters may have DIP switches that you may have to set in order to get the right settings. If you try to configure an adapter, for example an X.25 adapter that has not been installed, and there are no parameter conflicts you will be given a message as follows:

```
ampx0 Defined
Method error (/usr/lib/methods/cfgc1x):
0514-047 Cannot access a device.
[busquery]ioctl(): Function not implemented
ampx0 deleted
```

This shows that you have configured the adapter correctly except that you still must actually install it.

3. Select the adapter you want to add (assume that you are trying to configure a Multiport Model 2 adapter) and press **Enter**. A screen similar to Figure 24 is shown:

```
                    Add a Multiport Model 2 Adapter

Type or select values in entry fields.
Press Enter AFTER making all desired changes.

                                                 [Entry Fields]
  Description                                   Multiport Model 2 Adap>
  Parent Device                                 bus1
  ISA Interrupt Level                          [7]                      +#
  Bus IO Address                               [0x6A0]                  +X
  Bus Memory Address                           [0xE2000]                +X
  Define device only, do not configure          no                      +









F1=Help            F2=Refresh          F3=Cancel          F4=List
F5=Reset           F6=Command          F7=Edit            F8=Image
F9=Shell           F10=Exit            Enter=Do
```

Figure 24. Adding an ISA Adapter - Step 2

4. Change any input fields required and press **Enter** once you are done. If your given values conflict with some other ISA device, a message similar to Figure 25 will be shown:

```
                            COMMAND STATUS

Command: failed        stdout: yes          stderr: no

Before command completion, additional instructions may appear below.

apm1 Defined
lsresource : The attribute(s) for some device(s) in the system
could not be resolved.  To resolve conflicts, attribute(s) need to be
modified.  A suggested value for each attribute is provided.

DEVICE ATTRIBUTE    CURRENT SUGGESTED DESCRIPTION
apm1   bus_intr_lvl 7       9
apm1   bus_io_addr  0x6a0   0xaa0
apm1   bus_mem_addr 0xe2000 0xe4000
apm1  deleted




F1=Help             F2=Refresh          F3=Cancel           F6=Command
F8=Image            F9=Shell            F10=Exit            /=Find
n=Find Next
```

Figure 25. ISA Adapter Resource Conflict

5. Go back to the previous screen and correct the values accordingly.

You have successfully configured an ISA adapter.

4.4.3 128-Port Asynchronous Adapter Considerations

The 128-port asynchronous adapter subsystem meets the multiuser requirements for workstations in the open system environment. The subsystem can support up to 128 devices and offers higher speeds to the end user. It is an intelligent adapter with the ability to offload line protocol processing from the operating system.

The 128-port product consists of an adapter card, up to eight remote asynchronous node (RAN) units, each supporting 16 devices, for a total of 128 devices per adapter. The 128-port asynchronous adapter card resides in the system unit, and is connected by either EIA 422, direct cabling, EIA 422/EIA 232 synchronous modems, or Data Service Unit/Channel Service Units (DSU/CSUs) to the RAN. The number of 128-port asynchronous adapters that can be installed is dependent on the number of slots available in the system with a hardware limit of seven adapters per bus (an optional I/O bus can provide eight additional slots).

Each 128-port asynchronous adapter has two synchronous lines. Up to four RANs can be connected to a single synchronous line in daisy-chain fashion.

That is, the first RAN is connected to one of the adapter's lines, the second RAN is connected to the first RAN, and so on (up to four RANs).

The RANs can be attached to the 128-port adapter with a direct local connection, a synchronous modem connection, or a combination of the two. Figure 26 shows some of the possible connection types.

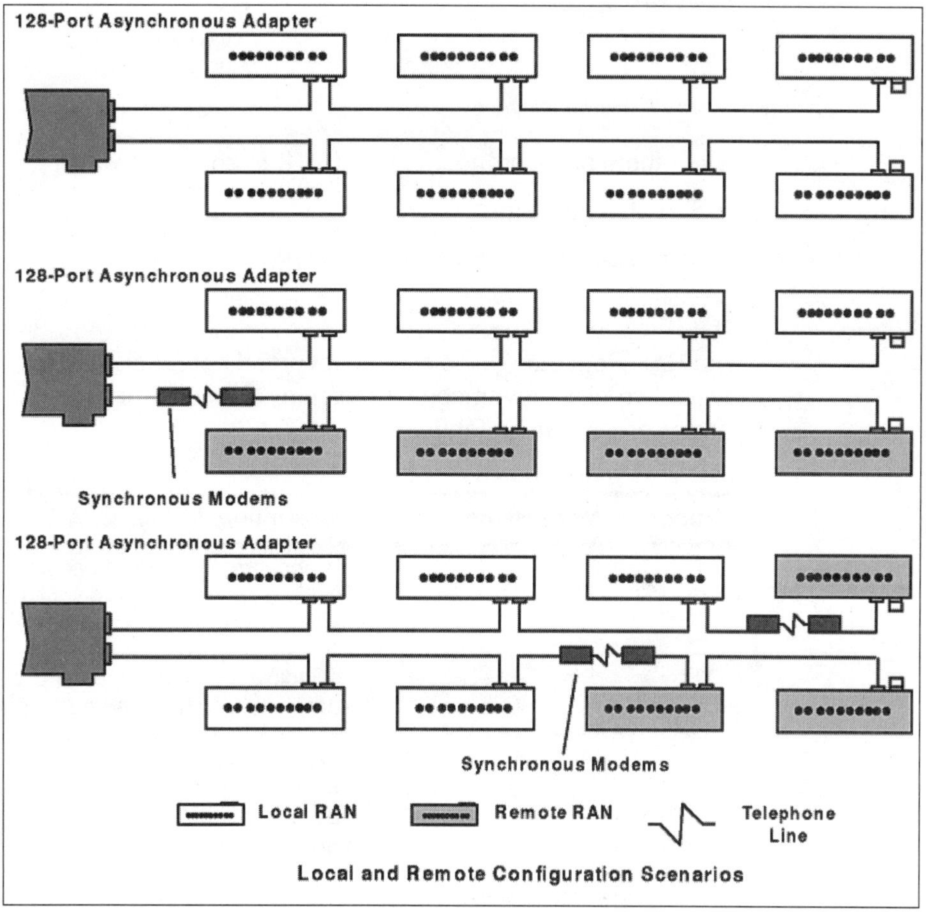

Figure 26. 128-Port Asynchronous Adapter Connection Combinations

The adapter identifies RANs by their node numbers. Each RAN in a daisy chain must have a unique node number (1n through 4n), which must be set during installation. The node numbers must be assigned in ascending order with the lowest number assigned to the RAN closest to the adapter. You can skip node numbers (to facilitate insertion of additional RANs at a later date), as long as the ascending sequence is maintained. Figure 27 summarizes the node number assignment.

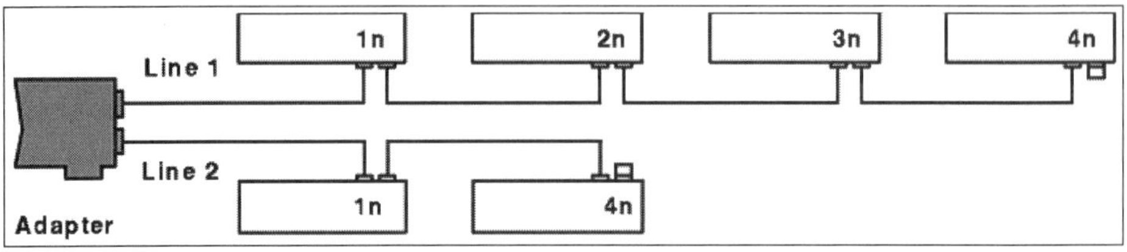

Figure 27. RAN Numbering

The remote asynchronous node (RAN) is equipped with:

- Ten LED indicators
- Two-digit, seven-segment LED display
- Two push buttons

The RAN front panel display has several different display modes as indicated by the two-digit, seven-segment display. Some of the RAN front panel display modes are shown in Table 3.

Table 3. RAN Activity Codes

Mode	Mode Name	Description
P1	POST Complete	P1 appears on the seven-segment display. Power-on self-test is complete, relays are open waiting for connection.
P2	Ping Packet Receive	P2 indicates that the operating system successfully transmitted a ping packet to RAN.
AC	Activity	AC appears on the seven-segment display. The 10 LEDs turn on sequentially from left to right. The speed of this *chase light* display increases with the overall activity level of the RAN.
En	Error Node	En appears on the seven-segment display. It indicates that a valid ping packet was received but the node number in EEPROM is incorrect.

In the case of duplicate node numbers, the RAN farthest from the host adapter will display En, instead of AC, when the system is started.

The configuration for a 128-port Asynchronous adapter follows the same sequence of steps for a normal ISA adapter; however, you can customize your adapter port-wise. That is, you can set different characteristics for your lines and the corresponding nodes.

4.5 Adding a TTY Device

In order to add a TTY, use the following procedure:

1. Issue `smitty tty` and select **Add a TTY** or `smitty maktty`.
2. The system will ask you for the TTY type and the parent adapter. Select both and press **Enter**.

   A screen similar to Figure 28 will be shown:

```
                                  Add a TTY

Type or select values in entry fields.
Press Enter AFTER making all desired changes.

[TOP]                                                   [Entry Fields]
  TTY type                                            tty
  TTY interface                                       rs232
  Description                                         Asynchronous Terminal
  Parent adapter                                      sa0
* PORT number                                        []                     +
  Enable LOGIN                                        disable               +
  BAUD rate                                          [9600]                 +
  PARITY                                             [none]                 +
  BITS per character                                 [8]                    +
  Number of STOP BITS                                [1]                    +
  TIME before advancing to next port setting         [0]                    +#
  TERMINAL type                                      [dumb]
  FLOW CONTROL to be used                            [xon]                  +
[MORE...31]

F1=Help             F2=Refresh          F3=Cancel           F4=List
F5=Reset            F6=Command          F7=Edit             F8=Image
F9=Shell            F10=Exit            Enter=Do
```

Figure 28. Adding a TTY

3. Select the port number you want this TTY to be added to in the **PORT number** parameter. For RANs, follow the location code rules to select the appropriate port number.
4. Change the **TERMINAL Type** parameter to the type of terminal you are using. This parameter is very important since you might not be able to use all the keys on your terminal if this parameter is set incorrectly. The TERM environment variable stores this setting. You can change the terminal emulation setting by using your TERM environment variable and using the `export` command to store the terminal emulation you want to use. For example, in order to use ibm3151 terminal emulation use the command:

```
export $TERM=ibm3151.
```

5. Set the line speed and the kind of communication (1/8/N or 1/7/E) for your terminal and press **Enter**.

   This will create a device special file in the /dev directory, add an entry to the /etc/inittab file in order to run the getty process on your terminal so that your terminal is available at system startup. It also adds another entry to the customized ODM (CuDv) database for the terminal you have just added.

You can also add a TTY directly on the command line. In order to add an ibm3151 RS232 terminal using adapter sa0 and port s1 with login enabled use the following command:

```
mkdev -c tty -t tty -s rs232 -p sa0 -w s1 -a login=enable -a term=ibm3151
```

You can remove a terminal by using the command:

```
rmdev -l <tty name> -d
```

Where `<tty name>` can be determined by using the command `tty` or by listing all the TTYs and then selecting the TTY you want to remove.

4.6 Adding a Tape Drive

Generally, a tape drive attached on a SCSI interface is automatically configured once you run the `cfgmgr` command or at the system start-up. There may be occasions when you want to add a new tape drive to your system. In order to add a tape drive, use the SMIT fastpath:

1. `smitty tape`
2. Select **Add a Tape Drive**

   A screen similar to Figure 29 on page 53 will be shown.

```
                              Tape Drive

Mo ┌──────────────────────────────────────────────────────────────────────┐
   │                         Tape Drive Type                              │
   │                                                                      │
   │ Move cursor to desired item and press Enter.                         │
   │                                                                      │
   │ [TOP]                                                                │
   │   1200mb-c  scsi 1.2 GB 1/4-Inch Tape Drive                          │
   │   150mb     scsi 150 MB 1/4-Inch Tape Drive                          │
   │   3490e     scsi 3490E Autoloading Tape Drive                        │
   │   4mm2gb    scsi 2.0 GB 4mm Tape Drive                               │
   │   4mm2gb2   scsi 2.0 GB 4mm Tape Drive                               │
   │   4mm4gb    scsi 4.0 GB 4mm Tape Drive                               │
   │   525mb     scsi 525 MB 1/4-Inch Tape Drive                          │
   │   8mm       scsi 2.3 GB 8mm Tape Drive                               │
   │   8mm5gb    scsi 5.0 GB 8mm Tape Drive                               │
   │   8mm7gb    scsi 7.0 GB 8mm Tape Drive                               │
   │ [MORE...3]                                                           │
   │                                                                      │
   │ F1=Help                 F2=Refresh              F3=Cancel            │
   │ F8=Image                F10=Exit                Enter=Do             │
F1 │ /=Find                  n=Find Next                                  │
F9 └──────────────────────────────────────────────────────────────────────┘
```

Figure 29. Adding a Tape Drive - Step 1

3. Choose the type of tape drive that you want to add and press **Enter**.
4. Select the parent adapter on which the tape will be attached and press **Enter**. A screen similar to Figure 30 on page 54 will be shown:

```
                              Add a Tape Drive

Type or select values in entry fields.
Press Enter AFTER making all desired changes.

                                                    [Entry Fields]
  Tape Drive type                                   8mm5gb
  Tape Drive interface                              scsi
  Description                                       5.0 GB 8mm Tape Drive
  Parent adapter                                    scsi0
* CONNECTION address                               []                        +
  BLOCK size (0=variable length)                   [1024]                    +#
  Use DEVICE BUFFERS during writes                  yes                      +
  Use EXTENDED file marks                           no                       +
  DENSITY setting #1                                140                      +
  DENSITY setting #2                                20                       +
  Use data COMPRESSION                              yes                      +



F1=Help             F2=Refresh          F3=Cancel           F4=List
F5=Reset            F6=Command          F7=Edit             F8=Image
F9=Shell            F10=Exit            Enter=Do
```

Figure 30. Adding a Tape Drive - Step 2

5. Enter the SCSI address in the `CONNECTION address` field.
6. The `BLOCK size` parameter is very important, since a tape is a block device. By default, the block size is 1024 bytes. If you save a file on a tape with block size of 512 bytes you will not be able to read it with a tape drive of block size equal to 1024 bytes on older AIX releases. It is recommended that you keep the block size 0, which is a variable block size. A variable block size automatically finds out the block size of your media and then reads the media accordingly. If the block sizes of the media and the tape drive are different you can encounter an error similar to this when you try to read something from a tape:

```
restore: 0511-160 Cannot read the backup media
/dev/rmt0.1:There is an input or output error
```

7. Press **Enter** to complete the process.

Alternatively, you can add a new tape drive on the command line. For example, in order to create device for an 8 mm tape attached on adapter scsi0 using 5 as the SCSI address use the command:

```
mkdev -c tape -t '8mm' -s 'scsi' -p 'scsi0' -w '5,0' -a block_size='0'
```

4.7 References

See the following publications for related information.

- *A Technical Introduction to PCI-based RS/6000 Servers*, SG24-4690
- *AIX Versions 3.2 and 4 Asynchronous Communications Guide*, SC23-2488

4.8 Quiz

1. What command can be run from the command line to permanently remove tty5 from the system?

   A. `rmdev -l tty5`

   B. `rmdev -dl tty5`

   C. `mkdev -dl tty5`

   D. `odmdelete -q "name=tty5" -o PdAt`

2. A client is setting up an 128-port asynchronous adapter with two remote RANs. The two SA devices (RANs) are not available to the system. In addition, node 1's LEDs is displaying AC and node 2's LEDs is displaying En. What is the most likely cause of the problem?

   A. There are 2 RANs with the same node number.

   B. The adapter itself is not being recognized by the system.

   C. The serial line in SMIT is defined with the wrong speed.

   D. The serial line in SMIT is defined with the wrong cable type.

4.8.1 Answers

1. B
2. A

4.9 Exercises

1. You have just purchased a new RS/6000. Find out the type of your RS/6000 system using the `bootinfo` command. Also, find out the number of processors you have.
2. You need to add a new ISA adapter to your system. Using the guidelines in the chapter, configure the ISA adapter correctly in your system.
3. Remove a TTY permanently from your system, also configure all of your TTYs to have ibm3151 as the default emulation setting.

4. Familiarize yourself with the various adapters available to RS/6000.

Chapter 5. Storage Management, LVM, and File Systems

In this chapter, storage management, Logical Volume Management (LVM), and file system support issues are covered. The basic tasks that require understanding are broken down into separate sections.

5.1 Logical Volume Storage Concepts

The five basic logical storage concepts are physical volumes, volume groups, physical partitions, logical volumes, and logical partitions. The relationships among these concepts is provided in Figure 31.

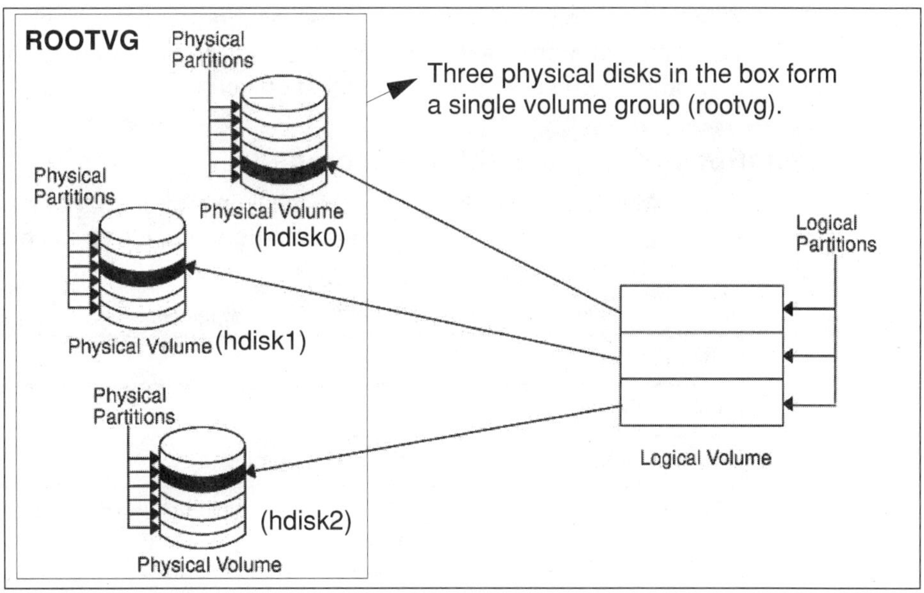

Figure 31. Relationship between Logical Storage Components

The following can be said regarding Figure 31:

- Each individual fixed-disk drive is called a physical volume (PV) and has a name. For example: hdisk0, hdisk1, or hdisk2.
- All physical volumes belong to one volume group (VG) named rootvg.
- All of the physical volumes in a volume group are divided into physical partitions (PPs) of the same size.
- Within each volume group, one or more logical volumes (LVs) are defined. Logical volumes are groups of information located on physical volumes.

Data on logical volumes appear as contiguous to the user, but can be discontiguous on the physical volume.

- Each logical volume consists of one or more logical partitions (LPs). Each logical partition corresponds to at least one physical partition. If mirroring is specified for the logical volume, additional physical partitions are allocated to store the additional copies of each logical partition.
- Logical volumes can serve a number of system purposes, for example paging, but each logical volume that holds ordinary systems, user data, or programs contains a single journaled file system (JFS). Each JFS consists of a pool of page-size (4 KB) blocks. In AIX 4.1, a given file system can be defined as having a fragment size of less than 4 KB (512 bytes, 1 KB, 2 KB).

After installation, the system has one volume group (the rootvg volume group) consisting of a base set of logical volumes required to start the system and any others you specify to the installation script.

5.1.1 Limitations of Logical Volume Storage

The LVM in AIX provides a lot of flexibility in disk management, however, similar to all other operating system components, it has its limitations. Table 4 lists the limitations on the logical storage in AIX.

Table 4. Limitations for Logical Volume Storage Management

Storage Components	Limitations
Volume Group	255 per system
Physical Volume	32 per volume group
Physical Partition	1016 per physical volume up to 256 MB each in size. A multiple of 1016 may be used on AIX 4.3.1 or later systems, provided the factor is set to a non-default value.
Logical volume	256 per volume group
Logical partition	35,512 per logical volume

5.2 Managing Physical Volumes

The following sections discuss adding a new disk drive, changing physical volume characteristics, and monitoring the physical volumes.

5.2.1 Configuration of Physical Volume

The following three methods can be used to configure a new disk drive. If the LVM will use this disk, it must also be made of a physical volume.

5.2.1.1 Method 1

This method is used when it is possible to shut down and power off the system prior to attaching the disk.

When the system is booted after adding a disk drive, the `cfgmgr` command is run by the system during booting, which will automatically configure the disk. After boot-up is complete, log in as root and run `lspv`, and look for a new disk entry in the output as shown in the following example.

```
hdisk1   none                       none
```

or

```
hdisk1   00005264d21adb2e           none
```

The 16-digit number in the second column of the preceding example is the physical volume identifier (PVID).

If the output shows the new disk with a PVID, it can be used by LVM for configuration. If the new disk does not have a PVID, then use the procedure 5.2.2, "Making an Available Disk a Physical Volume" on page 60 to allow the disk to be used by the LVM.

5.2.1.2 Method 2

This method may be used when it is not possible to shut down or power off the system prior to attaching the disk. Perform the following tasks.

1. Run `lspv` to list the physical disks already configured on the system as shown in the following example.

   ```
   # lspv
   hdisk0          000005265ac63976     rootvg
   ```

2. To configure all newly detected devices on the system (including the new disk) use the following command.

   ```
   cfgmgr
   ```

3. Run `lspv` again, and look for a new disk entry in the output as shown in the following example.

   ```
   hdisk1     none                  none
   ```

   or

   ```
   hdisk1     00005264d21adb2e      none
   ```

Once you have determined the name of the newly configured disk, use the procedure described in 5.2.2, "Making an Available Disk a Physical Volume" on page 60 to allow the disk to be utilized by the Logical Volume Manager.

5.2.1.3 Method 3

This method may be used when it is not possible to shut down or power off the system prior to attaching the disk. This method requires the following information about the new disk.

- How the disk is attached (subclass)
- The type of the disk (type)
- Which system attachment the disk is connected to (parent name)
- The logical address of the disk (where connected)

Use the following command to configure the disk and ensure that it is available as a physical volume by using the `pv=yes` attribute.

```
mkdev -c disk -s subclass -t type -p parentname \ -w whereconnected
-a pv=yes
```

The `pv=yes` attribute makes the disk a physical volume and writes a boot record with a unique physical volume identifier onto the disk (if it does not already have one).

5.2.2 Making an Available Disk a Physical Volume

A new disk drive can only be assigned to volume groups. To be used by the LVM, a disk must be configured as a physical volume. The following command will change an available disk (hdisk1) to a physical volume by assigning a physical volume identifier (PVID) if it does not already have one.

```
chdev -l hdisk1 -a pv=yes
```

This command has no effect if the disk is already a physical volume.

5.2.3 Modifying Physical Volume Characteristics

This section discusses the two characteristics which can be changed for a physical volume to control the use of physical volumes using the `chpv` command.

5.2.3.1 Setting Allocation Permission for a Physical Volume

The allocation permission for a physical volume determines if physical partitions contained on this disk, which are not allocated to a logical volume yet, can be allocated for use by logical volumes. Setting the allocation permission defines whether or not the allocation of new physical partitions is permitted for the specified physical volume.

The following command is used to turn off the allocation permission for physical volume hdisk1.

```
chpv -a n hdisk1
```

To turn the allocation permission back on, use the following command.

```
chpv -a y hdisk1
```

5.2.3.2 Setting the Availability of a Physical Volume

The availability of a physical volume defines whether any logical input/output operations can be performed to the specified physical volume. Physical volumes should be made unavailable when they are to be removed from the system or are lost due to failure.

The following command is used to set the state of a physical volume to unavailable.

```
chpv -v r pvname
```

This will quiesce all VGDA and VGSA copies on the physical volume, and the physical volume will not take part in future vary on quorum checking. Also, information about the specified volume will be removed from the VGDAs of the other physical volumes in that volume group.

The following command will make a physical volume available to the system.

```
chpv -v a pvname
```

Note

The `chpv` command uses space in the /tmp directory to store information while it is executing. If it fails, it could be due to lack of space in the /tmp directory. Create more space in that directory and try again.

5.2.4 Removing Physical Volumes

The physical volume must be unconfigured before it can be removed from the system. The following example shows how to unconfigure a physical volume (hdisk1) and change its state from available to defined using the `rmdev` command.

```
rmdev -l hdisk1
```

The definition of this physical volume will remain in the ODM.

5.2.5 Listing Information about Physical Volumes

A physical volume correctly installed on the system can be assigned to a volume group and can subsequently be used to hold file systems and logical volumes.

The information about free physical partitions and their availability within different sectors on the disk can be very useful. The following section will discuss using the `lspv` command to obtain such information pertinent to physical volumes.

5.2.5.1 Listing Physical Volumes on the System

The `lspv` command executed without any flag will produce output that will identify the physical volumes by name that are known to the system as shown in the following example.

```
# lspv
hdisk0          00615147ce54a7ee    rootvg
hdisk1          00615147a877976a    rootvg
#
```

The `lsdev` command with option with the `-C` option and `-c` class will also list the physical volumes on the system along with the status of each physical volume as shown in the following example.

```
# lsdev -C -c disk
hdisk0 Available 40-58-00-0,0 16 Bit SCSI Disk Drive
hdisk1 Available 40-58-00-1,0 16 Bit SCSI Disk Drive
hdisk2 Available 20-68-L      SSA Logical Disk Drive
hdisk3 Available 20-68-L      SSA Logical Disk Drive
hdisk4 Available 20-68-L      SSA Logical Disk Drive
hdisk5 Available 20-68-L      SSA Logical Disk Drive
hdisk6 Available 20-68-L      SSA Logical Disk Drive
#
```

5.2.5.2 Listing Physical Volume Characteristics

The following example shows the use of the `lspv` command to retrieve more detailed information about a physical volume.

```
# lspv hdisk1
PHYSICAL VOLUME:    hdisk1                   VOLUME GROUP:     rootvg
PV IDENTIFIER:      00615147a877976a         VG IDENTIFIER     00615147b27f2b40
PV STATE:           active
STALE PARTITIONS:   0                        ALLOCATABLE:      yes
PP SIZE:            4 megabyte(s)            LOGICAL VOLUMES:  13
TOTAL PPs:          238 (952 megabytes)      VG DESCRIPTORS:   1
FREE PPs:           71 (284 megabytes)
```

```
USED PPs:            167 (668 megabytes)
FREE DISTRIBUTION:   48..02..00..00..21
USED DISTRIBUTION:   00..46..47..47..27
#
```

The left hand pair of columns holds information about the physical volume itself. The right hand pair displays information concerning the volume group of which the physical volume is a member.

Following are the meanings of various fields in the preceding example.

PHYSICAL VOLUME	The name of the specified physical volume.
PV IDENTIFIER	The physical volume identifier (unique to the system).
PV STATE	The state of the physical volume. This defines whether or not the physical volume is available for logical input/output operations. It can be changed using the chpv command.
STALE PARTITIONS	The number of stale partitions.
PP SIZE	The size of a physical partition. This is a characteristic of the volume group and is set only at the creation of the volume group as an argument to the mkvg command. The default size is 4 MB.
TOTAL PPs	The total number of physical partitions, including both free and used partitions available on the physical volume.
FREE PPs	The number of free partitions available on the physical volume.
USED PPs	The number of used partitions on the physical volume.
FREE DISTRIBUTION	This field summarizes the distribution of free physical partitions across the physical volume, according to the sections of the physical volume on which they reside.
USED DISTRIBUTION	Same as free distribution, except that it displays the allocation of used physical partitions.
VOLUME GROUP	The name of the volume group to which the physical volume is allocated.
VG IDENTIFIER	The numerical identifier of the volume group to which the physical volume is allocated.

VG STATE — State of the volume group. If the volume group is activated with the `varyonvg` command, the state is either active/complete (indicating all physical volumes are active) or active/partial (indicating some physical volumes are not active). If the volume group is not activated with the `varyonvg` command, the state is inactive.

ALLOCATABLE — Whether the system is permitted to allocate new physical partitions on this physical volume.

LOGICAL VOLUMES — The number of the logical volumes in the volume group.

VG DESCRIPTORS — The number of VGDAs for this volume group which reside on this particular physical volume.

5.2.5.3 Listing Logical Volume Allocation within a PV

The following example shows the `lspv` command with the `-l` option to list the physical volume `hdisk1`. The output shows the name of all the logical volumes on the physical volume, the number of physical and logical partitions allocated, the distribution across the physical volume, and the mount point, if it exists.

```
# lspv -l hdisk1
hdisk1:
LV NAME          LPs   PPs   DISTRIBUTION          MOUNT POINT
rawlv            1     1     01..00..00..00..00    N/A
hd4              2     2     02..00..00..00..00    /
hd9var           1     1     01..00..00..00..00    /var
hd3              8     8     01..00..07..00..00    /tmp
lv06             5     5     00..05..00..00..00    /home2
lv07             13    13    00..13..00..00..00    /backfs
rawlv1           2     2     00..02..00..00..00    N/A
copied           2     2     00..02..00..00..00    N/A
newlv            1     1     00..01..00..00..00    N/A
fslv00           1     1     00..01..00..00..00    N/A
hd6              1     1     00..01..00..00..00    N/A
mytest           1     1     00..01..00..00..00    N/A
#
```

5.2.5.4 Listing Physical Partition Allocation by PV Region

The example provided in Figure 32 shows how to retrieve more detailed information about the range of physical partitions allocated to a logical volume and the region of disk used for those partitions.

```
# lspv -p hdisk1
hdisk1:
PP RANGE  STATE   REGION        LV NAME             TYPE       MOUNT POINT
  1-2     used    outer edge    hd5                 boot       N/A
  3-19    free    outer edge
 20-30    used    outer edge    hd2                 jfs        /usr
 31-31    used    outer edge    hd4                 jfs        /
 32-103   used    outer edge    hd2                 jfs        /usr
104-143   used    outer middle  paging01            paging     N/A
144-170   used    outer middle  hd2                 jfs        /usr
171-173   free    outer middle
174-174   used    outer middle  hd6                 paging     N/A
175-179   free    outer middle
180-184   used    outer middle  paging02            paging     N/A
185-192   used    outer middle  hd1                 jfs        /home
193-195   used    outer middle  lv01                jfs        /var/dce
196-205   used    outer middle  lv02                jfs        /var/dce/adm/dfs/
cache
206-206   used    outer middle  hd2                 jfs        /usr
207-207   used    center        hd8                 jfslog     N/A
208-208   used    center        hd4                 jfs        /
209-217   used    center        hd2                 jfs        /usr
218-218   used    center        hd9var              jfs        /var
219-221   used    center        hd3                 jfs        /tmp
222-222   used    center        hd1                 jfs        /home
223-285   used    center        hd2                 jfs        /usr
286-286   used    center        hd3                 jfs        /tmp
287-309   used    center        hd2                 jfs        /usr
310-412   used    inner middle  hd2                 jfs        /usr
413-447   used    inner edge    hd6                 paging     N/A
448-515   free    inner edge
#
```

Figure 32. Status and Characteristics of hdisk1 by Physical Partitions

The following is the description of the fields shown in the preceding example.

Field	Description
PP RANGE	The range of physical partitions for which the current row of data applies.
STATE	Whether or not the partitions have been allocated. Value can be either used or free.
REGION	Notional region of the disk within which the partitions are located.
LV NAME	Name of the logical volume to which the partitions in question have been allocated.
TYPE	Type of file system residing on the logical volume.
MOUNT POINT	Mount point of the file system, if applicable.

5.2.5.5 Listing Physical Partition Allocation Table

To determine the degree of contiguity of data on the system in order to improve the I/O performance of a logical volume you can use the `lspv` command with the `-M` option as shown in Figure 33. You may decide to reorganize the system after analyzing the output.

```
# lspv -M hdisk0
hdisk0:1-17
hdisk0:18       lv03:1
hdisk0:19       lv03:2
hdisk0:20       lv03:3
hdisk0:21       lv03:4
hdisk0:22-33
hdisk0:34       paging00:1
hdisk0:35       paging00:2
hdisk0:36       paging00:3
hdisk0:37       paging00:4
hdisk0:38       paging00:5
hdisk0:39       paging00:6
hdisk0:40       paging00:7
hdisk0:41       paging00:8
hdisk0:42       paging00:9
hdisk0:43       paging00:10
hdisk0:44       paging00:11
hdisk0:45       paging00:12
hdisk0:46       paging00:13
hdisk0:47       paging00:14
hdisk0:48       paging00:15
hdisk0:49       paging00:16
hdisk0:50       paging00:17
hdisk0:51       paging00:18
hdisk0:52       paging00:19
hdisk0:53       paging00:20
hdisk0:54       paging00:21
hdisk0:55       paging00:22
hdisk0:56       paging00:23
hdisk0:57       paging00:24
hdisk0:58-81
#
```

Figure 33. Physical Partition Allocation by Disk Region

The first column indicates the physical partition (if a group of contiguous partitions are free, it will indicate a range of partitions) for a particular hard disk. The second column indicates which logical partition of which logical volume is associated with that physical partition.

5.2.6 Migrating the Contents of a Physical Volume

The physical partitions belonging to one or more specified logical volumes can be moved from one physical volume to one or more other physical volumes within a volume group using the `migratepv` command.

Note

The `migratepv` command cannot move data between different volume groups, as shown in Figure 34.

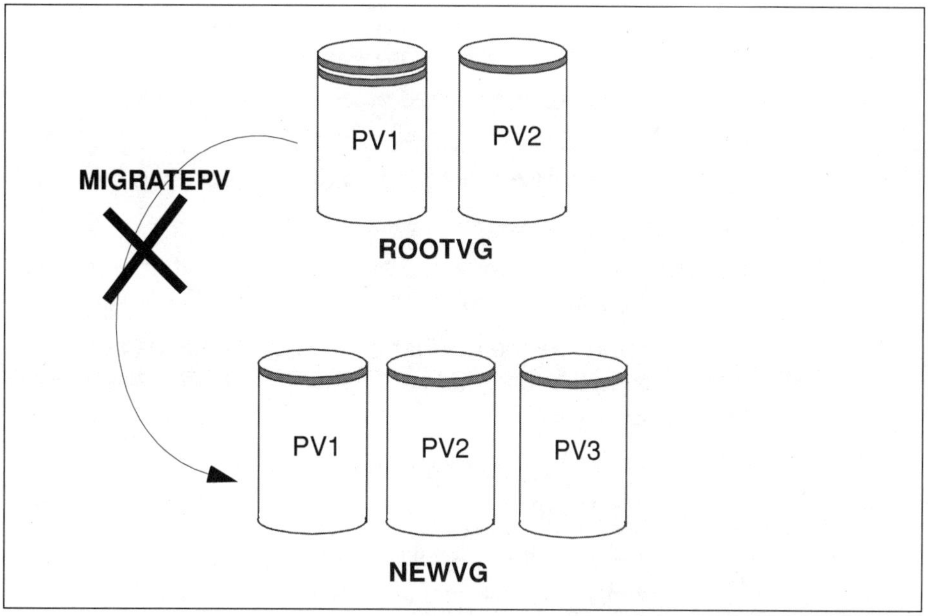

Figure 34. migratepv Does Not Work across Volume Groups

The following procedure describes how to move the data from a failing disk before it is removed for repair or replacement.

1. Determine which disks are in the volume group. Make sure that the source and destination physical volumes are in the same volume group. If the source and destination physical volumes are in the same volume group, proceed to step 3.

```
# lsvg -p hdisk0
rootvg:
    PV_NAME    PV STATE    TOTAL PPs    FREE PPs    FREE DISTRIBUTION
    hdisk0     active      159          0           00..00..00..00..00
```

2. If you are planning to migrate to a new disk, such as when you have a failing disk, perform the following steps:

   a. Make sure the disk is available by entering the following.

   ```
   # lsdev -Cc disk
   ```

```
hdisk0  Available  00-08-00-30  670 MB  SCSI  Disk Drive
hdisk1  Available  00-08-00-20  857 MB  SCSI  Disk Drive
```

b. If the disk is listed and in the available state, make sure it does not belong to another volume group using the following command. (In the following example, `hdisk1` can be used as a destination disk.)

```
# lspv
hdisk0      0000078752249812   rootvg
hdisk1      000000234ac56e9e   none
```

c. If the disk is not listed or is not available, you need to check or install the disk.

d. Add the new disk to the volume group using the command:

```
extendvg VGName hdiskNumber
```

3. Make sure that you have enough room on the target disk for the source that you want to move.

a. Determine the number of physical partitions on the source disk by using the following command. (SourceDiskNumber will be of the form `hdiskNumber`.)

```
lspv SourceDiskNumber | grep "USED PPs"
```

The output will look similar to the following:

```
USED PPs:      159 (636 megabytes)
```

In this example, you would need 159 free PPs on the destination disk to successfully complete the migration.

b. Determine the number of free physical partitions on the destination disk or disks using the following command for each destination disk (DestinationDiskNumber will be of the form `hdiskNumber`.)

```
lspv DestinationDiskNumber | grep "FREE PPs"
```

Add the free PPs from all of the destination disks. If the sum is larger than the number of USED PPs from step 3, you will have enough space for the migration.

4. Follow this step only if you are migrating data from a disk in the rootvg volume group. If you are migrating data from a disk in a user-defined volume group, proceed to step 5.

Check to see if the boot logical volume (`hd5`) is on the source disk:

```
lspv -l SourceDiskNumber | grep hd5
```

If you get no output, the boot logical volume is not located on the source disk. Continue to step 5.

If you get output similar to the following:

```
hd5              2   2   02..00..00..00..00   /blv
```

then run the following command:

`migratepv -l hd5 SourceDiskNumber DestinationDiskNumber`

Note

- This `migratepv` command is not allowed if the volume group is varied on in concurrent mode.
- The `migratepv` command cannot migrate striped logical volumes. To move data from one physical volume to another, use the `cplv` command to copy the data and then use the `rmlv` command to remove the old copy.
- You must either have root user authority or be a member of the system group to execute the `migratepv` command.

Next, you will get a message warning you to perform the `bosboot` command on the destination disk.

Note

When the boot logical volume is migrated from a physical volume, the boot record on the source should be cleared. Failure to clear this record may result in a system hang. When you execute the `bosboot` command, you must also execute `mkboot -c`.

Execute the `mkboot -c` command to clear the boot record on the source. Do the following:

```
bosboot -a -d /dev/DestinationDiskNumber
```

then:

```
bootlist -m normal DestinationDiskNumber
```

then:

```
mkboot -c -d /dev/SourceDiskNumber
```

5. Executing the SMIT fast path command `smitty migratepv` to migrate the data will show a screen similar to Figure 35 on page 70.

```
                         Move Contents of a Physical Volume

Type or select values in entry fields.
Press Enter AFTER making all desired changes.

                                                        [Entry Fields]
* SOURCE physical volume name                          hdisk1
* DESTINATION physical volumes                         [hdisk4]                +
  Move only data belonging to this                     []                      +
    LOGICAL VOLUME?










F1=Help             F2=Refresh          F3=Cancel           F4=List
F5=Reset            F6=Command          F7=Edit             F8=Image
F9=Shell            F10=Exit            Enter=Do
```

Figure 35. smitty migratepv Command

6. List the physical volumes (**PF4**), and select the source physical volume you examined previously.
7. Go to the DESTINATION physical volume field. If you accept the default, all the physical volumes in the volume group are available for the transfer. Otherwise, select one or more disks with adequate space for the partitions you will be moving (from step 4).
8. If you wish, go to the Move only data belonging to this LOGICAL VOLUME field, and list and select a logical volume. You will move only the physical partitions allocated to the logical volume specified that are located on the physical volume selected as the source physical volume.
9. Press **Enter** to move the physical partitions.
10. To remove the source disk from the volume group, such as when it is failing, enter the following command:

    ```
    reducevg VGNname SourceDiskNumber
    ```

11. To physically remove the source disk from the system, such as when it is failing, enter the following command:

    ```
    rmdev -l SourceDiskNumber -d
    ```

Following are a few more examples of using the `migratepv` command.

- Use the following command to move physical partitions from `hdisk1` to `hdisk6` and `hdisk7`. All physical volumes are in one volume group.

```
migratepv hdisk1 hdisk6 hdisk7
```

- Use the following command to move physical partitions in logical volume `lv02` from `hdisk1` to `hdisk6`.

```
migratepv -l lv02 hdisk1 hdisk6
```

5.3 Managing Volume Groups

This section discusses the functions that can be performed on volume groups. As with physical volumes, volume groups can be created and removed, and their characteristics can be modified. Additional functions such as activating and deactivating volume groups can also be performed.

5.3.1 Adding a Volume Group

Before a new volume group can be added to the system, one or more physical volumes, not used in other volume groups, and in an available state, must exist on the system.

It is important to decide upon certain information such as the volume group name and the physical volumes to use prior to adding a volume group.

New volume groups can be added to the system by using the `mkvg` command or by using SMIT. Of all the characteristics set at creation time of the volume group, the following are essentially the most important:

- Volume group name shall be unique on the system
- Names of all physical volumes to be used in the new volume group
- Maximum number of physical volumes that can exist in the volume group
- Physical partition size for the volume group
- Flag to activate the volume group automatically at each system restart

The following example shows the use of the `mkvg` command to create a volume group, `myvg`, using the physical volumes `hdisk1` and `hdisk5`, with a physical partition size of 8 KB. The volume group is limited to a maximum of 10 physical volumes.

```
mkvg -y myvg -d 10 -s 8 hdisk1 hdisk5
```

Alternatively, you can use the SMIT fast path command, `smitty mkvg` to obtain the screen shown in Figure 36 and enter the characteristics of the volume group to be created in the fields.

```
                              Add a Volume Group

Type or select values in entry fields.
Press Enter AFTER making all desired changes.

                                                      [Entry Fields]
  VOLUME GROUP name                                 []
  Physical partition SIZE in megabytes               4                       +
* PHYSICAL VOLUME names                             []                       +
  Activate volume group AUTOMATICALLY                yes                     +
    at system restart?
  Volume Group MAJOR NUMBER                         []                      +#
  Create VG Concurrent Capable?                      no                      +
  Auto-varyon in Concurrent Mode?                    no                      +




F1=Help            F2=Refresh          F3=Cancel          F4=List
F5=Reset           F6=Command          F7=Edit            F8=Image
F9=Shell           F10=Exit            Enter=Do
```

Figure 36. smitty mkvg Command

The `smitty mkvg` command will automatically activate the volume group by calling the `varyonvg` command. Moreover, the SMIT command limits the followings function as compared to command line.

- `smitty mkvg` does not provide the -d flag to set the maximum number of physical volumes. It uses a default value of 32.
- `smitty mkvg` does not provide the -m flag to set the maximum size of the physical volume. This flag will determine how many physical partitions are used. It uses a default value of 1016 partitions.
- `smitty mkvg` always uses the -f flag to force creation of the volume group.

Note

For a new volume group to be successfully added to the system using the `mkvg` command, the root file system should have about 2 MB of free space. Check this using the `df` command. This free space is required because a file is written in the directory /etc/vg each time a new volume group is added.

5.3.2 Modifying Volume Group Characteristics

The following sections discuss the tasks required to modify a volume group's characteristics.

5.3.2.1 Adding a Physical Volume

It may be necessary to increase the free space available in a volume group so that existing file systems and logical volumes within the volume group can be extended, or new ones can be added. To do this requires additional physical volumes be made available within the volume group.

It is possible to add physical volumes to a volume group, up to the maximum specified at creation time. A physical volume can be added using the `extendvg` command. The following example shows the command to add the physical volume, `hdisk3`, to volume group `newvg`.

```
extendvg newvg hdisk3
```

> **Note**
>
> The `extendvg` command will fail if the physical volume being added already belongs to a varied on volume group on the current system. Also, if the physical volume being added belongs to a volume group that is currently not varied on, the user will be asked to confirm whether or not to continue.

Alternatively, you can use the SMIT fast path command `smitty vgsc` and select the option **Add a Physical Volume to a Volume Group**.

5.3.2.2 Removing a Physical Volume

The volume group must be varied on before it can be reduced. The following example shows how to remove a physical volume, `hdisk3`, from a volume group, `myvg`.

```
reducevg myvg hdisk3
```

Alternatively, you can use the SMIT fast path command `smitty reducevg` to remove a physical volume from a volume group.

> **Note**
>
> The `reducevg` command provides the -d and -f flags.
>
> - The -d flag can be dangerous because it automatically deletes all logical volume data on the physical volume before removing the physical volume from the volume group. If a logical volume spans multiple physical volumes, the removal of any of those physical volumes may jeopardize the integrity of the entire logical volume.
> - The -f flag makes the -d flag even more dangerous by suppressing interaction with a user requesting confirmation that the logical volume should be deleted.

If the logical volumes on the physical volume specified to be removed also span other physical volumes in the volume group, the removal operation may destroy the integrity of those logical volumes, regardless of the physical volume on which they reside.

When you remove all physical volumes in a volume group, the volume group itself is also removed.

5.3.2.3 Removing a Physical Volume Reference

Sometimes a disk is removed from the system without first running `reducevg VolumeGroup PhysicalVolume`. The VGDA still has the removed disk's reference, but the physical volume name no longer exists or has been reassigned. To remove references to the disk which has been removed, you can still use the `reducevg` command using the PVID of the physical volume removed. The following command will remove the reference of a physical volume (with PVID of 000005265ac63976) from the volume group newvg.

```
reducevg VolumeGroup PVID
```

5.3.3 Importing and Exporting a Volume Group

There may be times when a volume group needs to be moved from one RISC System/6000 system to another, so that logical volume and file system data in the volume group can be accessed directly on the target system.

To remove the system definition of a volume group from the ODM database, the volume group needs to be exported using the `exportvg` command. This command will not remove any user data in the volume group, but will only remove its definition from the ODM database.

Similarly, when a volume group is moved, the target system needs to add the definition of the new volume group. This can be achieved by importing the volume group using the `importvg` command, which will add an entry to the ODM database.

The following example shows the export of a volume group `myvg`.

```
exportvg myvg
```

And the following example shows the import of a volume group `myvg`.

```
importvg myvg
```

You can also use SMIT fast path commands, `smitty exportvg` or `smitty importvg`, to export or import a volume group.

If the specified volume group name is already in use, the `importvg` command will fail with an appropriate error message, since duplicate volume group names are not allowed. In this instance, the command can be rerun with a unique volume group name specified, or it can be rerun without the -y flag or the volume group name, which gives the imported volume group a unique system default name. It is also possible that some logical volume names may also conflict with those already on the system. The `importvg` command will automatically reassign these with system default names. The important thing to remember when moving volume groups from system to system, is that the `exportvg` command is always run on the source system prior to importing the volume group to the target system. Consider that a volume group is imported on system Y without actually performing an `exportvg` on system X. If system Y makes a change to the volume group, such as removing a physical volume from the volume group, and the volume group is imported back onto system X, the ODM database on system X will not be consistent with the changed information for this volume group.

It is, however, worth noting that a volume group can be moved to another system without first being exported on the source system.

Note

- The `importvg` command changes the name of an imported logical volume if there currently is a logical volume with the same name already on the system. An error message is printed to standard error if an imported logical volume is renamed. The `importvg` command also creates file mount points and entries in /etc/filesystems if possible (if there are no conflicts).
- A volume group that has a paging space volume on it cannot be exported while the paging space is active. Before exporting a volume group with an active paging space, ensure that the paging space is not activated automatically at system initialization by running the following command:

  ```
  chps -a n paging_space name
  ```

  Then, reboot the system so that the paging space is inactive.
- If you do not activate the volume group through `smitty importvg`, you must run the `varyonvg` command to enable access to the file systems and logical volumes.
- If you imported a volume group that contains file systems, or if you activated the volume group through `smitty importvg`, it is highly recommended that you run the `fsck` command before you mount the file systems. If you are moving the volume group to another system, be sure to unconfigure the disks before moving them.
- The `smitty exportvg` command deletes references to file systems in /etc/filesystems, but it leaves the mount points on the system.

5.3.4 Varying On and Varying Off Volume Groups

Once a volume group exists, it can be made available for use for system administrative activities using the `varyonvg` command. This process involves the following steps.

1. Each VGDA on each physical volume in a volume group is read.
2. The header and trailer time stamps within each VGDA are read. These time stamps must match for a VGDA to be valid.
3. If a majority of VGDAs (called the quorum) are valid, then the vary on process proceeds. If they are not, then the vary on fails.

4. The system will take the most recent VGDA (the one with the latest time stamp) and write it over all other VGDAs so they match.
5. The `syncvg` command is run to resynchronize any stale partition present (in the case where mirroring is in use).

The `varyonvg` command has the following options that can be used to overcome damage to the volume group structure or give status information.

- The -f flag can be used to force a volume group to be varied on even when inconsistencies are detected. These inconsistencies are generally differences between the configuration data for each volume group held in the ODM database and VGDA.
- The -n flag will suppress the invocation of the `syncvg` command at vary on time. When a volume group is varied on, and stale partitions are detected, the vary on process will invoke the `syncvg` command to synchronize the stale partitions. This option is of value when you wish to carefully recover a volume group and you want to ensure that you do not accidentally write bad mirrored copies of data over good copies.
- The -s flag allows a volume group to be varied on in maintenance or systems management mode. Logical volume commands can operate on the volume group, but no logical volume can be opened for input or output.

The following example shows the command to activate a volume group, `newvg`.

```
varyonvg newvg
```

You can also use SMIT fast path command, `smitty varyonvg`, to obtain the screen shown in Figure 37 and enter the name of volume group to be varied on along with all the options.

```
                        Activate a Volume Group

Type or select values in entry fields.
Press Enter AFTER making all desired changes.

                                                        [Entry Fields]
* VOLUME GROUP name                                   []                      +
  RESYNCHRONIZE stale physical partitions?             yes                    +
  Activate volume group in SYSTEM                      no                     +
    MANAGEMENT mode?
  FORCE activation of the volume group?                no                     +
   Warning--this may cause loss of data
   integrity.
  Varyon VG in Concurrent Mode?                        no                     +







F1=Help             F2=Refresh          F3=Cancel           F4=List
F5=Reset            F6=Command          F7=Edit             F8=Image
F9=Shell            F10=Exit            Enter=Do
```

Figure 37. smitty varyonvg Command

The `varyoffvg` command will deactivate a volume group and its associated logical volumes. This requires that the logical volumes be closed which requires that file systems associated with logical volumes be unmounted. The `varyoffvg` also allows the use of the -s flag to move the volume group from being active to being in maintenance or systems management mode.

Note

In AIX Version 4, when a volume group is imported it is automatically varied on, whereas, in AIX Version 3, the volume group has to be varied on separately.

The following example shows the command to deactivate a volume group, `myvg`.

```
varyoffvg myvg
```

You can also use SMIT fast path command, `smitty varyoffvg`, which will show a screen as in Figure 38 on page 79. You can enter the name of volume group to be varied off and you can also put the volume group in system management mode.

```
                    Deactivate a Volume Group

Type or select values in entry fields.
Press Enter AFTER making all desired changes.

                                                    [Entry Fields]
* VOLUME GROUP name                               []                  +
  Put volume group in SYSTEM                       no                 +
    MANAGEMENT mode?













F1=Help             F2=Refresh          F3=Cancel           F4=List
F5=Reset            F6=Command          F7=Edit             F8=Image
F9=Shell            F10=Exit            Enter=Do
```

Figure 38. smitty varyoffvg Command

5.3.5 Monitoring Volume Groups

The `lsvg` command interrogates the ODM database for all volume groups currently known to the system. The following are a few examples showing the use of the `lsvg` command to monitor volume groups.

5.3.5.1 Listing the Volume Groups

The following example shows the use of the `lsvg` command without any flag to list all the volume groups known to the system.

```
# lsvg
rootvg
altinst_rootvg
datavg
testvg
#
```

The following example shows how to list the volume groups which are currently active (varied on).

```
# lsvg -o
testvg
datavg
rootvg
```

5.3.5.2 Listing the Characteristics of a Volume Group

The example in Figure 39 shows the command to list detailed information and status about volume group characteristics.

```
# lsvg rootvg
VOLUME GROUP:     rootvg                VG IDENTIFIER:   00615151e5394126
VG STATE:         active                PP SIZE:         4 megabyte(s)
VG PERMISSION:    read/write            TOTAL PPs:       596 (2384 megabytes)
MAX LVs:          256                   FREE PPs:        146 (584 megabytes)
LVs:              14                    USED PPs:        450 (1800 megabytes)
OPEN LVs:         13                    QUORUM:          2
TOTAL PVs:        2                     VG DESCRIPTORS:  3
STALE PVs:        0                     STALE PPs:       0
ACTIVE PVs:       2                     AUTO ON:         yes
MAX PPs per PV:   1016                  MAX PVs:         32
#
```

Figure 39. lsvg rootvg Command

5.3.5.3 Listing the Logical Volumes in a Volume Group

The example in Figure 40 shows the command used to display the names, characteristics, and status of all the logical volumes in volume group `rootvg`.

```
# lsvg -l rootvg
rootvg:
LV NAME       TYPE     LPs   PPs   PVs  LV STATE       MOUNT POINT
hd5           boot     2     2     1    closed/syncd   N/A
hd6           paging   36    36    1    open/syncd     N/A
hd8           jfslog   1     1     1    open/syncd     N/A
hd4           jfs      2     2     1    open/syncd     /
hd2           jfs      309   309   1    open/syncd     /usr
hd9var        jfs      1     1     1    open/syncd     /var
hd3           jfs      4     4     1    open/syncd     /tmp
hd1           jfs      9     9     1    open/syncd     /home
paging00      paging   24    24    1    open/syncd     N/A
paging01      paging   40    40    1    open/syncd     N/A
lv01          jfs      3     3     1    open/syncd     /var/dce
lv02          jfs      10    10    1    open/syncd     /var/dce/adm/dfs/c
lv03          jfs      4     4     1    open/syncd     /usr/vice/cache
paging02      paging   5     5     1    open/syncd     N/A
#
```

Figure 40. lsvg -l rootvg Command

5.3.5.4 List the Physical Volume Status within a Volume Group

The example shown in Figure 41 on page 81 shows the use of the `lsvg` command with the -p flag to display a list of physical volumes contained in a volume group, as well as some status information including physical partition allocation. This form of the lsvg command is useful for summarizing the concentrations of free space on the system.

```
# lsvg -p rootvg
rootvg:
PV_NAME          PV STATE    TOTAL PPs   FREE PPs    FREE DISTRIBUTION
hdisk1           active      515         93          17..08..00..00..68
hdisk0           active      81          53          17..12..00..08..16
#
```

Figure 41. lsvg -p vgname Command

Following is the description of the various fields shown in the preceding example.

PV_NAME
: The name of the physical volume.

PV STATE
: Whether or not this physical volume is active.

TOTAL PPs
: The total number of physical partitions on this physical volume.

FREE PPs
: The total number of unused physical partitions on this physical volume.

FREE DISTRIBUTION
: The location of the free physical partitions on the physical volumes. There are five columns, one for each disk region, in the following order: Outside edge, Outside middle, Center, Inside middle, Inside edge.

5.3.6 Reorganizing Volume Groups

The reorgvg command is used to reorganizes the physical partition allocation for a volume group according to the allocation characteristics of each logical volume.

Following is the syntax of the reorgvg command.

```
reorgvg [ -i ] VolumeGroup [ LogicalVolume ... ]
```

The volume group must be varied on and must have free partitions before you can use the reorgvg command. The relocatable flag of each logical volume must be set to y using the chlv -r command for the reorganization to take effect; otherwise, the logical volume is ignored.

Note

1. The `reorgvg` command does not reorganize the placement of allocated physical partitions for any striped logical volumes.
2. At least one free physical partition must exist on the specified volume group for the `reorgvg` command to run successfully.
3. If you enter the `reorgvg` command with the volume group name and no other arguments, it will only reorganize the first logical volume in the volume group. The first logical volume is the one listed by the `lsvg -l VolumeName` command.

In AIX Version 4.2 or later, if you enter the `reorgvg` command with the volume group name and no other arguments, the entire volume group is reorganized.

You can also use the SMIT fast path command, `smitty reorgvg` to do the same task. See Table 5 for details on the flags for the `reorgvg` command.

Table 5. reorgvg Command Flags

Flag	Description
-i	Specifies physical volume names read from standard input. Only the partitions on these physical volumes are organized.

- The following command reorganizes the logical volumes lv03, lv04, and lv07 on volume group vg02.

  ```
  reorgvg vg02 lv03 lv04 lv07
  ```

  Only the listed logical volumes are reorganized on vg02.

- The following example shows how to reorganize the partitions located on physical volumes `hdisk04` and `hdisk06` that belong to logical volumes `lv203` and `lv205`.

  ```
  echo "hdisk04 hdisk06" | reorgvg -i vg02 lv203 lv205
  ```

  Only the partitions located on physical volumes `hdisk04` and `hdisk06` of volume group `vg02`, which belong to logical volumes `lv203` and `lv205`, are reorganized.

5.3.7 Synchronizing the Volume Group

The `syncvg` command is used to synchronize logical volume copies that are not current (stale).

Following is the syntax of `syncvg` command.

```
syncvg [ -f ] [ -i ] [ -H ] [ -P NumParallelLps ] { -l | -p | -v }
Name ...
```

The `syncvg` command synchronizes the physical partitions, which are copies of the original physical partition that are not current. The `syncvg` command can be used with logical volumes, physical volumes, or volume groups, with the Name parameter representing the logical volume name, physical volume name, or volume group name. The synchronization process can be time consuming, depending on the hardware characteristics and the amount of data.

When the -f flag is used, an uncorrupted physical copy is chosen and propagated to all other copies of the logical partition, whether or not they are stale.

Unless disabled, the copies within a volume group are synchronized automatically when the volume group is activated by the `varyonvg` command. The commonly used flags with the `syncvg` command are shown in Table 6.

Table 6. Key Flags for the syncvg Command

Flag	Description
-p	Specifies that the Name parameter represents a physical volume device name.
-v	Specifies that the Name parameter represents a volume group device name.

The following examples show the use of the `syncvg` command.

- To synchronize the copies on physical volumes `hdisk04` and `hdisk05`, execute the following command.

  ```
  syncvg -p hdisk04 hdisk05
  ```

- To synchronize the copies on volume groups `vg04` and `vg05`, execute the following command.

  ```
  syncvg -v vg04 vg05
  ```

5.3.8 Creating a New Partition on a Disk That Already Has a Partition

This section describes how to move a volume group from one disk onto another disk. A problem faced will be that the new disk already has a volume group.

To migrate the information from the physical volume `hdisk4` to the physical volume `hdisk3` enter:

```
# migratepv hdisk4 hdisk3
0516-806 migratepv: Destination physical volume hdisk3 belongs
        to wrong volume group.
# lspv
hdisk0          000919746edab91f    rootvg
hdisk1          0009197459d92f2e    None
hdisk2          00091974d381d097    uservg
hdisk3          00091974d81ff431    newvg
hdisk4          00091974de731316    uservg
```

The easiest option is to move `hdisk4` to `hdisk1`. The command for this is:

```
migratepv hdisk4 hdisk1
```

The other option is to delete the volume group newvg. Any file systems associated with newvg and any logical volumes associated with newvg must be removed.

List the file system information and look for the `newlv` logical volume. Notice it is mounted on /u1.

```
# lsfs
Name                Nodename   Mount Pt                VFS   Size    Options
Auto Accounting
/dev/hd4            --         /                       jfs   32768   --       yes
no
/dev/hd1            --         /home                   jfs   3276800 --       yes
no
/dev/hd2            --         /usr                    jfs   4702208 --       yes
no
/dev/hd9var         --         /var                    jfs   16384   --       yes
no
/dev/hd3            --         /tmp                    jfs   32768   --       yes
no
/dev/userlv         --         /u                      jfs   3276800 rw       yes
no
/dev/newlv          --         /u1                     jfs   3276800 rw       yes
no
```

List the volume group to find the logical volume information. Notice the `newlv` and `loglv01` LV names.

```
# lsvg -o | lsvg -l newvg
newvg:
LV NAME        TYPE    LPs   PPs   PVs  LV STATE      MOUNT POINT
newlv          jfs     200   200   1    open/syncd    /u1
loglv01        jfslog  1     1     1    open/syncd    N/A
```

List the mount information to check if `newlv` is mounted. Notice that /u is mounted.

```
# mount
  node       mounted        mounted over    vfs       date        options
-------- ---------------  ---------------  ------ ------------ ---------------
         /dev/hd4         /                jfs    Nov 16 18:45 rw,log=/dev/hd8
         /dev/hd2         /usr             jfs    Nov 16 18:45 rw,log=/dev/hd8
         /dev/hd9var      /var             jfs    Nov 16 18:45 rw,log=/dev/hd8
         /dev/hd3         /tmp             jfs    Nov 16 18:45 rw,log=/dev/hd8
         /dev/hd1         /home            jfs    Nov 16 18:46 rw,log=/dev/hd8
         /dev/userlv      /u               jfs    Nov 17 14:12 rw,log=/dev/loglv00
         /dev/newlv       /u1              jfs    Nov 17 14:13 rw,log=/dev/loglv01
```

To unmount the `/dev/newlv` logical volume enter:

```
umount /dev/newlv
```

Type `mount` to check if `/dev/newlv` has ben unmounted. If successful type:

```
smitty lvm
```

At the Logical Volume Manager menu select **Logical Volumes**, as displayed in Figure 42.

```
                              Logical Volume Manager

Move cursor to desired item and press Enter.

  Volume Groups
  Logical Volumes
  Physical Volumes
  Paging Space

F1=Help              F2=Refresh           F3=Cancel            F8=Image
F9=Shell             F10=Exit             Enter=Do
```

Figure 42. Logical Volume Manager Menu

From the Logical Volumes Menu select **Remove a Logical Volume** as displayed in Figure 43 on page 86.

```
                          Logical Volumes

Move cursor to desired item and press Enter.

  List All Logical Volumes by Volume Group
  Add a Logical Volume
  Set Characteristic of a Logical Volume
  Show Characteristics of a Logical Volume
  Remove a Logical Volume
  Copy a Logical Volume








F1=Help            F2=Refresh         F3=Cancel          F8=Image
F9=Shell           F10=Exit           Enter=Do
```

Figure 43. Logical Volumes Menu

From the Remove a Logical Volume menu, enter the Logical volume name you want removed, as displayed in Figure 44.

```
                       Remove a Logical Volume

Type or select values in entry fields.
Press Enter AFTER making all desired changes.

                                                      [Entry Fields]
  LOGICAL VOLUME name                               [newlv]              +








F1=Help            F2=Refresh         F3=Cancel          F4=List
F5=Reset           F6=Command         F7=Edit            F8=Image
F9=Shell           F10=Exit           Enter=Do
```

Figure 44. Remove a Logical Volume Menu

In Figure 45 is the confirmation screen to continue. Press **Enter** to continue.

```
                         Remove a Logical Volume

Type or select values in entry fields.
Press Enter AFTER making all desired changes.

                                                         [Entry Fields]
  LOGICAL VOLUME name                                   [newlv]          +



  ┌──────────────────────────────────────────────────────────────────────┐
  │                           ARE YOU SURE?                              │
  │                                                                      │
  │ Continuing may delete information you may want                       │
  │ to keep.  This is your last chance to stop                           │
  │ before continuing.                                                   │
  │     Press Enter to continue.                                         │
  │     Press Cancel to return to the application.                       │
  │                                                                      │
F1│ F1=Help                  F2=Refresh               F3=Cancel          │
F5│ F8=Image                 F10=Exit                 Enter=Do           │
F9└──────────────────────────────────────────────────────────────────────┘
```

Figure 45. Remove a Logical Volume - Confirmation Screen

Once completed, the system will display the command status as in Figure 46 on page 88.

```
                                COMMAND STATUS

Command: OK            stdout: yes           stderr: no

Before command completion, additional instructions may appear below.

rmlv: Logical volume newlv is removed.
















F1=Help             F2=Refresh          F3=Cancel           F6=Command
F8=Image            F9=Shell            F10=Exit            /=Find
n=Find Next
```

Figure 46. Command Status Window - Remove a Logical Volume

Once the Logical Volume has been removed, the Volume Group must be removed. Press **F3** until you get to the Logical Volume Manager menu, then select **Volume Groups** as displayed in Figure 47.

```
                           Logical Volume Manager

Move cursor to desired item and press Enter.

  Volume Groups
  Logical Volumes
  Physical Volumes
  Paging Space
















F1=Help             F2=Refresh          F3=Cancel           F8=Image
F9=Shell            F10=Exit            Enter=Do
```

Figure 47. Logical Volume Manager Menu

In the Volume Groups menu select **Remove a Volume Group** as displayed in Figure 48.

```
                              Volume Groups

Move cursor to desired item and press Enter.

  List All Volume Groups
  Add a Volume Group
  Set Characteristics of a Volume Group
  List Contents of a Volume Group
  Remove a Volume Group
  Activate a Volume Group
  Deactivate a Volume Group
  Import a Volume Group
  Export a Volume Group
  Mirror a Volume Group
  Unmirror a Volume Group
  Synchronize LVM Mirrors
  Back Up a Volume Group
  Remake a Volume Group
  List Files in a Volume Group Backup
  Restore Files in a Volume Group Backup


F1=Help             F2=Refresh          F3=Cancel           F8=Image
F9=Shell            F10=Exit            Enter=Do
```

Figure 48. Volume Groups Menu

From the Remove a Volume Group menu, select the VOLUME GROUP name to be removed as displayed in Figure 49 on page 90.

```
                          Remove a Volume Group

Type or select a value for the entry field.
Press Enter AFTER making all desired changes.

                                                  [Entry Fields]
* VOLUME GROUP name                              [newvg]                +















F1=Help             F2=Refresh          F3=Cancel           F4=List
F5=Reset            F6=Command          F7=Edit             F8=Image
F9=Shell            F10=Exit            Enter=Do
```

Figure 49. Remove a Volume Group Menu

After a selection has been entered for the Volume Group to remove, a confirmation screen is displayed as in Figure 50. Press **Enter** to continue.

```
                          Remove a Volume Group

Type or select a value for the entry field.
Press Enter AFTER making all desired changes.

                                                  [Entry Fields]
* VOLUME GROUP name                              [newvg]                +




  ---------------------------------------------------------------------
  |                         ARE YOU SURE?                             |
  |                                                                   |
  | Continuing may delete information you may want                   |
  | to keep.  This is your last chance to stop                        |
  | before continuing.                                                |
  |     Press Enter to continue.                                      |
  |     Press Cancel to return to the application.                    |
  |                                                                   |
F1| F1=Help               F2=Refresh              F3=Cancel           |
F5| F8=Image              F10=Exit                Enter=Do            |
F9---------------------------------------------------------------------
```

Figure 50. Remove a Volume Group Confirmation Window

Figure 51 is the COMMAND STATUS screen confirming a successful removal of the Volume Group.

```
                              COMMAND STATUS

Command: OK            stdout: yes           stderr: no

Before command completion, additional instructions may appear below.

rmlv: Logical volume loglv01 is removed.
ldeletepv: Volume Group deleted since it contains no physical volumes.










F1=Help             F2=Refresh          F3=Cancel           F6=Command
F8=Image            F9=Shell            F10=Exit            /=Find
n=Find Next
```

Figure 51. Command Status Screen for Removal of a Volume Group

Press **F10** to exit to the command prompt.

To check the status of your Physical Volumes enter:

```
# lspv
hdisk0          000919746edab91f    rootvg
hdisk1          0009197459d92f2e    None
hdisk2          00091974d381d097    uservg
hdisk3          00091974d81ff431    None
hdisk4          00091974de731316    uservg
hdisk5          00091974e4f3d56e    None
```

To add the physical volume `hdisk3` to the volume group `uservg` enter:

```
smitty vg
```

From the Volume Groups menu select the **Set Characteristics of a Volume Group** option as displayed in Figure 52 on page 92.

```
                              Volume Groups

Move cursor to desired item and press Enter.

  List All Volume Groups
  Add a Volume Group
  Set Characteristics of a Volume Group
  List Contents of a Volume Group
  Remove a Volume Group
  Activate a Volume Group
  Deactivate a Volume Group
  Import a Volume Group
  Export a Volume Group
  Mirror a Volume Group
  Unmirror a Volume Group
  Synchronize LVM Mirrors
  Back Up a Volume Group
  Remake a Volume Group
  List Files in a Volume Group Backup
  Restore Files in a Volume Group Backup


F1=Help             F2=Refresh          F3=Cancel           F8=Image
F9=Shell            F10=Exit            Enter=Do
```

Figure 52. Volume Groups Menu

From the Set Characteristics of a Volume Group menu, select the **Add a Physical Volume to a Volume Group** option as displayed in Figure 53 on page 93.

```
                         Set Characteristics of a Volume Group

Move cursor to desired item and press Enter.

  Change a Volume Group
  Add a Physical Volume to a Volume Group
  Remove a Physical Volume from a Volume Group
  Reorganize a Volume Group









F1=Help              F2=Refresh           F3=Cancel            F8=Image
F9=Shell             F10=Exit             Enter=Do
```

Figure 53. Set Characteristics of a Volume Group Menu

In the Add a Physical Volume to a Volume Group field, enter the **VOLUME GROUP name** and the **PHYSICAL VOLUME names** as displayed in Figure 54.

```
                        Add a Physical Volume to a Volume Group

Type or select values in entry fields.
Press Enter AFTER making all desired changes.

                                                          [Entry Fields]
* VOLUME GROUP name                                     [uservg]                +
* PHYSICAL VOLUME names                                 [hdisk3]                +








F1=Help              F2=Refresh           F3=Cancel            F4=List
F5=Reset             F6=Command           F7=Edit              F8=Image
F9=Shell             F10=Exit             Enter=Do
```

Figure 54. Add a Physical Volume to a Volume Group Menu

Figure 55 displays the confirmation screen in the Add a Physical Volume to a Volume Group menu. Press **Enter** to continue.

```
                    Add a Physical Volume to a Volume Group

Type or select values in entry fields.
Press Enter AFTER making all desired changes.

                                                        [Entry Fields]
* VOLUME GROUP name                                    [uservg]              +
* PHYSICAL VOLUME names                                [hdisk3]              +




  ARE YOU SURE?

  Continuing may delete information you may want
  to keep.  This is your last chance to stop
  before continuing.
      Press Enter to continue.
      Press Cancel to return to the application.

F1  F1=Help               F2=Refresh              F3=Cancel
F5  F8=Image              F10=Exit                Enter=Do
F9
```

Figure 55. Add a Physical Volume to a Volume Group Confirmation Screen

Once the command has completed, you will see Command: OK as displayed in Figure 56.

```
                                COMMAND STATUS

Command: OK              stdout: no             stderr: no

Before command completion, additional instructions may appear below.





F1=Help              F2=Refresh           F3=Cancel            F6=Command
F8=Image             F9=Shell             F10=Exit             /=Find
n=Find Next
```

Figure 56. Add a Physical Volume to a Volume Group Command Status Screen

Press **F10** to exit to the command prompt. At the command prompt, check the status of your Physical Volume. Enter:

```
# lspv
hdisk0          000919746edab91f    rootvg
hdisk1          0009197459d92f2e    None
hdisk2          00091974d381d097    uservg
hdisk3          00091974d81ff431    uservg
hdisk4          00091974de731316    uservg
hdisk5          00091974e4f3d56e    None
```

To move the information from `hdisk4` to `hdisk3` enter:

```
migratepv hdisk4 hdisk3
```

To remove `hdisk4` from the volume group `uservg` enter:

```
# reducevg uservg hdisk4
# lspv
hdisk0          000919746edab91f    rootvg
hdisk1          0009197459d92f2e    None
hdisk2          00091974d381d097    uservg
hdisk3          00091974d81ff431    uservg
hdisk4          00091974de731316    None
hdisk5          00091974e4f3d56e    None
```

5.3.9 Creating a Volume Group Without Running chdev

In this section, there exists a volume group called `uservg` on hdisk2. You are going to install a new disk and try to extend a `uservg` to use that drive.

List the volume groups to check what is available:

```
# lsvg
rootvg
uservg
newvg
```

List the disk devices on your system by entering:

```
# lsdev -Cc disk
hdisk0 Available 40-58-00-0,0 16 Bit SCSI Disk Drive
hdisk1 Available 40-58-00-1,0 16 Bit SCSI Disk Drive
hdisk2 Available 20-68-L      SSA Logical Disk Drive
hdisk3 Available 20-68-L      SSA Logical Disk Drive
```

Shut the system down and install the new device, boot the machine, log into root and then enter the following:

```
# lsdev -Cc disk
hdisk0 Available 40-58-00-0,0 16 Bit SCSI Disk Drive
hdisk1 Available 40-58-00-1,0 16 Bit SCSI Disk Drive
hdisk2 Available 20-68-L      SSA Logical Disk Drive
hdisk3 Available 20-68-L      SSA Logical Disk Drive
hdisk4 Defined   20-68-L      SSA Logical Disk Drive
```

To check the volume group `uservg`, enter:

```
# lsvg uservg
VOLUME GROUP:   uservg         VG IDENTIFIER:  000919742f85e776
VG STATE:       active         PP SIZE:        8 megabyte(s)
VG PERMISSION:    read/write      TOTAL PPs:       537 (4296 megabytes)
MAX LVs:          256             FREE PPs:        336 (2688 megabytes)
LVs:              2               USED PPs:        201 (1608 megabytes)
OPEN LVs:       2              QUORUM:         2
TOTAL PVs:      1              VG DESCRIPTORS: 2
STALE PVs:      0              STALE PPs:      0
ACTIVE PVs:     1              AUTO ON:        yes
MAX PPs per PV: 1016           MAX PVs:        32
```

To extend the volume group `uservg`, enter the following:

```
smitty vg
```

Select the **Set Characteristics of a Volume Group** option from the Volume Groups menu as displayed in Figure 57.

```
                               Volume Groups

Move cursor to desired item and press Enter.

  List All Volume Groups
  Add a Volume Group
  Set Characteristics of a Volume Group
  List Contents of a Volume Group
  Remove a Volume Group
  Activate a Volume Group
  Deactivate a Volume Group
  Import a Volume Group
  Export a Volume Group
  Mirror a Volume Group
  Unmirror a Volume Group
  Synchronize LVM Mirrors
  Back Up a Volume Group
  Remake a Volume Group
  List Files in a Volume Group Backup
  Restore Files in a Volume Group Backup


F1=Help              F2=Refresh           F3=Cancel            F8=Image
F9=Shell             F10=Exit             Enter=Do
```

Figure 57. The Volume Groups Menu

Select the **Add a Physical Volume to a Volume Group** option in the Set Characteristics of a volume group menu as displayed in Figure 58 on page 98.

```
                    Set Characteristics of a Volume Group

Move cursor to desired item and press Enter.

  Change a Volume Group
  Add a Physical Volume to a Volume Group
  Remove a Physical Volume from a Volume Group
  Reorganize a Volume Group




F1=Help              F2=Refresh          F3=Cancel           F8=Image
F9=Shell             F10=Exit            Enter=Do
```

Figure 58. Set Characteristics of a Volume Group Menu

From the Add a Physical Volume to a Volume Group menu, insert the Volume Group name and the Physical Volume names as displayed in Figure 59.

```
                    Add a Physical Volume to a Volume Group

Type or select values in entry fields.
Press Enter AFTER making all desired changes.

                                                      [Entry Fields]
* VOLUME GROUP name                                [uservg]               +
* PHYSICAL VOLUME names                            [hdisk4]               +




F1=Help              F2=Refresh          F3=Cancel           F4=List
F5=Reset             F6=Command          F7=Edit             F8=Image
F9=Shell             F10=Exit            Enter=Do
```

Figure 59. Add a Physical Volume to a Volume Group Menu

Once the Volume Group and Physical Volume information has been entered, the system will display a confirmation message as displayed in Figure 60.

```
                     Add a Physical Volume to a Volume Group

Type or select values in entry fields.
Press Enter AFTER making all desired changes.

                                                        [Entry Fields]
* VOLUME GROUP name                                   [uservg]                +
* PHYSICAL VOLUME names                               [hdisk4]                +


  ┌──────────────────────────────────────────────────────────────────────────┐
  │                             ARE YOU SURE?                                │
  │                                                                          │
  │ Continuing may delete information you may want                           │
  │ to keep.  This is your last chance to stop                               │
  │ before continuing.                                                       │
  │     Press Enter to continue.                                             │
  │     Press Cancel to return to the application.                           │
  │                                                                          │
F1│ F1=Help                 F2=Refresh              F3=Cancel                │
F5│ F8=Image                F10=Exit                Enter=Do                 │
F9└──────────────────────────────────────────────────────────────────────────┘
```

Figure 60. Add a Physical Volume to a Volume Group Confirmation Display

Figure 61 on page 100 shows the screen for the failed operation. The reason for the failure is that the disk is defined but not available.

```
                              COMMAND STATUS

Command: failed          stdout: yes            stderr: no

Before command completion, additional instructions may appear below.

0516-024 hdisk4: Unable to open physical volume.
        Either PV was not configured or could not be opened. Run
        diagnostics.
0516-792 extendvg: Unable to extend volume group.










F1=Help              F2=Refresh           F3=Cancel            F6=Command
F8=Image             F9=Shell             F10=Exit             /=Find
n=Find Next
```

Figure 61. Command Status for the Add Physical Volume Option

Press **F10** to exit SMIT and then type the following:

```
# mkdev -l 'hdisk4'
hdisk4 Available
```

The device `hdisk4` is now available for the system to create a volume group on.

Go back into the SMIT Volume Group Menu and enter:

```
smitty vg
```

Select the **Set Characteristics of a Volume Group** as displayed in Figure 57 on page 97.

Select the **Add a Physical Volume to a Volume Group** as displayed in Figure 58 on page 98.

Enter the **Volume Group name** and the **Physical Volume names** as displayed in Figure 59 on page 98. At the confirmation window press **Enter** to continue, as displayed in Figure 60 on page 99.

Once the process is complete, the Command Status screen will display `OK` for the successful completion of the command as shown in Figure 62 on page 101.

```
                              COMMAND STATUS

Command: OK              stdout: no              stderr: no

Before command completion, additional instructions may appear below.

F1=Help              F2=Refresh           F3=Cancel            F6=Command
F8=Image             F9=Shell             F10=Exit             /=Find
n=Find Next
```

Figure 62. Successful Completion of Physical Volume Addition to Volume Group

To check the volume group named uservg, enter:

```
# lsvg uservg
VOLUME GROUP:    uservg           VG IDENTIFIER:  000919742f85e776
VG STATE:        active           PP SIZE:        8 megabyte(s)
VG PERMISSION:   read/write       TOTAL PPs:      1074 (8592 megabytes)
MAX LVs:         256              FREE PPs:       873 (6984 megabytes
LLVs:            2                USED PPs:       201 (1608 megabytes)
OPEN LVs:        2                QUORUM:         2
TOTAL PVs:       2                VG DESCRIPTORS: 3
STALE PVs:       2                STALE PPs:      0
ACTIVE PVs:      2                AUTO ON:        yes
MAX PPs per PV:  1016             MAX PVs:        32
```

5.4 Managing Logical Volumes

Physical volumes and volume groups are normally not addressed directly by users and applications to access data, and they cannot be manipulated to provide disk space for use by users and applications. However, logical volumes provide the mechanism to make disk space available for use, giving users and applications the ability to access data stored on them.

When you create a logical volume, you specify the number of logical partitions for the logical volume. A logical partition maps to one, two, or three physical partitions, depending on the number of copies of your data you want to maintain. For example, you can specify a logical volume to be mirrored and have more than one copy as shown in Figure 63. One copy of the logical volume (the default) indicates that there is a direct mapping of one logical partition to one physical partition.

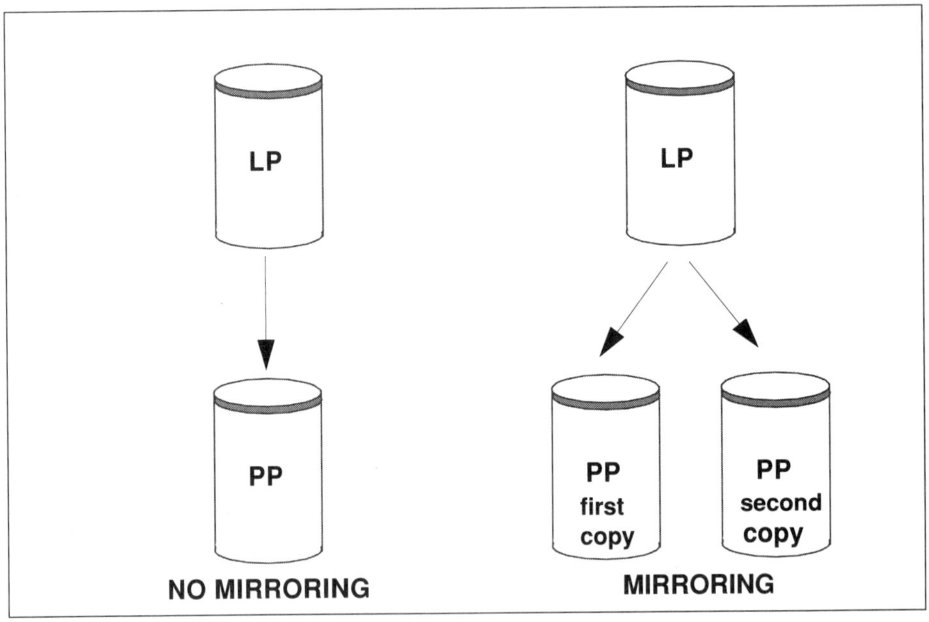

Figure 63. Mapping of LP to PP for Mirrored and Unmirrored Data

The management of logical volumes is, therefore, the management of disk space that is available for use. This section will review the functions that can be performed by users on logical volumes.

5.4.1 Adding a Logical Volume

You can create additional logical volumes with the `mklv` command. This command allows you to specify the name of the logical volume and define its characteristics, including the number and location of logical partitions to allocate for it. The default maximum size for a logical volume at creation is 128 logical partitions, unless specified to be larger.

5.4.1.1 Creating a Logical Volume Using Command Line

The `mklv` command is used to create a new logical volume. Following is the al syntax of the command and the most commonly used flags are shown in Table 7.

```
mklv [ -a Position ] [ -b BadBlocks ] [ -c Copies ] [ -d Schedule ] [ -e
Range ] [ -i ] [ -L Label ] [ -m MapFile ] [ -r Relocate ] [ -s Strict ] [
-t Type ] [ -u UpperBound ] [ -v Verify ] [ -w MirrorWriteConsistency ] [ -x
Maximum ] [ -y NewLogicalVolume | -Y Prefix ] [ -S StripeSize ] [ -U Userid
] [ -G Groupid ] [-P Modes ] VolumeGroup Number [ PhysicalVolume ... ]
```

Table 7. mklv Command Flags

Flag	Description
-c copies	Sets the number of physical partitions allocated for each logical partition. The copies variable can be set to a value from 1 to 3; the default is 1.
-i	Reads the PhysicalVolume parameter from standard input. Use the -i flag only when PhysicalVolume is entered through standard input.
-L	Sets the logical volume label. The default label is None. The maximum size of the label file is 127 characters. If the logical volume is going to be used as a journaled file system (JFS), then the JFS will use this field to store the mount point of the file system on that logical volume for future reference.
-P Modes	Specifies permissions (file modes) for the logical volume special file.
-t Type	Sets the logical volume type. The standard types are JFS (file systems), JFSLOG (journal file system logs), and paging (paging spaces), but a user can define other logical volume types with this flag. You cannot create a striped logical volume of type boot. The default is JFS. If a log is manually created for a file system, the user must run the `logform` command to clean out the new JFSLOG before the log can be used. Use the following command to format the logical volume `logdev`. `logform /dev/logdev` where `/dev/logdev` is the absolute path to the logical volume.
-y NewLogicalVolume	Specifies the logical volume name to use instead of using a system-generated name. Logical volume names must be unique systemwide names, and can range from 1 to 15 characters. If the volume group is varied on in concurrent mode, the new name should be unique across all the concurrent nodes the volume group is varied on. The name cannot begin with a prefix already defined in the PdDv class in the Device Configuration Database for other devices.

The following example shows the use of `mklv` command to create a new logical volume, `newlv`. This will create a logical volume called `newlv` in the `rootvg` and it will have 10 logical partitions and each logical partition consists of two physical partitions.

```
mklv -y newlv -c 2 rootvg 10
```

5.4.1.2 Creating a Logical Volume Using SMIT

You can use the following SMIT hierarchy to create a logical volume.

1. Execute `smitty mklv`.
2. Press **F4** to get a list of all the volume groups that are defined in the system. A screen similar to Figure 64 will be shown:

```
                              Add a Logical Volume

Type or select a value for the entry field.
Press Enter AFTER making all desired changes.

                                                     [Entry Fields]
* VOLUME GROUP name                                 []                      +



   ------------------------------------------------------------------------
   |                          VOLUME GROUP name                           |
   |                                                                      |
   | Move cursor to desired item and press Enter.                         |
   |                                                                      |
   |   rootvg                                                             |
   |                                                                      |
   | F1=Help                 F2=Refresh              F3=Cancel            |
F1 | F8=Image                F10=Exit                Enter=Do             |
F5 | /=Find                  n=Find Next                                  |
F9 ------------------------------------------------------------------------
```

Figure 64. mklv - Step 2

3. Use the arrow keys to select the volume group in which you want to create your new logical volume and press **Enter**. A screen similar to Figure 65 will be shown:

```
                              Add a Logical Volume

Type or select values in entry fields.
Press Enter AFTER making all desired changes.

[TOP]                                                   [Entry Fields]
  Logical volume NAME                                 []
* VOLUME GROUP name                                    rootvg
* Number of LOGICAL PARTITIONS                        []                     #
  PHYSICAL VOLUME names                               []                     +
  Logical volume TYPE                                 []
  POSITION on physical volume                          middle                +
  RANGE of physical volumes                            minimum               +
  MAXIMUM NUMBER of PHYSICAL VOLUMES                  []                     #
    to use for allocation
  Number of COPIES of each logical                     1                     +
    partition
  Mirror Write Consistency?                            yes                   +
  Allocate each logical partition copy                 yes                   +
[MORE...11]

F1=Help             F2=Refresh          F3=Cancel           F4=List
F5=Reset            F6=Command          F7=Edit             F8=Image
F9=Shell            F10=Exit            Enter=Do
```

Figure 65. mklv - Step 3

4. In the Logical volume NAME parameter, enter the name of the logical volume you are creating (`newlv` in this case).
5. In the Number of LOGICAL PARTITIONS parameter, enter the number of logical partitions you want to assign to your new logical volume (10 in this case). Each logical partition corresponds to one or more physical partitions depending upon the number of copies of data you want to keep.
6. In the PHYSICAL VOLUME names parameter, enter the physical volumes that you want to use for this logical volume. If you do not specify any names, the first PV in the system will be used to place all the data on.
7. In the Number of COPIES of each logical partition parameter, enter the number of copies that you want for your data. If you want to mirror your data change, the default is from 1 to a maximum of 3.
8. Press **Enter** to create the logical volume.

5.4.2 Removing a Logical Volume

You may need to remove a logical volumes if it is no longer in use for storage purposes by users and applications. The `rmlv` command can be used to remove a logical volume.

5.4.2.1 Removing a Logical Volume Using Command Line

The `rmlv` command is used to remove a logical volume. Following is the general syntax of the command and its commonly used flags are shown in Table 8.

```
rmlv [ -f ] [ -p Physical Volume ] LogicalVolume ...
```

Table 8. rmlv Command Flags

Flag	Description
-f	Removes the logical volumes without requesting confirmation.
-p PhysicalVolume	Removes only the logical partition on the PhysicalVolume. The logical volume is not removed unless there are no other physical partitions allocated.

The following example shows the command to remove a logical volume, `newlv`.

```
# rmlv newlv
Warning, all data on logical volume newlv will be destroyed.
rmlv: Do you wish to continue? y(es) n(o) y
#
```

Entering a `y` as the response to this dialogue and pressing **Enter** will complete the process of deletion of a logical volume.

5.4.2.2 Removing a Logical Volume Using SMIT

Alternatively, you can use the SMIT fast path command, `smitty rmlv`, to remove a logical volume.

5.4.2.3 Removing a Logical Volume When rootvg is Full

In this section, you will attempt to remove the Logical Volume `templv`, but with a few surprises when the `rootvg` is full.

Unmount the Logical Volume:

```
umount /dev/templv
```

Unmount the logical volume that will be removed:

```
# rmlv templv
Warning, all data contained on logical volume templv will be destroyed.
rmlv: Do you wish to continue? y(es) n(o)? y
/tmp/lvmap11780: There is not enough space in the file system.
0516-912 rmlv: Unable to remove logical volume templv.
```

While removing the logical volume, you receive the preceding error message. Check disk space by entering the following:

```
# df
Filesystem     512-blocks      Free %Used    Iused %Iused Mounted on
/dev/hd4            32768         0  100%     1868    16% /
/dev/hd2          4702208         0  100%    51167     9% /usr
/dev/hd9var         16384         0  100%      183     9% /var
/dev/hd3            32768         0  100%       34     1% /tmp
/dev/hd1            16384         8  100%       49     3% /home
/dev/userlv      16793600   9968728   41%       21     1% /u
```

The file systems /, /usr, /var, /tmp, and /home are full. There are two options to fix this problem.

1. Check the file systems and find unused or obsolete files that can be removed.
2. Increase the size of the file systems if you have enough disk space, or add an additional drive and use the extendvg command to add the drive to the rootvg.

After investigation you will find that there is a file called bigfile, which is an unused file that is taking up space on the file system /tmp and /home. Delete this file from the two file systems. The other file systems will be resized using the chfs command.

To delete the obsolete files from /tmp and /home, do the following:

```
# cd /tmp
# rm bigfile
# cd /home
# rm bigfile
# cd /
# df
Filesystem     512-blocks      Free %Used    Iused %Iused Mounted on
/dev/hd4            49152         0  100%     1868    16% /
/dev/hd2          4702208         0  100%    51167     9% /usr
/dev/hd9var         16384         0  100%      183     9% /var
/dev/hd3            32768     31568    4%       33     1% /tmp
/dev/hd1            16384     15656    5%       48     3% /home
/dev/userlv      16793600   9968728   41%       21     1% /u
```

To resize the other three file systems enter:

```
smitty jfs
```

From the Journaled File Systems menu select, the **Change / Show Characteristics of a Journaled File System** option as displayed in Figure 66.

```
                         Journaled File Systems

Move cursor to desired item and press Enter.

  Add a Journaled File System
  Add a Journaled File System on a Previously Defined Logical Volume
  Change / Show Characteristics of a Journaled File System
  Remove a Journaled File System
  Defragment a Journaled File System










F1=Help            F2=Refresh          F3=Cancel           F8=Image
F9=Shell           F10=Exit            Enter=Do
```

Figure 66. Journaled File Systems Menu

Once the Change / Show Characteristics of a Journaled File System option has been taken, a File System Name submenu will appear. Select the file system to which changes will be made as displayed in Figure 67 on page 109.

```
                          Journaled File Systems

Move cursor to desired item and press Enter.

  Add a Journaled File System
  +----------------------------------------------------------------------+
  |                        File System Name                              |
  |                                                                      |
  | Move cursor to desired item and press Enter.                         |
  |                                                                      |
  |   /                                                                  |
  |   /home                                                              |
  |   /usr                                                               |
  |   /var                                                               |
  |   /tmp                                                               |
  |   /export/lpp_source                                                 |
  |   /export/spot                                                       |
  |   /richfs                                                            |
  |   /testfs                                                            |
  |                                                                      |
  | F1=Help               F2=Refresh              F3=Cancel              |
  | F8=Image              F10=Exit                Enter=Do               |
F1| /=Find                n=Find Next                                    |
F9+----------------------------------------------------------------------+
```

Figure 67. File System Name Submenu

Figure 68 shows the original characteristics of the / (root) file systems. Go down to the **Size of file system (in 512-byte blocks)** option.

```
            Change / Show Characteristics of a Journaled File System

Type or select values in entry fields.
Press Enter AFTER making all desired changes.

                                                     [Entry Fields]
  File system name                                  /
  NEW mount point                                  [/]
  SIZE of file system (in 512-byte blocks)         [32768]
  Mount GROUP                                      [bootfs]
  Mount AUTOMATICALLY at system restart?            yes                    +
  PERMISSIONS                                       read/write             +
  Mount OPTIONS                                    []                      +
  Start Disk Accounting?                            no                     +
  Fragment Size (bytes)                             4096
  Number of bytes per inode                         2048
  Compression algorithm                             no
  Large File Enabled                                false
  Allocation Group Size (MBytes)                    8

F1=Help             F2=Refresh          F3=Cancel           F4=List
F5=Reset            F6=Command          F7=Edit             F8=Image
F9=Shell            F10=Exit            Enter=Do
```

Figure 68. Original Change / Show Characteristics of a JFS Menu

Figure 69 shows the same menu as Figure 68, except the Size of file system (in 512-byte blocks) has been changed. The size can only be increased.

```
              Change / Show Characteristics of a Journaled File System

Type or select values in entry fields.
Press Enter AFTER making all desired changes.

                                                         [Entry Fields]
  File system name                                        /
  NEW mount point                                        [/]
  SIZE of file system (in 512-byte blocks)               [49152]
  Mount GROUP                                            [bootfs]
  Mount AUTOMATICALLY at system restart?                  yes                +
  PERMISSIONS                                             read/write         +
  Mount OPTIONS                                          []                  +
  Start Disk Accounting?                                  no                 +
  Fragment Size (bytes)                                   4096
  Number of bytes per inode                               2048
  Compression algorithm                                   no
  Large File Enabled                                      false
  Allocation Group Size (MBytes)                          8

F1=Help              F2=Refresh           F3=Cancel            F4=List
F5=Reset             F6=Command           F7=Edit              F8=Image
F9=Shell             F10=Exit             Enter=Do
```

Figure 69. New Change / Show Characteristics of a Journaled File System Menu

In Figure 70 on page 111, the Command Status window displaying the success of the operation to increase the size of a file system is shown.

```
                                COMMAND STATUS

Command: OK            stdout: yes            stderr: no

Before command completion, additional instructions may appear below.

Filesystem size changed to 40960













F1=Help              F2=Refresh           F3=Cancel            F6=Command
F8=Image             F9=Shell             F10=Exit             /=Find
n=Find Next
```

Figure 70. Command Status Window

Press **F10** to exit out of the SMIT system and go back to the command line.

To check the new size of the file system, enter:

```
# df
Filesystem    512-blocks      Free %Used    Iused %Iused Mounted on
/dev/hd4           49152     25856   48%     1867    16% /
/dev/hd2         4702208         0  100%    51167     9% /usr
/dev/hd9var        16384         0  100%      183     9% /var
/dev/hd3           32768     31568    4%       33     1% /tmp
/dev/hd1           16384     15656    5%       48     3% /home
/dev/userlv     16793600   9968728   41%       21     1% /u
```

To change the size of the file system `/usr` and `/var` from the command line enter:

```
# chfs -a size='5000000' /usr
Filesystem size changed to 5013504
# chfs -a size='32768' /var
Filesystem size changed to 32768
```

To check the size of the file systems enter:

```
# df
Filesystem    512-blocks      Free %Used    Iused %Iused Mounted on
/dev/hd4           49152     25848   48%     1867    16% /
/dev/hd2         5013504    301520   94%    51167     9% /usr
/dev/hd9var        32768     15864   52%      183     5% /var
/dev/hd3           32768     31568    4%       33     1% /tmp
/dev/hd1           16384     15656    5%       48     3% /home
/dev/userlv     16793600   9968728   41%       21     1% /u
```

The file systems now all have additional space. Remove the logical volume by entering the following:

```
# rmlv templv
Warning, all data contained on logical volume templv will be destroyed.
rmlv: Do you wish to continue? y(es) n(o)? y
rmlv: Logical volume templv is removed.
```

The logical volume has been removed. To remove the volume group enter:

```
# reducevg -df tempvg hdisk4
rmlv: Logical volume loglv01 is removed.
ldeletepv: Volume Group deleted since it contains no physical volumes.
```

The volume group has been removed and the physical volume made available for use on another volume group. To verify this, enter:

```
# lspv
hdisk0         000919746edab91f    rootvg
hdisk1         0009197459d92f2e    None
hdisk2         00091974d381d097    uservg
hdisk3         00091974d81ff431    uservg
hdisk4         00091974de731316    None
hdisk5         00091974e4f3d56e    None
hdisk6         0009197425444544    raidvg
```

5.4.3 Reducing the Size of Logical Volume

The following steps could be performed to reduce the size of a logical volume to free up the excess logical partition allocation.

1. Back up all data in the logical volume.
2. Remove the logical volume.
3. Recreate the logical volume with the reduced logical partition allocation.
4. Restore the data.

The resulting free space could be put to better use by allocating it to other logical volumes requiring it.

5.4.4 Increasing the Size of Logical Volume

An existing logical volume can be increased in size by using the `extendlv` command or SMIT.

If the logical volume is used by a journaled file system, you can also use the `chfs` command or SMIT fast path command `smitty chjfs` to increase the size of the logical volume.

5.4.4.1 Extending a Logical Volume Using Command Line

The `extendlv` command is used to increase the size of a logical volume. Following is the general syntax of the command and its commonly used flags.

```
extendlv [ -a Position ] [ -e Range ] [ -u Upperbound ] [ -s Strict ]
LogicalVolume Partitions [ PhysicalVolume ... ]
```

The following example shows the use of the `extendlv` command to add three more logical partitions to the logical volume you created:

```
extendlv newlv 3
```

5.4.4.2 Extending a Logical Volume Using SMIT

The following SMIT fast path command can be used to increase the size of a logical volume:

```
smitty extendlv
```

5.4.5 Copying a Logical Volume

Logical volumes may need to be copied for a number of reasons. If a disk is to be removed and replaced with a new disk, the logical volumes on that disk will need to be copied to the new disk. Logical volumes can be copied to new logical volumes or to existing logical volumes which are then overwritten.

5.4.5.1 Copying a Logical Volume Using Command Line

The following example shows the use of `cplv` command to copy a logical volume:

```
cplv -v myvg -y newlv oldlv
```

This copies the contents of `oldlv` to a new logical volume called `newlv` in the volume group `myvg`. If the volume group is not specified, the new logical volume will be created in the same volume group as the old logical volume. This command creates a new logical volume.

The following example demonstrates how to copy a logical volume to an existing logical volume.

```
cplv -e existinglv oldlv
```

This copies the contents of `oldlv` to the logical volume `existinglv`. Confirmation for the copy will be requested as all data in `existinglv` will be overwritten.

If `existinglv` is smaller than `oldlv`, then data will be lost, probably resulting in corruption.

Copying a logical volume can also be done through smit using the `smit cplv` fastpath.

> **Note**
>
> Do not copy from a larger logical volume containing data to a smaller one. Doing so results in a corrupted file system because some data (including the superblock) is not copied. This command will fail if the `cplv` creates a new logical volume and the volume group is varied on in concurrent mode.

5.4.5.2 Copying a Logical Volume Using SMIT

Alternatively, you can use the SMIT fast path command, `smitty cplv` to obtain a screen as shown in Figure 71.

```
                          Copy a Logical Volume

Move cursor to desired item and press Enter.

  Copy over an existing logical volume
  Copy to a user created logical volume
  Copy to a system created logical volume


F1=Help             F2=Refresh          F3=Cancel           F8=Image
F9=Shell            F10=Exit            Enter=Do
```

Figure 71. cplv - Step 1

1. Select **Copy over an existing logical volume**. A screen similar to Figure 72 will be shown.

```
                     Copy over an existing logical volume

Type or select values in entry fields.
Press Enter AFTER making all desired changes.

                                                          [Entry Fields]
* SOURCE logical volume name                          []                     +
* DESTINATION logical volume                          []                     +









F1=Help               F2=Refresh            F3=Cancel             F4=List
F5=Reset              F6=Command            F7=Edit               F8=Image
F9=Shell              F10=Exit              Enter=Do
```

Figure 72. cplv - Step 2

2. Enter the name of the logical volume you want to copy in the SOURCE logical volume name parameter
3. Enter the name of the logical volume on which you want to copy your existing logical volume to in the DESTINATION logical volume name field. This name can be of an existing logical volume that you have already created or it can be a new logical volume that you want to create. Press **Enter** to complete this step.

Note

You might encounter the following error.

```
cplv : Destination logical volume must have type set to copy
```

If this is the case, use the following command.

```
chlv -t copy <Destination Logical Volume Name>
```

Return to your SMIT session. Now the system will allow you to copy the logical volume. This has been done to ensure extra security so that you do not overwrite your data accidently.

5.4.6 Listing Logical Volumes

The following logical volumes are automatically created at the system installation time.

`hd5` This is the boot logical volume that holds the boot code. It is available only at the system startup time.

`hd6` This is the default paging space logical volume that is used by the system to perform paging.

`hd8` This logical volume is used as the default logging space for the journaled file systems.

`hd4` This logical volume in used by the /, root file system.

`hd2` This logical volume is used by the /usr file system.

`hd9var` This logical volume is used by the /var file system.

`hd3` This logical volume used by the /tmp file system.

`hd1` This logical volume is used by the /home file system.

The following example will list all the logical volumes defined on the system as shown in Figure 73.

```
lsvg | lsvg -il
```

```
rootvg:
LV NAME             TYPE       LPs   PPs   PVs  LV STATE      MOUNT POINT
hd5                 boot       2     2     1    closed/syncd  N/A
hd6                 paging     32    32    1    open/syncd    N/A
hd8                 jfslog     1     1     1    open/syncd    N/A
hd4                 jfs        4     4     1    open/syncd    /
hd2                 jfs        123   123   1    open/syncd    /usr
hd9var              jfs        1     1     1    open/syncd    /var
hd3                 jfs        4     4     1    open/syncd    /tmp
hd1                 jfs        1     1     1    open/syncd    /home
lv00                jfs        4     4     1    closed/syncd  /usr/vice/cache
lv01                jfs        3     3     1    open/syncd    /var/dce
lv02                jfs        10    10    1    closed/syncd  /var/dce/adm/dfs/c
ache
lvtest              ???        3     6     1    open/syncd    /test
lvbkup              ???        3     3     1    closed/syncd  N/A
lv03                jfs        108   108   1    closed/syncd  /export/lpp_source
_1
lv04                jfs        53    53    1    closed/syncd  /export/spot_1
lv05                jfs        158   158   1    closed/syncd  /work
lv06                jfs        5     5     1    closed/syncd  /home2
lv07                jfs        1     1     1    open/syncd    /auto1
lv08                jfs        1     1     1    closed/syncd  /auto2
Standard input
```

Figure 73. Logical Volume Listing

The `lslv` command can be used to view all the attributes related to a logical volume (`newlv`) as shown in Figure 74.

```
# lslv newlv
LOGICAL VOLUME:     newlv                  VOLUME GROUP:   rootvg
LV IDENTIFIER:      00615147b27f2b40.26    PERMISSION:     read/write
VG STATE:           active/complete        LV STATE:       closed/syncd
TYPE:               jfs                    WRITE VERIFY:   off
MAX LPs:            512                    PP SIZE:        4 megabyte(s)
COPIES:             1                      SCHED POLICY:   parallel
LPs:                1                      PPs:            1
STALE PPs:          0                      BB POLICY:      relocatable
INTER-POLICY:       minimum                RELOCATABLE:    yes
INTRA-POLICY:       middle                 UPPER BOUND:    32
MOUNT POINT:        N/A                    LABEL:          None
MIRROR WRITE CONSISTENCY: on
EACH LP COPY ON A SEPARATE PV ?: yes
#
```

Figure 74. Logical Volume Attributes

5.4.7 Logical Volume Size

The size of a logical volume is the space that is allocated to the logical volume and is a factor of the number of logical partitions that are allocated to the logical volume and the number of copies that you have told the system to maintain.Therefore, the total space taken up by the logical volume is determined by the following formula.

Total LV size=PP size * LPs assigned to LV * Number of copies of the LV

The following example shows how to calculate the logical volume size.

If PP size is 4 MB, LPs assigned to the logical volume are 10, and the number of copies of the logical volume are 2, then the total space that will be allocated to this logical volume will be 80 MB (4*10*2).

5.4.8 Logical Volume Striping

Striping is a technique for spreading the data in a logical volume across several disk drives in such a way that the I/O capacity of the disk drives can be used in parallel to access data on the logical volume. The primary objective of striping is for high-performance reading and writing of large sequential files.

In an ordinary logical volume, the data addresses correspond to the sequence of blocks in the underlying physical partitions. In a striped logical volume, the data addresses follow the sequence of stripe units. A complete stripe consists of one stripe unit on each of the physical devices that contains part of the striped logical volume. The LVM determines which physical blocks on which physical drives correspond to a block being read or written. If more than one drive is involved, the necessary I/O operations are scheduled for all drives simultaneously.

The way you would set up the logical volume striping is by using the `vmtune` command.

The `vmtune` command changes operational parameters of the Virtual Memory Manager (VMM) and other AIX components.

The `vmtune` command can only be executed by root. Changes made by the `vmtune` command persist until the next reboot of the system. If a permanent change in VMM parameters is needed, an appropriate `vmtune` command should be put in inittab.

The `vmtune` command syntax is as follows:

```
vmtune [ -b numfsbuf ] [ -B numpbuf ] [ -c numclust ] [ -f minfree ] [ -F
maxfree ] [ -k npskill ] [ -l lrubucket ] [ -M maxpin ] [ -N pd_npages ] [
-p minperm ] [ -P maxperm ] [ -r minpgahead ] [ -R maxpgahead ] [-u
lvm_budcnt] [ -w npswarn ] [-W maxrandwrt]
```

Provided in Table 9 are the flags and their descriptions for the `vmtune` command.

Table 9. vmtune Command Flags and Flag Descriptions

Flag	Flag Description
-b numfsbu*f*	Specifies the number of file system bufstructs. The default value is 64.
-B numpbu*f*	Specifies the number of pbufs used by the LVM. The maximum value is 128. In AIX Version 3, the number of pbufs may need to be increased in systems doing many large, sequential I/O operations.
-c numclust	Specifies the number of 16 KB clusters processed by write behind. The default value is 1.
-f minfree	Specifies the minimum number of frames on the free list. This number can range from 8 to 204800.
-F maxfree	Specifies the number of frames on the free list at which page stealing is to stop. This number can range from 16 to 204800, but must be greater than the number specified by the minfree parameter by at least the value of maxpgahead.
-k npskill	Specifies the number of free paging-space pages at which AIX begins killing processes. The default value is 128.
-l lrubucket	Specifies the size (in 4 KB pages) of the least-recently used (LRU) page-replacement bucket size. This is the number of page frames which will be examined at one time for possible pageouts when a free frame is needed. A lower number will result in lower latency when looking for a free frame, but will also result in behavior that is not similar to a true lru alogorithm. The default value is 512 MB and the minimum is 256 MB. Tuning this option is not recommended.
-M maxpin	Specifies the maximum percentage of real memory that can be pinned. The default value is 80. If this value is changed, the new value should ensure that at least 4 MB of real memory will be left unpinned for use by the kernel.

Flag	Flag Description
-N pd_npages	Specifies the number of pages that should be deleted in one chunk from RAM when a file is deleted. The default value is the largest possible file size divided by the page size (currently 4096). If the largest possible file size is 2 GB, then pd_npages is by default 524288. Tuning this option is really only useful for real-time applications.
-p minperm	Specifies the point below which file pages are protected from the repage algorithm. This value is a percentage of the total real-memory page frames in the system. The specified value must be greater than or equal to five.
-P maxperm	Specifies the point above which the page stealing algorithm steals only file pages. This value is expressed as a percentage of the total real-memory page frames in the system. The specified value must be greater than or equal to five.
-r minpgahead	Specifies the number of pages with which sequential read-ahead starts. This value can range from 0 through 4096. It should be a power of two.
-R maxpgahead	Specifies the maximum number of pages to be read ahead. This value can range from 0 through 4096. It should be a power of two and should be greater than or equal to minpgahead.
-u lvm_bufcnt	Specifies the number of LVM buffers for raw physical I/Os. The default value is nine. The possible values can range between 1 and 64. This option is only available in AIX Version 4.
-w npswarn	Specifies the number of free paging-space pages at which AIX begins sending the SIGDANGER signal to processes. The default value is 512.
-W maxrandwrt	Specifies a threshold (in 4 KB pages) for random writes to accumulate in RAM before these pages are sync'd to disk via a write-behind algorithm. This threshold is on a per file basis.

The recommended values for logical volume striping are:

minpgahead 2

maxpgahead 16 x number of disk drives

I/O requests Equal to maxpgahead

The maxfree and minfree settings should be done after doing some investigation into the `vmstat` command and then setting the system according to your system requirements. For a better understanding of tuning your AIX system, consult the *AIX Versions 3.2 and 4 Performance Tuning Guide*, SC23-2365. For this example, use a value of 128:

minfree 128

maxfree minfree + maxpgahead

For this section, assume the following devices exist:

```
# lspv
hdisk0        000919746edab91f    rootvg
hdisk1        0009197459d92f2e    uservg
hdisk2        00091974d381d097    uservg
```

Your system has three disk drives, using the recommended values described for logical volume striping, your values would be:

```
minpgahead 2
maxpgahead 48 (3x16)
minfree 128
maxfree 176 (48 + 128)
```

To set the system up with these parameters enter:

```
/usr/lpp/bos/samples/vmtune -f 128 -F 144 -r 2 -R 176
```

To make these changes permanent, enter the above line into /etc/inittab.

5.5 Managing Journaled File Systems

A file system is a set of files, directories, and other structures. File systems maintain information and identify of the location of a file or directory's data. In addition to files and directories, file systems contain a boot block, a superblock, bitmaps, and one or more allocation groups. An allocation group contains disk i-nodes and fragments.

The following three types of file systems are supported on an AIX system.

Journaled File System This native file system type is called the journaled file system (JFS). Each journaled file system resides on a separate logical volume. The operating system mounts journaled file systems during initialization.

Network File System The network file system (NFS) is a distributed file system that allows users to access files and directories located on remote computers and use those files and directories as if they are local.

CD-ROM File System The CD-ROM file system (CDRFS) is a file system type that allows you to access the contents of a CD-ROM through the normal file system interfaces.

The Journaled File System (JFS) divides the logical volume into a number of fixed size units called logical blocks. The logical blocks in the file system are organized as follows:

Logical Block 0 The first logical block in the file system is reserved and available for a bootstrap program or any other required information; this block is unused by the file system.

Superblock The first and thirty-first logical blocks are reserved for the superblock (logical block 31 being a backup copy). The super block contains information such as the overall size of the file system in 512 byte blocks, the file system name, file system log device address (logs will be covered later in this section), version number, and file system state.

Allocation Groups The rest of the logical blocks in the file system are divided into a number of allocation groups. An allocation group consists of data blocks and i-nodes to reference those data blocks when they are allocated to directories or files.

5.5.1 Characteristics of Journaled File System

The size for a journaled file system (JFS) is defined when the file system is created considering the following parameters:

- Number of i-nodes
- Allocation group size
- File system fragment addressability
- Journaled file system log size
- Maximum journaled file system size

5.5.1.1 Number of I-nodes

The total number of i-nodes in a file system limits the total number of files and the total size of the file system. The JFS provides the nbpi (number of bytes per i-node) parameter that affects the number of i-nodes in a file system. JFS supports nbpi values of 512, 1024, 2048, 4096, 8192, 16384, 32768, 65536, and 131072. The values 32768, 65536, and 131072 only apply to AIX Version 4.2 or later.

For example, to create an 8 MB file system with an nbpi value of 4096, an i-node will be generated for each 4096 bytes of data. This would result in a maximum of 2048 i-nodes for an 8 MB file system, which means that if every file in the file system is ideally 4 KB in length, a maximum of 2048 files can be created in the file system.

The JFS restricts all file systems to 16 MB (224) i-nodes.

5.5.1.2 Allocation Group Size

AIX Version 4.2 or later supports various allocation group sizes. The JFS segregates file system space into groupings of i-nodes and disk blocks for user data. These groupings are called allocation groups. The allocation group size can be specified when the file system is created. The allocation group sizes are 8 MB, 16 MB, 32 MB, and 64 MB. Each allocation group size has an associated nbpi range. The ranges are defined by the following table:

Table 10. Allowable nbpi Values

Allocation Group size in MB	Maximum number of i-nodes
8	512,1024,2048,4096,8192,16384
16	1024,2048,4096,8192,16384, 32768
32	2048,4096,8192,16384,32768,65536
64	4096,8192,16384,32768,65536,131072

5.5.1.3 File System Fragment Addressability

The JFS supports four fragment sizes: 512, 1024, 2048, and 4096 byte units of contiguous disk space. The JFS maintains fragment addresses in i-nodes and indirect blocks as 28-bit numbers. Each fragment must be addressable by a number from 0 to (228).

5.5.1.4 Journaled File System Log Size

Multiple journaled file systems use a common log, called a JFS log, configured to be 4 MB in size. For example, after initial installation, all file systems within the root volume group use logical volume hd8 as a common JFS log. The default logical volume partition size is 4 MB, and the default log size is one partition, therefore, the root volume group normally contains a 4 MB JFS log. When file systems exceed 2 GB or when the total amount of file system space using a single log exceeds 2 GB, the default log size needs to be increased. The JFS log is limited to a maximum size of 256 MB.

5.5.1.5 Maximum Journaled File System Size

The maximum JFS size is defined when the file system is created. For example, selecting an nbpi ratio of 512 will limit the file system to a size of 8 GB (512 * 228 = 8 GB). When creating a JFS file system, the factors listed (nbpi, fragment size, and allocation group size) need to be weighed carefully. The file system size limitation is the minimum of NPBI * 224 or Fragment Size * 228.

5.5.2 Creating a File System

Every file system in AIX corresponds to a logical volume. In order to create a journaled file system use the following SMIT hierarchy.

1. Executing the SMIT fast path command `smitty crjfs` will show a screen similar to Figure 75 on page 125.

```
                    Add a Journaled File System

Move cursor to desired item and press Enter.

  Add a Standard Journaled File System
  Add a Compressed Journaled File System
  Add a Large File Enabled Journaled File System









F1=Help            F2=Refresh         F3=Cancel          F8=Image
F9=Shell           F10=Exit           Enter=Do
```

Figure 75. smitty crjfs - Step 1

2. Select **Add a Standard Journaled File System** to add a new journaled file system. A screen similar to Figure 76 is displayed.

```
                    Add a Journaled File System

Move cursor to desired item and press Enter.

  Add a Standard Journaled File System
  Add a Compressed Journaled File System
  Add a Large File Enabled Journaled File System


   ┌──────────────────────────────────────────────────────────────┐
   │                      Volume Group Name                       │
   │                                                              │
   │ Move cursor to desired item and press Enter.                 │
   │                                                              │
   │   rootvg                                                     │
   │                                                              │
   │ F1=Help              F2=Refresh           F3=Cancel          │
   │ F8=Image             F10=Exit             Enter=Do           │
F1 │ /=Find               n=Find Next                             │
F9 └──────────────────────────────────────────────────────────────┘
```

Figure 76. crjfs - Step 2

3. Select the volume group you want to add this new file system to by using the arrow keys. In this case, since there is only one volume group (rootvg), only rootvg is displayed. Select **rootvg** as your target volume group by pressing the **Enter** key.
4. Once you select the target volume group, a screen similar to Figure 77 is displayed.

```
                        Add a Standard Journaled File System

Type or select values in entry fields.
Press Enter AFTER making all desired changes.

                                                         [Entry Fields]
  Volume group name                                     rootvg
* SIZE of file system (in 512-byte blocks)             []                        #
* MOUNT POINT                                          []
  Mount AUTOMATICALLY at system restart?                no                       +
  PERMISSIONS                                           read/write               +
  Mount OPTIONS                                        []                        +
  Start Disk Accounting?                                no                       +
  Fragment Size (bytes)                                 4096                     +
  Number of bytes per inode                             4096                     +
  Allocation Group Size (MBytes)                        8                        +




F1=Help             F2=Refresh          F3=Cancel           F4=List
F5=Reset            F6=Command          F7=Edit             F8=Image
F9=Shell            F10=Exit            Enter=Do
```

Figure 77. crjfs - Step 3

5. In the Size of file system (in 512 byte blocks) parameter, enter the size of the file system you want to create. For example if you want to create a file system of 4 MB size, you can simply multiply the number of megabytes (4 in this case) with 2048 to get 512-byte blocks you will need to create a file system this large (8192 in this case).

Note

In AIX, all of the I/O is in 4 KB blocks, however, space is allocated in multiples of 512 byte blocks. This is done just to remain consistent with other UNIX systems. The smallest file system that you can create is equal to one PP, therefore, even if you mention the number of blocks to be less than one PP, the system will still create a file system equal to one PP. The following example shows how to calculate the number of blocks for a given amount of space in MB.

Since	512 bytes = 1 block
Therefore	1024 bytes = 2 blocks
and	1 MB = 2*1024 blocks
Therefore	x MB = x * 2048 blocks (Answer)

This indicates that the equivalent number of blocks for a file system of 2 MB are 4096 (Enter this number in the Size of File System field).

6. Next, in the MOUNT POINT parameter enter the full path where you want your file system to attach itself to the file system hierarchy. A mount point is a directory or file at which the new file system, directory, or file is made accessible.

7. Press **Enter** to create the journaled file system. The screen shown in Figure 78 indicates the successful completion of the process.

```
                              COMMAND STATUS

Command: OK            stdout: yes           stderr: no

Before command completion, additional instructions may appear below.

Based on the parameters chosen, the new /dummy JFS file system
is limited to a maximum size of 134217728 (512 byte blocks)

New File System size is 8192









F1=Help              F2=Refresh           F3=Cancel            F6=Command
F8=Image             F9=Shell             F10=Exit             /=Find
n=Find Next
```

Figure 78. crjfs- Step 4

Alternatively, you can achieve the same task on the command line using the following command:

```
crfs -v jfs -g rootvg -a size=8192 -m /dummy
```

This will create a journaled file system of 8 MB with `/dummy` as the mount point in the `rootvg` volume group.

5.5.3 Mounting a File System

Mounting is a concept that makes file systems, files, directories, devices, and special files available for use at a particular location. It is the only way a file system is made accessible. Once you have created the file system, the next task is to make it available to your users. In order to do that, you must know how AIX manages the patching of the newly created file systems into its file tree using the mount points.

Figure 79 on page 129 shows a file system mount point (/u/dick) before a file system is mounted over it.

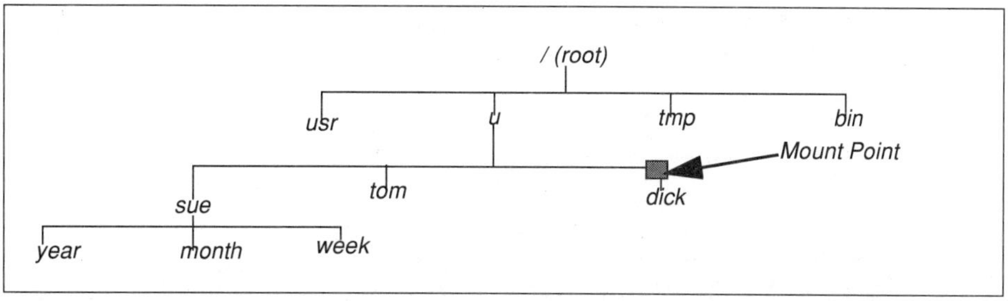

Figure 79. File Tree View before Mounting

Figure 80 shows a mounted file system /u/dick over the /u/dick mount point.

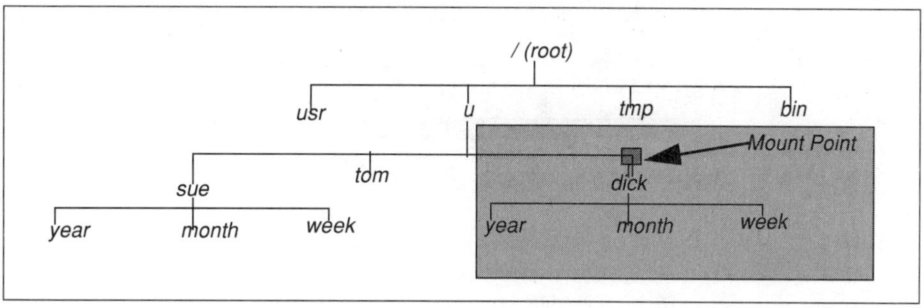

Figure 80. File Tree View after Mounting

Note

- When a file system is mounted over a directory, the permissions of the root directory of the mounted file system take precedence over the permissions of the mount point.
- A common problem is failure of the `pwd` command. Without search permission in the mounted-over directory, the `pwd` command returns the following message.

  ```
  pwd: Permission denied
  ```

  This problem can be avoided by always setting the permissions of the mounted-over directory to at least 111.

5.5.3.1 Mounting a File System through Command Line

The following command shows how to mount a file system (`/FileSystemX`).

```
mount /FileSystemX
```

Alternatively, if you know the name of the device associated with your file system you can use the device name to mount your newly created file system.

If you want to mount all the file systems, you can use the following command to mount all the file systems at one time.

```
mount {-a|all}
```

5.5.3.2 Mounting a File System through SMIT

A file system can be also be mounted using the following SMIT fast path hierarchy.

1. Executing `smitty mount` will display the screen shown in Figure 81.

```
                              Mount a File System

Move cursor to desired item and press Enter.

  List All Mounted File Systems
  Mount a File System
  Mount a Group of File Systems

F1=Help              F2=Refresh           F3=Cancel            F8=Image
F9=Shell             F10=Exit             Enter=Do
```

Figure 81. Mount File System - Step 1

2. Use the arrow keys to move the cursor down and select **Mount a File System** by pressing the **Enter** key. A screen similar to Figure 82 on page 131 is shown:

```
                              Mount a File System

Type or select values in entry fields.
Press Enter AFTER making all desired changes.

                                                      [Entry Fields]
  FILE SYSTEM name                                  []                      +
  DIRECTORY over which to mount                     []                      +
  TYPE of file system                                                       +
  FORCE the mount?                                   no                     +
  REMOTE NODE containing the file system            []
    to mount
  Mount as a REMOVABLE file system?                  no                     +
  Mount as a READ-ONLY system?                       no                     +
  Disallow DEVICE access via this mount?             no                     +
  Disallow execution of SUID and sgid programs       no                     +
    in this file system?

F1=Help             F2=Refresh          F3=Cancel           F4=List
F5=Reset            F6=Command          F7=Edit             F8=Image
F9=Shell            F10=Exit            Enter=Do
```

Figure 82. Mount File System - Step 2

3. Use the arrow keys to move down to DIRECTORY over which to mount.
4. Press **F4** to get a list of the mount points that you have defined for your file system. (Refer to 5.5.2, “Creating a File System” on page 124, to see how you created a file system, and notice that you created a mount point for your file system. You will use the same mount point to make your file system available to the users). Pressing **F4** shows a screen similar to Figure 83 on page 132.

```
                         Mount a File System

Ty ┌─────────────────────────────────────────────────────────────┐
Pr │                DIRECTORY over which to mount                │
   │                                                             │
   │ Move cursor to desired item and press Enter.                │ +
   │                                                             │ +
   │ [TOP]                                                       │ +
   │   /                                                         │ +
   │   /home                                                     │
   │   /usr                                                      │
   │   /var                                                      │ +
   │   /tmp                                                      │ +
   │   /usr/vice/cache       /dev/lv00          jfs      32768   │ +
   │   /var/dce                                                  │ +
   │   /var/dce/adm/dfs/cache                                    │
   │   /test                 /dev/lvtest        jfs      24576   │
   │   /export/lpp_source_1                                      │
   │ [MORE...8]                                                  │
   │                                                             │
   │ F1=Help              F2=Refresh           F3=Cancel         │
F1 │ F8=Image             F10=Exit             Enter=Do          │
F5 │ /=Find               n=Find Next                           │
F9 └─────────────────────────────────────────────────────────────┘
```

Figure 83. Mount FIle System - Step 3

5. Use the arrow keys to select the file system you want to mount. Press **Enter** to make the selection. This will display the mount point you just selected in the DIRECTORY over which to mount field.

6. Press **Enter** again and wait for the SMIT ok prompt, which indicates the successful completion of the process.

5.5.3.3 Automatic Mounting

Mounts can be set to occur automatically during system initialization. There are two types of automatic mounts:

- Those mounts that are required to boot and run the system. These file systems are explicitly mounted by the boot process. The stanzas of such file systems in the /etc/filesystems file have mount =automatic. When the multi-user initialization starts, the /etc/rc script does not try to mount these file systems again when it executes the `mount all` command. Similarly, when the `umount all` command is executed, these file systems are not unmounted.

- The second type of automatic mount is user-controlled. These file systems are mounted by the /etc/rc script when it issues the `mount all` command. The stanzas of user-controlled automatic mounts have mount = true in /etc/filesystems.

You can specify a file system to be mounted automatically when you either use the `mount all` command or the by the /etc/rc script at the initialization time. You can achieve this by setting the Mount AUTOMATICALLY at system restart parameter to TRUE when you are creating a file system. (See Figure 77 on page 126)

5.5.3.4 Displaying Mounted File Systems

The following example shows the use of command `mount` without a flag to display information about all the currently mounted file systems.

```
# mount
node       mounted          mounted over     vfs      date          options
-------- --------------- ---------------  ------ ------------ ---------------
         /dev/hd4        /                jfs    Oct 25 18:20 rw,log=/dev/hd8
         /dev/hd2        /usr             jfs    Oct 25 18:20 rw,log=/dev/hd8
         /dev/hd9var     /var             jfs    Oct 25 18:20 rw,log=/dev/hd8
         /dev/hd3        /tmp             jfs    Oct 25 18:20 rw,log=/dev/hd8
         /dev/lv01       /var/dce         jfs    Oct 25 18:21 rw,log=/dev/hd8
         /dev/hd1        /home            jfs    Oct 27 15:14 rw,log=/dev/hd8
         /dev/lvtest     /test            jfs    Oct 27 15:17 rw,log=/dev/hd8
         /dev/lv07       /auto1           jfs    Oct 27 15:34 rw,log=/dev/hd8
```

5.5.4 Removing a File System

The following example shows the steps involved to remove a file system.

1. Using the `mount` command to check the file systems that are currently mounted will display the following screen.

```
# mount
node       mounted          mounted over     vfs      date          options
-------- --------------- ---------------  ------ ------------ ---------------
         /dev/hd4        /                jfs    Oct 25 18:20 rw,log=/dev/hd8
         /dev/hd2        /usr             jfs    Oct 25 18:20 rw,log=/dev/hd8
         /dev/hd9var     /var             jfs    Oct 25 18:20 rw,log=/dev/hd8
         /dev/hd3        /tmp             jfs    Oct 25 18:20 rw,log=/dev/hd8
         /dev/lv01       /var/dce         jfs    Oct 25 18:21 rw,log=/dev/hd8
         /dev/hd1        /home            jfs    Oct 27 15:14 rw,log=/dev/hd8
         /dev/lvtest     /test            jfs    Oct 27 15:17 rw,log=/dev/hd8
         /dev/lv07       /auto1           jfs    Oct 27 15:34 rw,log=/dev/hd8
```

2. Identify if the file system you want to remove is shown in the list.

   Yes Continue with Step 3.

   No Go to Step 5.

3. Unmount the file system by using the `umount` command.

   ```
   umount <filesystem name>
   ```

4. Repeat Step 1 to check whether the file system has successfully been unmounted.

Alternatively, using the SMIT fast path command `smitty rmjfs` to remove a journaled file system will display a screen similar to the one shown in Figure 84.

```
                         Remove a Journaled File System

Type or select values in entry fields.
Press Enter AFTER making all desired changes.

                                                        [Entry Fields]
* FILE SYSTEM name                                     []                      +
  Remove Mount Point                                   no                      +









F1=Help             F2=Refresh          F3=Cancel           F4=List
F5=Reset            F6=Command          F7=Edit             F8=Image
F9=Shell            F10=Exit            Enter=Do
```

Figure 84. rmjfs - Step 1

5. Press **F4** to get a list of all the file systems that are defined on the system. You will obtain a screen similar to Figure 85.

```
                       Remove a Journaled File System

Ty
Pr                            FILE SYSTEM name

     Move cursor to desired item and press Enter.
*                                                                       +
     [TOP]                                                              +
       /
       /home
       /usr
       /var
       /tmp
       /usr/vice/cache
       /var/dce
       /var/dce/adm/dfs/cache
       /test
       /export/lpp_source_1
     [MORE...6]

     F1=Help                F2=Refresh              F3=Cancel
F1   F8=Image               F10=Exit                Enter=Do
F5   /=Find                 n=Find Next
F9
```

Figure 85. rmjfs - Step 2

6. Select the file system to be removed using the arrow keys and press **Enter.**
7. The name of the file system you just selected will be shown in the FILE SYSTEM name parameter.
8. If you want to keep the directory name that was used to mount this file system, press **Enter** to complete the command, otherwise change the Remove Mount Point parameter to YES and press **Enter** to complete the process.

5.5.5 Increasing the Size of a File System

AIX provides you the facility to increase the size of a file system dynamically, provided you have enough free space available on your disk. File systems that are low on space might create unanticipated problems.

Note

Whenever a file system is full, the system cannot write to it and returns you the following error.

```
There is not enough room in the file system
```

5.5.5.1 Increasing File System Size Using the Command Line

A file system can be increased by using the `chfs` command as shown in the following steps.

1. Use the `df` command to find out the current size of the file system.
2. Calculate the number of blocks you need to add.
3. On the command line, enter the following command:

```
chfs -a size=<new size in 512-byte blocks> <file system name>
Filesystem size changed to <new size in 512-byte blocks>
```

5.5.5.2 Increasing the Size of a File System Using SMIT

To increase the file system size using the SMIT fast path command (`smitty chjfs`), do the following steps.

1. Executing the `smitty chjfs` will display a screen similar to Figure 86.

```
                          File System Name

Move cursor to desired item and press Enter.

[TOP]
  /
  /home
  /usr
  /var
  /tmp
  /usr/vice/cache
  /var/dce
  /var/dce/adm/dfs/cache
  /test
  /export/lpp_source_1
[MORE...6]

F1=Help                 F2=Refresh              F3=Cancel
F8=Image                F10=Exit                Enter=Do
/=Find                  n=Find Next
```

Figure 86. chjfs - Step 1

2. Use the arrow keys to select the file system you want to change, and press the **Enter** key. A screen similar to Figure 87 on page 137 will be shown, which will report the current file system attributes.

```
            Change / Show Characteristics of a Journaled File System

Type or select values in entry fields.
Press Enter AFTER making all desired changes.

                                                        [Entry Fields]
  File system name                                    /tmp
  NEW mount point                                    [/tmp]
  SIZE of file system (in 512-byte blocks)           [32768]
  Mount GROUP                                        []
  Mount AUTOMATICALLY at system restart?              yes              +
  PERMISSIONS                                         read/write       +
  Mount OPTIONS                                      []                +
  Start Disk Accounting?                              no               +
  Fragment Size (bytes)                               4096
  Number of bytes per inode                           4096
  Compression algorithm                               no
  Large File Enabled                                  false
  Allocation Group Size (MBytes)                      8


F1=Help             F2=Refresh          F3=Cancel           F4=List
F5=Reset            F6=Command          F7=Edit             F8=Image
F9=Shell            F10=Exit            Enter=Do
```

Figure 87. chjfs - Step 2

3. Enter the new file system size that you calculated in the SIZE of file system (in 512 byte block) field.
4. Press **Enter.** The SMIT OK prompt will indicate the successful completion of the process.

5.5.6 Checking the File System Consistency

The `fsck` command checks file system consistency and interactively repairs the file system. The general syntax of the `fsck` command is as follows:

```
fsck [ -n ] [ -p ] [ -y ] [ -dBlockNumber ] [ -f ] [ -ii-NodeNumber ] [ -o
Options ] [ -tFile ] [ -V VfsName ] [ FileSystem1 - FileSystem2 ... ]
```

The flags commonly used with the `fsck` command and their meanings are shown in the following table.

Table 11. fsck Command Flags

Flag	Description
-f	Performs a fast check. Under normal circumstances, the only file systems likely to be affected by halting the system without shutting down properly are those that are mounted when the system stops. The -f flag prompts the `fsck` command not to check file systems that were unmounted successfully. The `fsck` command determines this by inspecting the s_fmod flag in the file system superblock. This flag is set whenever a file system is mounted and cleared when it is unmounted successfully. If a file system is unmounted successfully, it is unlikely to have any problems. Because most file systems are unmounted successfully, not checking those file systems can reduce the checking time.
-p	Does not display messages about minor problems, but fixes them automatically. This flag does not grant the wholesale license that the -y flag does and is useful for performing automatic checks when the system is started normally. You should use this flag as part of the system startup procedures, whenever the system is being run automatically. Also allows parallel checks by group. If the primary superblock is corrupt, the secondary superblock is verified and copied to the primary superblock.
-tFile	Specifies a file parameter as a scratch file on a file system other than the one being checked, if the `fsck` command cannot obtain enough memory to keep its tables. If you do not specify the -t flag and the `fsck` command needs a scratch file, it prompts you for the name of the scratch file. However, if you have specified the -p flag, the `fsck` command is unsuccessful. If the scratch file is not a special file, it is removed when the `fsck` command ends.
-y	Assumes a yes response to all questions asked by the `fsck` command. This flag lets the `fsck` command take any action it considers necessary. Use this flag only on severely damaged file systems.

The `fsck` command checks and interactively repairs inconsistent file systems. You should run this command before mounting any file system. You must be able to read the device file on which the file system resides (for example, the /dev/hd0 device).

Normally, the file system is consistent and the `fsck` command merely reports on the number of files, used blocks, and free blocks in the file system. If the file system is inconsistent, the `fsck` command displays information about the inconsistencies found and prompts you for permission to repair them. If the file system cannot be repaired, restore it from backup.

Mounting an inconsistent file system may result in a system crash. If you do not specify a file system with the FileSystem parameter, the `fsck` command will check all the file systems with attribute check=TRUE in /etc/filesystems.

Note

By default, the /, /usr, /var, and /tmp file systems have the check attribute set to False (check=false) in their /etc/filesystem stanzas. The attribute is set to False for the following reasons:

1. The boot process explicitly runs the `fsck` command on the /, /usr, /var, and /tmp file systems.
2. The /, /usr, /var, and /tmp file systems are mounted when the /etc/rc file is executed. The `fsck` command will not modify a mounted file system and `fsck` results on mounted file systems are unpredictable

5.5.7 Initializing the JFS Log Device

The `logform` command initializes a logical volume for use as a JFS log device, which stores transactional information about file system metadata changes and can be used to roll back incomplete operations if the machine crashes. Following is the general syntax of the `logform` command.

```
logform LogName
```

Note

- The `logform` command is destructive; it wipes out all data in the logical volume.
- Accidentally running this on a file system completely destroys the file system's data. The `logform` command should only be run on CLOSED logical volumes. If a log device is open due to its use by a mounted file system, the file system should be unmounted prior to running `logform` against the log device.The `logform` command destroys all log records on existing log devices, which may result in file system data loss. You can check to ensure that the log device is closed by running the following:

  ```
  lsvg -l VGname
  ```

5.5.8 How to Add Additional JFS Logs

A file system log is a formatted list of file system transaction records. The log for this system is called the journaled file system (JFS) log and is used when the system goes down before the transactions have been completed. The JFS log ensures file system integrity, but not necessarily data integrity. A dedicated disk is created on hd8 for rootvg when the system is installed. The JFS log size is 4 MB. You can also create a JFS log on a separate disk for other volume groups, as shown in the following procedure.

In this example we will be using uservg as the volume group and userlv as the logical volume. First, determine the mounted file systems:

```
# mount
node       mounted        mounted over   vfs      date         options
------ -------------- -------------  ---- ----------- --------------
       /dev/hd4       /              jfs  Nov 16 18:45 rw,log=/dev/hd8
       /dev/hd2       /usr           jfs  Nov 16 18:45 rw,log=/dev/hd8
       /dev/hd9var    /var           jfs  Nov 16 18:45 rw,log=/dev/hd8
       /dev/hd3       /tmp           jfs  Nov 16 18:45 rw,log=/dev/hd8
       /dev/hd1       /home          jfs  Nov 16 18:46 rw,log=/dev/hd8
       /dev/userlv    /u             jfs  Nov 18 11:25 rw,log=/dev/loglv00
```

Notice that the log for the `/userlv` logical volume is the logical volume loglv00.

To check the `loglv00 LV` enter:

```
# lslv loglv00
LOGICAL VOLUME:  loglv00               VOLUME GROUP:  uservg
LV IDENTIFIER:   00091974342f2afa.2    PERMISSION:    read/write
VG STATE:        active/complete       LV STATE:      opened/syncd
TYPE:            jfslog                WRITE VERIFY:  off
MAX LPs:         512                   PP SIZE:       8 megabyte(s)
COPIES:          1                     SCHED POLICY:  parallel
LPs:             1                     PPs:           1
STALE PPs:       0                     BB POLICY:     relocatable
INTER-POLICY:    minimum               RELOCATABLE:   yes
INTRA-POLICY:    middle                UPPER BOUND:   32
MOUNT POINT:     N/A                   LABEL:         None
MIRROR WRITE CONSISTENCY: on
EACH LP COPY ON A SEPARATE PV ?: yes
```

Check the physical volumes (PVs) to look for a drive with no VG associated.

```
# lspv
hdisk0          000919746edab91f     rootvg
hdisk1          0009197459d92f2e     None
hdisk2          00091974d381d097     uservg
```

```
hdisk3          00091974d81ff431    uservg
hdisk4          00091974de731316    None
```

Notice that `hdisk1` and `hdisk4` have no VGs assigned to them. To extend the `uservg` volume group to incorporate hdisk4 type:

```
extendvg -f 'uservg' 'hdisk4'
```

To create the jfslog on `hdisk4` enter:

```
smitty mklv
```

In Figure 88, select **VOLUME GROUP name**. In this example it is `uservg`.

```
                              Add a Logical Volume

Type or select a value for the entry field.
Press Enter AFTER making all desired changes.

                                                        [Entry Fields]
* VOLUME GROUP name                                    [uservg]             +










F1=Help              F2=Refresh           F3=Cancel            F4=List
F5=Reset             F6=Command           F7=Edit              F8=Image
F9=Shell             F10=Exit             Enter=Do
```

Figure 88. Add a Logical Volume Menu

From the Add a Logical Volume menu, select the following options:

Logical volume NAME to create	`userlog`
Number of LOGICAL PARTITIONS	`1`
PHYSICAL VOLUME names	`hdisk4`
Logical volume TYPE	`jfslog`
POSITION on physical volume	`center`

as displayed in Figure 89 on page 142.

```
                         Add a Logical Volume

Type or select values in entry fields.
Press Enter AFTER making all desired changes.

[TOP]                                              [Entry Fields]
  Logical volume NAME                             [userlog]
  VOLUME GROUP name                                uservg
  Number of LOGICAL PARTITIONS                    [1]                #
  PHYSICAL VOLUME names                           [hdisk4]          +
  Logical volume TYPE                             [jfslog]
  POSITION on physical volume                      center           +
  RANGE of physical volumes                        minimum          +
  MAXIMUM NUMBER of PHYSICAL VOLUMES              []                 #
    to use for allocation
  Number of COPIES of each logical                 1                +
    partition
  Mirror Write Consistency?                        yes              +
  Allocate each logical partition copy             yes              +
[MORE...11]

F1=Help           F2=Refresh         F3=Cancel          F4=List
F5=Reset          F6=Command         F7=Edit            F8=Image
F9=Shell          F10=Exit           Enter=Do
```

Figure 89. Add a Logical Volume Selection Menu

Once completed, the COMMAND STATUS screen will display confirmation as displayed in Figure 90.

```
                              COMMAND STATUS

Command: OK            stdout: yes            stderr: no

Before command completion, additional instructions may appear below.

userlog













F1=Help           F2=Refresh         F3=Cancel          F6=Command
F8=Image          F9=Shell           F10=Exit           /=Find
n=Find Next
```

Figure 90. Add a Logical Volume Command Status

Press **F10** and exit SMIT to the command line and enter the following:

```
# /usr/sbin/logform /dev/userlog
logform: destroy /dev/userlog (y)?y
```

Note

The preceding command formats the JFS-log logical volume so that it can record file-system transactions. Nothing is destroyed despite the wording in the prompt.

Make sure the /userlv has been mounted by typing:

```
# mount
node       mounted        mounted over  vfs      date        options
------ -------------- -------------  ---- ----------- --------------
       /dev/hd4       /              jfs  Nov 16 18:45 rw,log=/dev/hd8
       /dev/hd2       /usr           jfs  Nov 16 18:45 rw,log=/dev/hd8
       /dev/hd9var    /var           jfs  Nov 16 18:45 rw,log=/dev/hd8
       /dev/hd3       /tmp           jfs  Nov 16 18:45 rw,log=/dev/hd8
       /dev/hd1       /home          jfs  Nov 16 18:46 rw,log=/dev/hd8
       /dev/userlv    /u             jfs  Nov 18 11:25 rw,log=/dev/userlog
```

Notice that the log is now `userlog` instead of `loglv00`.

To verify that you have set up the file system and log correctly, use the following command:

```
# lsvg -l uservg
uservg:
LV NAME           TYPE    LPs  PPs  PVs  LV STATE     MOUNT POINT
userlv            jfs     820  820  2    open/syncd   /u
userlog           jfslog  1    1    1    open/syncd   N/A#
```

There should be two logical volumes listed, as shown in the preceding example.

5.6 Troubleshooting File System Problems

This section will discuss some of the problems encountered while managing LVM and how to resolve them.

5.6.1 Recovering from Super Block Errors

If you receive one of the following errors from the `fsck` or `mount` commands, the problem may be a corrupted superblock.

```
fsck: Not an AIX3 file system
fsck: Not an AIXV3 file system
fsck: Not an AIX4 file system
fsck: Not an AIXV4 file system
fsck: Not a recognized file system type
mount: invalid argument
```

The problem can be resolved by restoring the backup of superblock over the primary superblock using one of the following commands.

```
dd count=1 bs=4k skip=31 seek=1 if=/dev/lv00 of=/dev/lv00
```

The following command works only for AIX 4.x.

```
fsck -p /dev/lv00
```

Once the restoration process is completed, check the integrity of the file system by issuing the `fsck` command.

```
fsck /dev/lv00
```

In many cases, restoration of the backup of superblock to the primary superblock will recover the file system. If this does not resolve the problem, recreate the file system, and restore the data from a backup.

5.6.2 Cannot Unmount File Systems

A file system cannot be unmounted if any references are still active within that file system and the following error message will be displayed.

```
Device busy
```

or

```
A device is already mounted or cannot be unmounted
```

The following situations can leave an open references to a mounted file system.

- Files are open within a file system. Close these <files> before the file system can be unmounted.The `fuser` command is often the best way to determine what is still active in this file system. The `fuser` command will return the process IDs for all processes that have open references within a specified file system as shown in the following example.

  ```
  fuser -xc /tmp
  /tmp: 2910 3466 11654 26400
  ```

  The process having an open reference can be killed by using the `kill` command and the unmount can be accomplished.

- If the file system is still busy and not getting unmounted, this could be due to a kernel extension that is loaded, but exists within the source file system. The `fuser` command will not show these kinds of references, since a user process is not involved. However the `genkex` command will report on all loaded kernel extensions.
- File systems are still mounted within that file system. Unmount those file systems before this file system can be unmounted. If any file system is mounted within a file system, this leaves open references in the source file system at the mount point of the other file system. Use the `mount` command to get a list of mounted file systems. Unmount all the file system which are mounted within the file system to be unmounted.

5.6.3 When the df Command Hangs

If the system hangs when you use the `df` command, the process described in this section may assist you.

Run the `df` command to check the file system. Note that the `raven:/u2` entry at the bottom is a remote file system that is locally mounted.

```
# df
Filesystem     512-blocks        Free %Used     Iused %Iused Mounted on
/dev/hd4            40960       19384   53%      1252    13% /
/dev/hd2           663552       13288   98%     13170    16% /usr
/dev/hd9var        401408      262528   35%     22288    45% /var
/dev/hd3            65536       35336   47%        70     1% /tmp
/dev/hd1           360448       19704   95%        98     1% /home
raven:/u2           16384           0  100%        18     1% /u2
```

If the remote system raven is down and you enter the `df` command, the following will be your response:

```
# df
Filesystem     512-blocks        Free %Used     Iused %Iused Mounted on
/dev/hd4            40960       19384   53%      1252    13% /
/dev/hd2           663552       13288   98%     13170    16% /usr
/dev/hd9var        401408      262528   35%     22288    45% /var
/dev/hd3            65536       35336   47%        70     1% /tmp
/dev/hd1           360448       19704   95%        98     1% /home
NFS server raven not responding still trying
```

Break out of the error by pressing **Ctrl-c**.

Correct the problem with the remote system and once communication has been reestablished, you can run the `df` command to completion.

Some tips to check the remote system follow.

- To check if the remote system is reachable through the network, enter:

```
# ping raven
PING raven.itsc.austin.ibm.com: (9.3.1.215): 56 data bytes
64 bytes from 9.3.1.215: icmp_seq=0 ttl=255 time=9 ms
64 bytes from 9.3.1.215: icmp_seq=1 ttl=255 time=1 ms
^C
----raven.itsc.austin.ibm.com PING Statistics----
2 packets transmitted, 2 packets received, 0% packet loss
round-trip min/avg/max = 1/5/9 ms
```

  This shows that the problem is on the remote machine. If ping failed, it could be a break in the network or a problem with the network adapters in either machine. Choose another address on the same network segment to test.

- Stop and restart the NFS daemon on the remote system:

```
# stopsrc -s nfsd
0513-044 The stop of the nfsd Subsystem was completed successfully.
# startsrc -s nfsd
0513-059 The nfsd Subsystem has been started. Subsystem PID is 10178.
```

5.6.4 Deleting an Application File That Is Locked

In this section, you are trying to delete an application file that is locked. When you try to delete the file, you receive an error message telling you that it cannot be deleted because the file is locked.

If you get an error trying to delete the file `/userdirectory/myfile` enter:

```
# fuser /userdiectory/myfile
myfile:    104772
```

The number `104772` is the process ID (PID) of the file. To kill the process ID enter:

```
kill -9 104772
```

Now, to delete the file and free the disk space for use by the file system enter:

```
rm myfile
```

5.7 Summary of LVM Commands

This section summarizes the key commands that have been used in different sections of this chapter.

5.7.1 PV Commands

The following commands are most commonly used with physical volume related tasks.

`lsdev`	Lists devices in the ODM
`chdev`	Changes the characteristics of a device
`mkdev`	Adds a device to the system
`chpv`	Changes the state of the physical volume
`lspv`	Displays information about a physical volume within a volume group
`migratepv`	Moves allocated physical partitions from one physical volume to one or more other physical volumes

5.7.2 VG Commands

The following commands are most commonly used with volume group related tasks.

`mkvg`	Creates a new volume group
`extendvg`	Adds a physical volume to a volume group
`reducevg`	Removes physical volume from a volume group
`chvg`	Changes a volume group
`lsvg`	Displays information about a volume group
`importvg`	Installs a volume group
`exportvg`	Removes a volume group
`reorgvg`	Reorganizes a volume group
`syncvg`	Synchronizes a volume group
`varyonvg`	Makes a volume group available for use
`varyoffvg`	Makes a volume group unavailable for use

5.7.3 LV Commands

Following are some of the most commonly used logical volume commands.

`mklv`	Creates a logical volume
`lslv`	Lists the characteristics of a logical volume
`rmlv`	Removes a logical volume

`extendlv` Increases the size of a logical volume

`chlv` Changes the characteristic of a logical volume

`mklvcopy` Adds copies to a logical volume

`rmlvcopy` Removes copies from a logical volume

5.7.4 File System Commands

Following is the list of file systems commands that have been discussed in this chapter:

`chfs` Changes the characteristics of a file system

`crfs` Adds a file system

`lsfs` Displays the characteristics of a file system

`rmfs` Removes a file system

`mount` Makes a file system available for use

`fsck` Checks file system consistency and interactively repairs the file system

`umount` Unmounts a previously mounted file system, directory, or file

`df` Reports information about space on file systems

`dd` Reads the InFile parameter or standard input, does the specified conversions, then copies the converted data to the *OutFile* parameter or standard output; the input and output block size can be specified to take advantage of raw physical I/O

5.8 References

The following publications contain more information about LVM concepts.

- *AIX Storage Management*, GG24-4484.
- *AIX Version 4.3 System Management Guide: Operating System and Devices*, SC23-4126.

  IBM Solution Developer Program,

  URL: `http://www.developer.ibm.com/library/aix4.3/64bit_43.html#BOS Commands`
- *RS/6000 Resource,*

  URL:`http://www.rs6000.ibm.com/resource/`

5.9 Quiz

1. Company XYZ has a standalone RS/6000 system they use to maintain an expanding customer database. The database is currently stored in the logical volume dblv in rootvg on hdisk4. Because of future growth, the customer decided to move the database to a new drive in a separate volume group. This new drive is hdisk5 in volume group datavg. Which of the following commands can be used to move the database logical volume, dblv, to the new volume group?

   A. `mklv -l dblv`

   B. `cplv -v datavg dblv`

   C. `migratelv dblv hdisk5`

   D. `migratepv -l dblv hdisk4 hdisk5`

2. While attempting to write a 200 MB file to the user data file system with 1 GB free space, the system responds with the message that it is out of space. Which of the following could be causing this?

   df output

Filesystem	1024-blocks	Free	%Used	Iused	%Iused	Mounted on
/dev/hd4	40960	3744	91%	2416	12%	/
/dev/hd2	1003520	35280	97%	37596	13%	/usr
/dev/hd9var	36864	24540	34%	1236	14%	/var
/dev/hd3	167936	8108	96%	844	2%	/tmp
/dev/hd1	40960	20232	51%	1364	14%	/home
/dev/datalv	1224704	1023952	16%	6309	7%	/user/data
/dev/datalv2	16384	5884	65%	1018	25%	/data2
/dev/userlv2	12288	11608	6%	49	2%	/user2
/dev/userlv	12288	5002	59%	643	7%	/user
/dev/foolv	12288	121	99%	49	2%	/foo

   A. The `/user/data` filesystem is mounted read only.

   B. The permissions on the `/user` filesystem is wrong.

   C. The permissions on the `/user/data` file system is wrong.

   D. `/user` is preventing you from reaching the `/user/data` file system.

1. The order-processing department of a company has complained of slow response times from their application. The system administrator has determined this is due to a disk I/O bottleneck on the physical volume where the application data file system is located. Which of the following could be used to help improve the application response times?

   A. Stripe the file system logical volume across multiple disks.

   B. Move the jfslog to the same physical volume as the file system.

   C. Increase the size of the application data file system.

D. Move the physical volume into a separate volume group.

2. Customer XYZ discovered that one of their hard drives, hdisk3, was bad. The drive contains volume group data3vg which was used by an application many years ago. Since they do not need to keep this information, they decided to simply remove the drive. After rebooting, the physical volume for hdisk3 is still listed in the volume group descriptor area (VGDA). Which of the following commands can be used to delete the physical volume from data3vg?

   A. `reducevg`

   B. `synclvodm`

   C. `reducelvodm`

   D. `syncvg`

5.9.1 Answers

1. B
2. D
3. A
4. A

5.10 Exercises

The following exercises will help you explore these topics in greater detail.

1. List all the physical volumes, volume groups, logical volumes, physical partitions and file systems on your system.
2. Determine which disks the rootvg volume group resides on.
3. Add a new physical volume to your system and check to make sure the drive is available.
4. Create a volume group named datavg on this new physical volume.
5. Create a file system named datafiles.
6. Unmount the datafiles file system.
7. Create a mirror of datavg.
8. Determine whether you have a disk quorum.
9. Increase the size of the file system datafiles.
10. Reduce the file system datafiles.

11. List the disks that a file system, datafiles, and a volume group, datavg, reside on.
12. Remove the mirror of datavg and check to make sure the device isn't mirrored.
13. Remove the datavg volume group.
14. Create multiple jfslogs on several PVs.
15. How do you erase a file that is being locked by an application?
16. Run `extendvg` to extend a volume group. What needs to be run first?
17. Stripe data to spread I/O.

Chapter 6. SMIT Fast Path Commands

System Management Interface Tool (SMIT) provides an alternative, natural-language, task-oriented interface for AIX system management. The SMIT facility runs in two interfaces, ASCII (nongraphical) or AIXwindows (graphical). After you enter SMIT using the `smit` command, the first screen displayed is the main menu which is shown in Figure 91. The main menu selections lead to submenus, helping to narrow the scope of choice to a particular task. Alternatively you can use the `smit` command with a *fast path* parameter which can save you time by allowing you to go directly to the menu or dialog for your task, bypassing the upper-level menus. For example, to change the characteristics of a user, enter the following command:

```
smit chuser
```

The `chuser` command is an example of a fast path parameter. The `smit` command plus the fast path parameter, chuser, takes you directly to the menu, Change User Attributes, which guides you through the steps to change a user's characteristics.

```
                              System Management

Move cursor to desired item and press Enter.

  Software Installation and Maintenance
  Software License Management
  Devices
  System Storage Management (Physical & Logical Storage)
  Security & Users
  Communications Applications and Services
  Print Spooling
  Problem Determination
  Performance & Resource Scheduling
  System Environments
  Processes & Subsystems
  Applications
  Using SMIT (information only)




F1=Help              F2=Refresh           F3=Cancel            F8=Image
F9=Shell             F10=Exit             Enter=Do
```

Figure 91. The First SMIT Screen

At any menu in SMIT, you can show the fast path to that menu by pressing **F8** or by choosing **Fast Path** from the Show menu.

6.1 Summary of SMIT Fast Path Commands

The following list provides a quick reference to many SMIT fast paths. In this list, a SMIT menu name is followed by its associated fast path in parentheses. Enter the word smit and the fast path shown to go directly to its associated menu.

- Software Installation and Maintenance (**install)**
  - Install and Update Software **(install_update**)
    - Install and Update from LATEST Available Software **(install_latest)**
    - Update Installed Software to Latest Level (Update All) **(install_all)**
    - Install and Update Software by Package Name (includes devices and printers) **(install_package)**
    - Install Software Bundle (Easy Install) **(install_bundle)**
    - Update Software by Fix (APAR) **(update_by_fix)**
    - Install and Update from ALL Available Software **(install_all)**
  - List Software and Related Information **(list_software)**
  - Software Maintenance and Utilities **(maintain_software)**
    - Commit Applied Software Updates (Remove Saved Files) **(commit)**
    - Reject Applied Software Updates (Use Previous Version) **(reject)**
    - Remove Installed Software **(remove)**
    - Copy Software to Hard Disk for Future Installation **(bffcreate**)
    - Check Software File Sizes After Installation **(check_files)**
    - Verify Software Installation and Requisites **(verify_install)**
  - Network Installation Management **(nim_client)**
  - System Backup Manager **(backsys)**
    - Back Up the System **(mksysb)**
    - List Files in a System Image **(lsmksysb)**
    - Restore Files in a System Image **(restmksysb)**
- Software License Management (**licences)**
  - Manage Nodelocked Licenses **(manage_nodelocked)**
  - Manage License Servers and License Databases **(manage_servers)**
  - Show License Usage on Servers **(show_server_status)**

- Devices **(dev)**
  - Install/Configure Devices Added After IPL **(cfgmgr)**
  - Printer/Plotter **(printer)**
    - Printer/Plotter Devices **(pdp)**

      Add a Printer/Plotter **(makprt)**

      Move a Printer/Plotter to Another Port **(movprt)**

      Change / Show Characteristics of a Printer/Plotter **(chgprt)**

      Remove a Printer/Plotter **(rmvprt)**

      Install Additional Printer/Plotter Software **(printerinst)**
    - Print Spooling **(spooler)**
  - TTY **(tty)**
  - PTY **(pty)**
  - Console **(console)**
  - Fixed Disk **(disk)**
  - CD ROM Drive **(cdrom)**
  - Read/Write Optical Drive **(rwopt)**
  - Diskette Drive **(diskette)**
  - Tape Drive **(tape)**
  - Communication **(commodev)**
  - Graphic Displays **(g_display)**
  - Graphic Input Devices **(input)**
  - Low Function Terminal (LFT) **(lft)**
  - SCSI Initiator Device **(scsiid)**
  - SCSI Adapter **(scsia)**
  - Asynchronous I/O **(aio)**
  - Multimedia **(mm)**
  - List Devices **(lsattr)**
  - Install Additional Device Software **(devinst)**
- System Storage Management (Physical & Logical Storage) (**storage)**
  - Logical Volume Manager **(lvm)**
    - Volume Groups **(vg)**

        - Logical Volumes **(lv)**
        - Physical Volumes **(pv)**
        - Paging Space **(pgsp)**

          Add Another Paging Space **(mkps)**

          Change / Show Characteristics of a Paging Space **(chps)**

          Remove a Paging Space **(rmps)**

          Activate a Paging Space **(swapon)**
    - File Systems **(fs)**
        - Add / Change / Show / Delete File Systems **(manfs)**
        - Mount a File System **(mountfs)**
        - Mount a Group of File Systems **(mountg**)
        - Unmount a File System **(umountfs)**
        - Unmount a Group of File Systems **(umountg)**
        - Verify a File System **(fsck)**
        - Backup a File System **(backfilesys)**
        - Restore a File System **(restfilesys)**
        - List Contents of a Backup **(listtoc)**
    - Files & Directories **(filemgr)**
        - Backup a File or Directory **(backfile**)
        - Restore a File or Directory **(restfile**)
    - System Backup Manager **(backsys)**
- Security & Users (**security)**
    - Users **(users)**
        - Add a User **(mkuser)**
        - Change a User's Password **(passwd)**
        - Change / Show Characteristics of a User **(chuser)**
        - Lock / Unlock a User's Account **(lockuser)**
        - Reset User's Failed Login Count **(failed_login)**
        - Remove a User **(rmuser)**
    - Groups **(groups)**
    - Passwords **(passwords)**

        - Login Controls **(login)**
        - Roles **(roles)**
- Communications Applications and Services **(commo)**
    - TCP/IP **(tcpip)**
        - Minimum Configuration & Startup **(mktcpip)**
        - Further Configuration **(configtcp)**
        - Use DHCP for TCPIP Configuration & Startup **(usedhcp)**
        - IPV6 Configuration **(configtcp6)**
    - NFS **(nfs_menu) (nfs)**
    - CIFS/SMB **(smb)**
- Print Spooling (**spooler)**
    - Start a Print Job **(qprt)**
    - Manage Print Jobs **(jobs)**
    - Manage Print Queues **(pqmanage)**
    - Add a Print Queue **(mkpq)**
    - Add an Additional Printer to an Existing Print Queue **(mkpqprt)**
    - Change / Show Print Queue Characteristics **(chpq)**
    - Change / Show Printer Connection Characteristics **(chprtcom)**
    - Remove a Print Queue **(rmpq)**
    - Manage Print Server **(server)**
    - Programming Tools **(pqtools)**
- Problem Determination (**problem)**
    - Error Log **(error)**
        - Generate Error Report **(errpt)**
        - Change / Show Characteristics of the Error Log **(errdemon)**
        - Clean the Error Log **(errclear)**
    - System Dump **(dump)**
        - Change the Primary Dump Device **(dumpchgp)**
        - Change the Secondary Dump Device **(dumpchgs)**
    - Alog **(alog)**
    - Hardware Diagnostics **(diag)**

    - Verify Software Installation and Requisites **(verify_install)**
- Performance & Resource Scheduling (**performance)**
    - Resource Status & Monitors **(monitors)**
    - Analysis Tools **(analysis)**
    - Resource Controls **(controls)**
    - Schedule Jobs **(at)**
- System Environments **(system)**
    - Stop the System **(shutdown)**
    - Assign the Console **(chcons)**
    - Change / Show Date and Time **(chtz_date)**
    - Manage Language Environment **(mlang)**
    - Change / Show Characteristics of Operating System **(cgsys)**
    - Change / Show Number of Licensed Users **(chlicense)**
    - Manage AIX Floating User Licenses for this Server **(netls_server)**
    - Broadcast Message to all Users **(wall)**
    - Manage System Logs **(logs)**
    - Change / Show Characteristics of System Dump **(dump)**
    - Internet and Documentation Services **(web_configure)**
    - Change System User Interface **(dt_config)**
    - Manage Remote Reboot Facility **(rrbtty)**
- Processes & Subsystems (**src)**
    - Processes **(process)**
    - Subsystems **(subsys)**
    - Subservers **(subserver)**

6.2 References

The following publication contains more information about the SMIT fast path commands.

- *AIX Version 4.3 System Management Guide: Operating System & Devices,* SC23-4126

6.3 Quiz

1. Company ABC recently ordered an HP Laserjet 5 printer. The system administrator needs to install the printer drivers for the printer. What SMIT installation screen fastpath can be used to perform the installation?

   A. `smit makprt`

   B. `smit printerinst`

   C. `smit install_commit`

   D. `smit maintain_software`

2. The system administrator wants to add a new printer queue for an EPSON dot matrix printer. What SMIT fast path command shall he use to perform the function?

   A. `smit qprt`

   B. `smit mkpq`

   C. `smit chpq`

   D. `smit mkpqrt`

6.3.1 Answers

1. B
2. B

6.4 Exercises

1. Perform the following functions using the SMIT fast path commands.
   - Update software by fix (APAR).
   - Verify the software installation and requisites.
   - Add a plotter.
   - Activate a paging space.
   - Add a paging space.
   - Change a user's password.
   - Add a print queue.
   - Show characteristics of error log.

Chapter 7. Problem Determination

This chapter provides information to assist you in solving problems with operating system, hardware, or other programs installed on the system using the following tools.

- Error Logging Facility
- System Dump Facility

7.1 Software Service Aids Package

AIX Version 4.1 base system (bos.rte) consists of errlog subroutines, errsave, and errlast kernel service, error device driver (/dev/error), error daemon, and the `errinstall`, `errupdate`, and `errstop` commands.

An optionally installable software service aids package (bos_sysmgt.serv_aid) which consists of the `errclear`, `errdead`, `errlogger`, `errmsg`, `errpt`, and `sysdumpstart` commands is required to generate reports from an error log using the `errpt` command and to delete entries from the error log using the `errclear` command.

7.2 Error Logging Facility

The error logging facility records hardware and software failures in the error log for informational purposes or for fault detection and corrective action. The error logging subsystem is composed of three components whose processing flow is shown in Figure 92. The type of tasks are defined as follows.

Error Log Programming Used by developers to create error templates and create messages.

Error Processing Invoked when an error occurs.

Error Log File Processing Used by administrators to diagnose a problem.

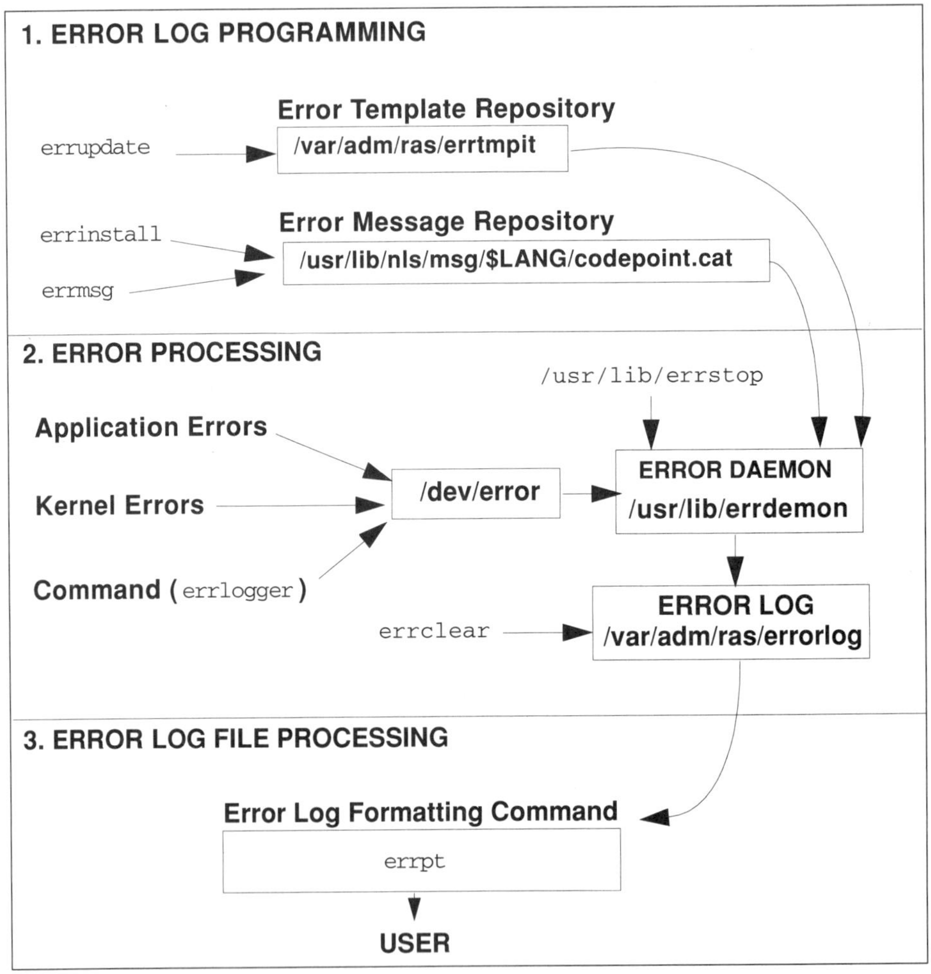

Figure 92. Error Logging Subsystem Overview

7.2.1 Managing Error Log

The following sections discuss various error log management related functions.

7.2.1.1 Configuring an Error Log File (/var/adm/ras/errlog)

This section discusses the use of `errdemon` command to customize the error log file.

- To list the current values for the error log file name, error log file size, and buffer size that are currently stored in the error log configuration database settings, use the following command.

```
# /usr/lib/errdemon -l
Error Log Attributes
--------------------------------------------
Log File                /var/adm/ras/errlog
Log Size                4096 bytes
Memory Buffer Size      8192 bytes
```

  The preceding example shows the default error log file attributes. The log file size cannot be made smaller than the hard-coded default of 4 KB and the buffer cannot be made smaller than the hard-coded default of 8 KB.

- To change the log file name to /var/adm/ras/errlog.test, use the following command.

```
/usr/lib/errdemon -i /var/adm/ras/errlog.test
```

- To change the log file size to 8 MB, use the following command.

```
/usr/lib/errdemon -s 8192
```

  If the log file size specified is smaller than the size of the log file currently in use, the current log file is renamed by appending .old to the file name and a new log file is created with the specified size limit. The amount of space specified is reserved for the error log file and is not available for use by other files. Therefore, you should be careful not to make the log excessively large. But, if you make the log too small, important information may be overwritten prematurely. When the log file size limit is reached, the file wraps. That is, the oldest entries are overwritten by new entries.

- To change the size of the error log device driver's internal buffer to 16 MB, use the following command.

```
# /usr/lib/errdemon -B 16384
0315-175 The error log memory buffer size you supplied will be rounded
up to a multiple of 4096 bytes.
```

  If the specified buffer size is larger than the buffer size currently in use, the in-memory buffer is immediately increased and if the specified buffer size is smaller than the buffer size currently in use, the new size is put into effect the next time the error daemon is started after the system is rebooted. The size you specify is rounded up to the next integral multiple of the memory page size (4 KB).

  You should be careful not to impact your system's performance by making the buffer excessively large. But, if you make the buffer too small, the buffer may become full if error entries are arriving faster than they are being read from the buffer and put into the log file. When the buffer is full, new entries are discarded until space becomes available in the buffer. When this situation occurs, an error log entry is created to inform you of the problem.

The following command shows the new attributes of error log file.

```
# /usr/lib/errdemon -l
Error Log Attributes
--------------------------------------------
Log File                /var/adm/ras/errlog.test
Log Size                8192 bytes
Memory Buffer Size      16384 bytes
```

7.2.1.2 Starting the Error Logging Daemon

To determine if error logging daemon is on or off, issue the `errpt` command. The `errpt` command output may contain entries as shown in Figure 93.

```
# errpt
IDENTIFIER TIMESTAMP  T C RESOURCE_NAME  DESCRIPTION
9DBCFDEE   1108182898 T O errdemon       ERROR LOGGING TURNED ON
192AC071   1108182898 T O errdemon       ERROR LOGGING TURNED OFF
AA8AB241   1108182798 T O OPERATOR       OPERATOR NOTIFICATION
# 
```

Figure 93. errpt Command

If the `errpt` command does not generate entries, error logging has been turned off. To activate the daemon use the following command.

```
/usr/lib/errdemon
```

The errdemon daemon starts error logging and writes error log entries in the system error log.

7.2.1.3 Stopping the Error Logging Daemon

To stop the error logging daemon from logging entries use the following command.

```
/usr/lib/errstop
```

7.2.1.4 Cleaning an Error Log

Cleaning of the error log implies deleting old or unnecessary entries from the error log. Cleaning is normally done as part of the daily `cron` command execution (see Chapter 14, “The cron Daemon and crontab” on page 299 for more information on cron). If it is not done automatically, you should probably clean the error log regularly.

To delete all the entries from the error log, use the following command:

```
errclear 0
```

To selectively remove entries from the error log, for example, to delete all software errors enteries use the following command:

```
errclear -d S 0
```

Alternatively, use the SMIT fast path command (`smit errclear`) that will display the screen as shown in Figure 94 and enter appropriate fields as per requirement to clean the error log.

```
                              Clean the error log

Type or select values in entry fields.
Press Enter AFTER making all desired changes.

                                                         [Entry Fields]
  Remove entries older than this NUMBER OF DAYS       [30]                  #
  Error CLASSES (default is all)                      []                    +
  Error TYPES   (default is all)                      []                    +
  Error LABELS (default is all)                       []                    +
  Error ID's      (default is all)                    []                    +X
  Resource CLASSES (default is all)                   []
  Resource TYPES   (default is all)                   []
  Resource NAMES  (default is all)                    []
  SEQUENCE numbers (default is all)                   []
  LOGFILE                                             [/var/adm/ras/errlog]
  TEMPLATE file                                       [/var/adm/ras/errtmplt]

F1=Help              F2=Refresh          F3=Cancel           F4=List
F5=Reset             F6=Command          F7=Edit             F8=Image
F9=Shell             F10=Exit            Enter=Do
```

Figure 94. SMT errclear Command

7.2.1.5 Generating an Error Report

The `errpt` command generates the default summary error report that contains one line of data for each error. It includes flags for selecting errors that match specific criteria. By using the default condition, you can display error log entries in the reverse order they occurred and were recorded. By using the - c (concurrent) flag, you can display errors as they occur. You can use flags to generate reports with different formats. Following is the syntax of the `errpt` command.

errpt [-a] [-c] [-d *ErrorClassList*] [-e *EndDate*] [-g] [-i *File*] [-j *ErrorID* [,*ErrorID*]] | [-k *ErrorID* [,*ErrorID*]] [-J *ErrorLabel* [,*ErrorLabel*]] | [-K *ErrorLabel* [,*ErrorLabel*]] [-l

SequenceNumber] [-m *Machine*] [-n *Node*] [-s *StartDate*] [-F *FlagList*] [-N *ResourceNameList*] [-R *ResourceTypeList*] [-S *ResourceClassList*] [-T *ErrorTypeList*] [-y *File*] [-z *File*]

The output of `errpt` command without any flag will display the error log enteries with the following fields.

IDENTIFIER Numerical identifier for the event.

TIMESTAMP Date and time of the event occurrence.

T Type of error. Depending upon the severity of the error, the following are the possible error types:

- PEND The loss of availability of device or component is imminent.
- PERF The performance of the device or component has degraded to below an acceptable level.
- PERM Most severe errors due to a condition that could not be recovered.
- TEMP Condition that was recovered after a number of unsuccessful attempts.
- UNKN Not possible to determine the severity of an error.
- INFO This is an informational entry.

C Class of error. The following are the possible error classes.

- H Hardware.
- S Software.
- O Informational message.
- U Undetermined.

RESOURCE_NAME Name of the failing resource.

DESCRIPTION Summary of the error.

Using `errpt` command without a flag will output all the enteries in the log as shown in the following example. Since the number of error log enteries may exceed a single page, you can use `errpt|pg` pipe to have a page-wise view.

```
# errpt
IDENTIFIER TIMESTAMP  T C RESOURCE_NAME  DESCRIPTION
0BA49C99   1106154298 T H scsi0          SCSI BUS ERROR
E18E984F   1106110298 P S SRC            SOFTWARE PROGRAM ERROR
2A9F5252   1106094298 P H tok0           WIRE FAULT
```

```
E18E984F    1102120498 P S SRC              SOFTWARE PROGRAM ERROR
E18E984F    1101105898 P S SRC              SOFTWARE PROGRAM ERROR
AD331440    1101104498 U S SYSDUMP          SYSTEM DUMP
E18E984F    1030182798 P S SRC              SOFTWARE PROGRAM ERROR
E18E984F    1030182698 P S SRC              SOFTWARE PROGRAM ERROR
E18E984F    1030182598 P S SRC              SOFTWARE PROGRAM ERROR
E18E984F    1023175198 P S SRC              SOFTWARE PROGRAM ERROR
E18E984F    1023175098 P S SRC              SOFTWARE PROGRAM ERROR
E18E984F    1023174898 P S SRC              SOFTWARE PROGRAM ERROR
2A9F5252    1022143498 P H tok0             WIRE FAULT
35BFC499    1022081198 P H hdisk0           DISK OPERATION ERROR
AD331440    1021185998 U S SYSDUMP          SYSTEM DUMP
0BA49C99    1021185798 T H scsi0            SCSI BUS ERROR
35BFC499    1021180298 P H hdisk0           DISK OPERATION ERROR
```

The preceding example shows that the resource name for a disk operation error is hdisk0. To obtain all the errors with resource name hdisk0 from the error log, use the `errpt` command with -N flag as shown in the following example:

```
# errpt -N hdisk0
IDENTIFIER TIMESTAMP  T C RESOURCE_NAME  DESCRIPTION
35BFC499   1022081198 P H hdisk0         DISK OPERATION ERROR
35BFC499   1021180298 P H hdisk0         DISK OPERATION ERROR
```

7.2.1.6 Reading an Error Log Report

To read the contents of an error log report, use the `errpt` command with the -a flag. For example, to read an error log report with resource name hdisk0, use the `errpt` command with the -a and -j flags with error identifier as shown in the following sample error report:

```
# errpt -a -j 35BFC499
---------------------------------------------------------------------------
LABEL:           DISK_ERR3
IDENTIFIER:      35BFC499

Date/Time:        Thu Oct 22 08:11:12
Sequence Number: 36
Machine Id:       006151474C00
Node Id:          sv1051c
Class:            H
Type:             PERM
Resource Name:    hdisk0
Resource Class:   disk
Resource Type:    scsd
Location:         04-B0-00-6,0
VPD:
```

```
        Manufacturer................IBM
        Machine Type and Model......DORS-32160     !#
        FRU Number..................
        ROS Level and ID............57413345
        Serial Number...............5U5W6388
        EC Level....................85G3685
        Part Number.................07H1132
        Device Specific.(Z0)........000002028F00001A
        Device Specific.(Z1)........39H2916
        Device Specific.(Z2)........0933
        Device Specific.(Z3)........1296
        Device Specific.(Z4)........0001
        Device Specific.(Z5)........16

Description
DISK OPERATION ERROR

Probable Causes
DASD DEVICE
STORAGE DEVICE CABLE

Failure Causes
DISK DRIVE
DISK DRIVE ELECTRONICS
STORAGE DEVICE CABLE

        Recommended Actions
        PERFORM PROBLEM DETERMINATION PROCEDURES

Detail Data
SENSE DATA
0A06 0000 2800 0000 0088 0002 0000 0000 0200 0200 0000 0000 0000 0000 0000
0000 0000 0000 0000 0000 0000 0000 0000 0000 0000 0000 0000 0000 0000 0000
0000 0000 0000 0000 0000 0000 0000 0000 0000 0000 0000 0000 0000 0000 0000
0000 0000 0000 0000 0000 0000 0000 0000 0000 0000 0000 0000 0000 0000 0000
0000 0000 0000 0000 0000 0000 0000 0000 0000 0000 0000 0000 0000 0000 0000
0001 0001 2FC0
```

7.2.1.7 Copying an Error Log to Diskette or Tape

You may need to send the error log to AIX System Support Center for analysis. To copy the error log to a diskette, place a formatted diskette into the diskette drive and use the following commands:

```
ls /var/adm/ras/errlog | backup -ivp
```

To copy the error log to tape, place a tape in the drive and enter:

```
ls /var/adm/ras/errlog | backup -ivpf/dev/rmt0
```

7.2.1.8 Log Maintenance Activities

The `errlogger` command allows the system administrator to record messages in the error log. Whenever you perform a maintenance activity, replace hardware, or apply a software fix, it is a good idea to record this activity in the system error log.

The following example shows the log enteries before and after a message (Error Log cleaned) was logged by an operator (using `errlogger` command) in the error log.

```
# errpt
IDENTIFIER TIMESTAMP  T C RESOURCE_NAME  DESCRIPTION
9DBCFDEE   1109164598 T O errdemon       ERROR LOGGING TURNED ON
192AC071   1109164598 T O errdemon       ERROR LOGGING TURNED OFF
# errlogger "Error Log cleaned"
# errpt
IDENTIFIER TIMESTAMP  T C RESOURCE_NAME  DESCRIPTION
AA8AB241   1109164698 T O OPERATOR       OPERATOR NOTIFICATION
9DBCFDEE   1109164598 T O errdemon       ERROR LOGGING TURNED ON
192AC071   1109164598 T O errdemon       ERROR LOGGING TURNED OFF
```

The identifier `AA8AB241` in the preceding example is the message record entry with description `OPEARATOR NOTIFICATION`.

7.3 System Dump Facility

The system dump copies selected kernel structures to the dump device when an unexpected system halt occurs. The dump device can be configured dynamically to either a tape or a logical volume on the hard disk to store the system dump. A primary dump device is a dedicated dump device, while a secondary dump device is shared.

While installing an operating system, the dump device is automatically configured. By default, AIX Version 4 configures /dev/hd6 (paging logical volume) as the primary dump device and /dev/sysdumpnull as the secondary dump device. If the system was migrated from AIX Version 3, /dev/hd7 (the default dump device for AIX Version 3) will continue to be the default dump device for AIX Version 4.

The dump can either be system initiated or user initiated, as shown in Figure 95. When the system dump completes, the system either halts or reboots, depending upon the setting of the autorestart attribute of sys0, which can be shown and altered using SMIT by selecting **System Environments**, and then

Change / Show Characteristics of Operating System. The Automatically REBOOT system after a crash option shows and sets the value of sys0 attribute.

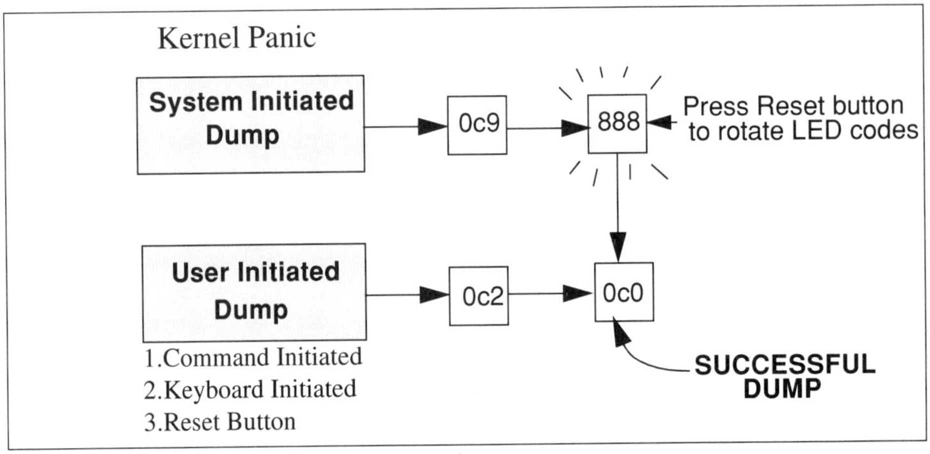

Figure 95. Successful System Dumps - LED Codes

7.3.1 Managing a Dump Device

The `sysdumpdev` command is used to dynamically configure the dump device as shown in the following examples.

- To list the current dump destination use the following command:

```
# sysdumpdev -l
primary              /dev/hd6
secondary            /dev/sysdumpnull
copy directory       /var/adm/ras
forced copy flag     TRUE
always allow dump    FALSE
```

- The following example shows the command to change the primary dump device from the default, /dev/hd6, to /dev/hd5:

```
# sysdumpdev -P -p /dev/hd5
primary              /dev/hd5
secondary            /dev/sysdumpnull
copy directory       /var/adm/ras
forced copy flag     TRUE
always allow dump    FALSE
```

- To estimate the dump size of the current system, use the following command:

```
# sysdumpdev -e
```

```
0453-041 Estimated dump size in bytes: 18227200
```

- The following example shows the command to display statistical information about the previous dump, and in this example, there is no dump record:

```
# sysdumpdev -L
0453-019 No previous dumps recorded.
```

- The following example shows running the `sysdumpdev -L` command after a successful dump has occurred on the system:

```
# sysdumpdev -L
0453-039

Device name:         /dev/hd6
Major device number: 10
Minor device number: 2
Size:                24202752 bytes
Date/Time:           Tue Nov 10 16:50:45 CST 1998
Dump status:         0
dump completed successfully
Dump copy filename: /var/adm/ras/vmcore.1
```

Alternatively, all the commands used in the preceding examples of this section can be executed using the SMIT fastpath command by executing `smit dump`, which will display the menu shown in Figure 96. Then select the appropriate option from the menu to do the desired function.

```
                              System Dump

Move cursor to desired item and press Enter.

  Show Current Dump Devices
  Show Information About the Previous System Dump
  Show Estimated Dump Size
  Change the Primary Dump Device
  Change the Secondary Dump Device
  Change the Directory to which Dump is Copied on Boot
  Start a Dump to the Primary Dump Device
  Start a Dump to the Secondary Dump Device
  Copy a System Dump from a Dump Device to a File
  Copy a System Dump from a Dump Device to Diskette
  Always ALLOW System Dump







F1=Help              F2=Refresh           F3=Cancel            F8=Image
F9=Shell             F10=Exit             Enter=Do
```

Figure 96. SMIT Dump Command

7.3.2 System Initiated Dump

A system dump initiated by a kernel panic is written to the primary dump device.

7.3.2.1 Understanding Flashing 888 Error Messages

A flashing 888 in a three digit hardware display indicates that a message is encoded as a string of three digit display values which can be read by pressing the reset button repeatedly and noting the changed three digit value every time until a flashing 888 is displayed again. Some RS/6000 systems use an advance button to perform this task.

An initial value of 102 after flashing 888 indicates an unexpected system halt as shown in Figure 97. The value of mmm indicates the cause of halt, crash code (see Table 12), and the value of ddd indicates the dump status, and dump code (see Table 13 on page 174).

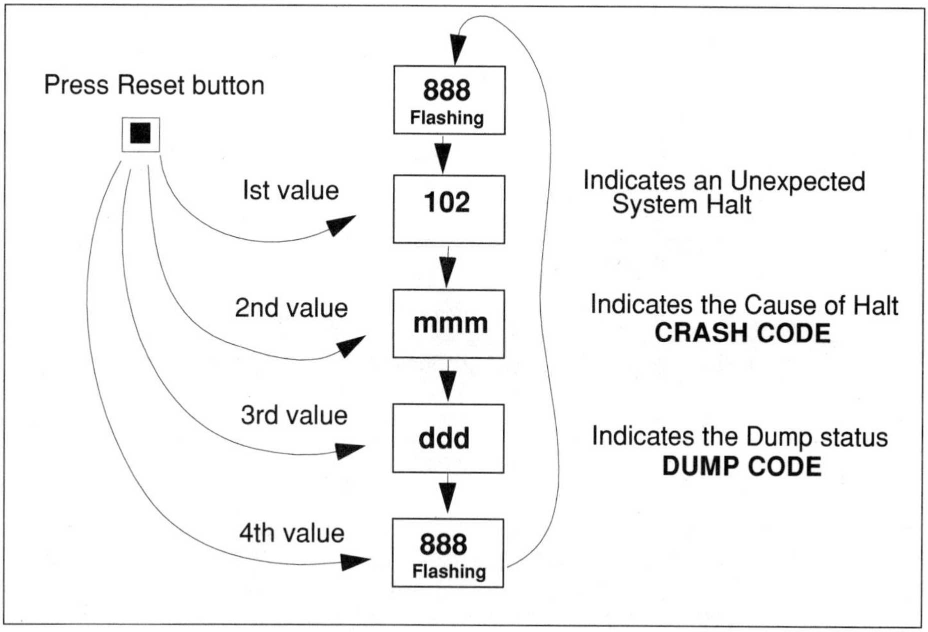

Figure 97. Unexpected System Halt - Three-Digit Display String

The following table lists various crash codes. The 2xx type codes describe a machine check are reporting hardware failure.

Table 12. Crash Codes

000	Unexpected system interrupt.
200	Machine check due to memory bus error (RAS/CAS parity).
201	Machine check due to memory time out.
202	Machine check due to memory card failure.
203	Machine check due to address exception: address out of range.
204	Machine check due to attempted store into R.
205	Machine check due to uncorrectable error correction code due to address parity.
206	Machine check due to uncorrectable error correction code.
207	Machine check due to undefined error.
208	Machine check due to an L2 uncorrectable ECC.
300	Data storage interrupt: processor type.

32x	Data storage interrupt: The number represented by x is the bus unit identification.
38x	Data storage interrupt: The number represented by x is the bus unit identification.
400	Instruction storage interrupt.
500	External interrupt.
52x	External interrupt.
53x	External interrupt because of IOCC bus timeout.
54x	External interrupt because of IOCC keyboard check.
700	Program interrupt.
800	Floating point unavailable.

The following table lists various system dump codes.

Table 13. System Dump Codes

0c0	Dump completed successfully.
0c2	Dump started.
0c3	The dump is inhibited.
0c4	Dump completed unsuccessfully. Not enough space available on dump device. Partial dump available.
0c5	Dump failed to start. Unexpected error occurred when attempting to write to dump device.
0c7	Network dump in progress.
0c8	Dump disabled. System configuration does not include a dump device.
0c9	System initiated dump started.

7.3.3 User Initiated Dump

There are three ways for a user to invoke a system dump depending upon the system condition as shown in Figure 98 on page 176. The following sections discuss the steps involved in initiating a system dump, verifying the dump, copying the dump onto a tape, and sending it to Service Support Center for analysis.

7.3.3.1 Check the Estimated Dump Size

The following command shows the estimated size of dump will be `20971520` bytes:

```
# sysdumpdev -e
0453-041 Estimated dump size in bytes: 20971520
```

7.3.3.2 Check the Size of Primary Dump Device

The primary dump device, in this case, is the paging logical volume (/dev/hd6). To display its size, use `lsps -a` command as shown in the following example. If the reported free space is less than estimated dump size (reported in the preceding section), you should increase the dump device size. The following example shows the 128 MB of primary dump device with 6% used:

```
# lsps -a
Page Space  Physical Volume   Volume Group    Size  %Used  Active  Auto  Type
hd6         hdisk0            rootvg         128MB      6     yes   yes    lv
```

7.3.3.3 Starting a Dump

If you initiate the system dump from the command line, use the `sysdumpstart` command with a -p flag to write to the primary device or a -s flag to write to the secondary device.

If the dump is initiated using the special key sequences, use the sequence Ctrl-Alt-NumPad1 to write to the primary dump device and use the sequence Ctrl-Alt-NumPad2 to write to the secondary dump device.

If you initiate a system dump by pressing the reset button, the system dump is written to the primary dump device.

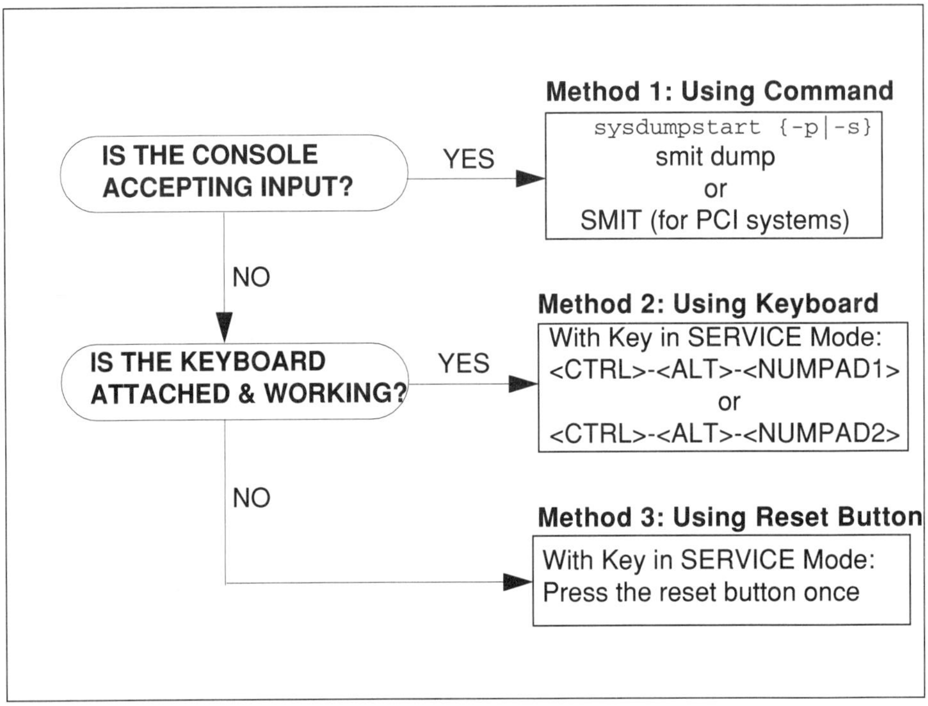

Figure 98. Method of User Initiated System Dump

7.3.3.4 Verifying a System Dump

The `crash` command is an interactive tool which is used to examine a system dump file. Checking that the dump is readable saves time by reducing callbacks from the support center.

To invoke the `crash` command on a system image file and kernel file, use the following command syntax:

```
crash SystemImageFile KernelFile
```

where SystemImageFile is either a file name or the name of the dump device and KernelFile is the default kernel /usr/lib/boot/unix.

The following example shows the commands to obtain the system dump file name (var/adm/ras/vmcore.1) and then uses the `crash` command on that dump file to verify the validity of dump.

```
# sysdumpdev -L
0453-039

Device name:          /dev/hd6
```

```
Major device number: 10
Minor device number: 2
Size:                24202752 bytes
Date/Time:           Tue Nov 10 16:50:45 CST 1998
Dump status:         0
dump completed successfully
Dump copy filename: /var/adm/ras/vmcore.1
#
# crash /var/adm/ras/vmcore.1
Using /unix as the default namelist file.
>
> stat
        sysname: AIX
        nodename: aix4xdev
        release: 3
        version: 4
        machine: 000044091C00
        time of crash: Tue Nov 10 16:50:45 CST 1998
        age of system: 1 day, 5 hr., 28 min.
        xmalloc debug: disabled
        abend code: 0
        csa: 0x0
>
> quit
#
```

If the crash command outputs the >, and the stat subcommand verifies the details of dump, the dump is successful. Any other output indicates the dump may not be successfully analyzed.

7.3.3.5 Compile and Copy a System Dump onto Tape

The snap command is used to gather configuration information of the system. It provides a convenient method of sending the lslpp and errpt output to the Service Support Center. It gathers the information and compresses the information to a tar file which can be downloaded to a tape or diskette or electronically transmitted.

The default directory for the output from the snap command is /tmp/ibmsupt. If you want to name an optional directory, use the -d option with the path of the desired output directory. Approximately 8 MB of temporary disk space is required when executing all of the snap command options. The cleanup option -r, should be used to remove the information saved by the snap command and to retrieve disk space.

Following are the commonly used options with snap command:

-g Gathers the output of the `lslpp -L` command and stores the information in /tmp/ibmsupt/general/lslpp.L. The `-g` flag also gathers general system information and outputs it to /tmp/ibmsupt/general/general.snap.

-D Gathers dump and /unix (assumes dump device to be /dev/hd7).

-a Gathers information for all of the groups.

-c Creates a compressed tar image of all files in the /tmp/ibmsupt directory tree (or other output directory).

-o Creates a tar file and downloads it to removable media.

-v Displays the output of the commands executed by the snap command.

-f Gather file system information.

-k Gather kernel information.

The following command copies the information on to tape device, rmt0:

```
/usr/sbin/snap -gfkD -o /dev/rmt0
```

Before executing the `snap -c` or `snap -o` commands, any additional information required by the Support Center should be copied to the /tmp/ibmsupt directory. For example, you may be asked by the Service Support Center to provide a test case that demonstrates the problem. The test case should be copied to the /tmp/ibmsupt directory. When the -c or -o option of the `snap` command is executed, the test case will be included.

Note

The `snap -c` and `snap -o` commands are mutually exclusive. Do not execute both during the same problem-determination session. The `snap -c` command should be used to transmit information electronically and the `snap -o` command should be used to transmit information on a removable output device.

7.3.3.6 Label the Dump Tape

You can label the dump tape with the following information.

- PMR number
- Command used to create the tape
- Block size of tape

7.4 References

The following publications contain more information about system problem determination tools.

- *AIX Version 4.3 Messages Guide and Reference*, SC23-4129
- *AIX Version Problem Solving Guide and Reference*, SC23-4123
- *AIX Version 4.3 Kernel Extensions and Device Support Programming Concepts*, SC23-4125
- *AIX Version 4.3 Installation Guide*, SC23-4112

7.5 Quiz

1. A system administrator is using installp to install the software for a new SSA adapter that was just added to an F50. The install seems to hang for an unusually long time and the LED display reads 0c9. What is most likely happening?

   A. The system has crashed and is dumping.

   B. The system is committing the SSA lpps.

   C. The system is running cfgmgr to add the device.

   D. The system is running diagnostics on the SSA subsystem.

2. Customer XYZ has been running with AIX V4 for several months with no problems. The system just crashed and they need assistance with determining what happened. By pressing the yellow reset button, they found that the crash codes displayed on the LEDs were: 888-102-700-0c0. These LED codes indicate that:

   A. It was a software problem and there is a partial dump for analysis.

   B. It was a hardware problem and there is a partial dump for analysis.

   C. It was a software problem and there is a complete dump for analysis.

   D. It was a hardware problem and there is a complete dump for analysis.

3. Analyzing the following error report listing, how would a system specialist find out detailed information on why the system shutdown?

```
IDENTIFIER TIMESTAMP  T C RESOURCE_NAME  DESCRIPTION
2A9F5252   1119151898 P H tok0           WIRE FAULT
2BFA76F6   1117101698 T S SYSPROC        SYSTEM SHUTDOWN BY USER
9DBCFDEE   1117101998 T O errdemon       ERROR LOGGING TURNED ON
192AC071   1117101598 T O errdemon       ERROR LOGGING TURNED OFF
AA8AB241   1116181498 T O CMDCRASH_EXIT  OPERATOR NOTIFICATION
AA8AB241   1116181498 T O CMDCRASH_ENTRY OPERATOR NOTIFICATION
2BFA76F6   1116173598 T S SYSPROC        SYSTEM SHUTDOWN BY USER
```

```
9DBCFDEE   1116174198 T O errdemon        ERROR LOGGING TURNED ON
192AC071   1116173498 T O errdemon        ERROR LOGGING TURNED OFF
2BFA76F6   1116164698 T S SYSPROC         SYSTEM SHUTDOWN BY USER
```

A. `errpt 2BFA76F6`

B. `errpt -j 2BFA76F6`

C. `errpt -a -j 2BFA76F6`

D. `errpt -a -j 2BFA76F6`

4. ABC Company has an employee time tracking application which has randomly stopped running several times over the last few months. The system administrator has written a script that monitors the status of the application. If the application is not running, the script restarts the application and adds an entry to the system error log reporting the time of the failure. What command is used in the monitor script to add the failure message to the system error log?

   A. `errpt`

   B. `errsave`

   C. `errorlog`

   D. `errlogger`

7.5.1 Answers

1. A
2. C
3. C
4. D

7.6 Exercises

1. Determine the status of an error logging daemon on the system.
2. Display the error log on the system. Delete all the software enteries from the error log.
3. Determine the size of error log file on the system.
4. Display only the errors with resource name hdisk0 from the error log.
5. Copy the error log on to a tape device (/dev/rmtx).
6. You have applied a new APAR. Log an entry into the error log to record this activity. With what resource name is the entry listed when you display the error log with `errpt` command?

7. Estimate the dump size for the system. Display your current dump device configuration. If the size of a dump device is less than the estimated dump size, increase the size of the dump device and initiate a dump on the system.
8. Verify the system dump taken in the preceding step using `crash` command.
9. Copy the dump on to a tape using `snap` command.

Chapter 8. System Backup and Restore

This chapter covers the backup and restore procedures and the common tasks that are carried out to ensure that you have backed up the proper information and that your backup media is reliable.

8.1 Saving Information

Data in AIX is divided in system and user parts. System data makes up the operating system and its extensions. It is kept in the root file system on root volume group. User data is mainly contained in user-defined file systems, but partly contained in root file system (/home file system).

In order to successfully backup your system to ensure availability of data at all times. AIX provides you with a number of commands to achieve this task. These commands are used depending on the type of information you are trying to save. Figure 99 on page 184 shows you the flow of the backup process, for example, in order to save rootvg you can adopt different approaches depending on what are you trying to save using the `mksysb` command. You can alternatively save individual files by using `tar`, `cpio`, `dd` and `backup` commands. You can also save entire user volume groups by using the `savevg` command.

The format of the `mksysb` tape that is produced is given in section 8.2, "The Data Layout of a mksysb Tape" on page 184.

Note

Keep following points in mind while running the `mksysb` command:

- Use /etc/exclude.rootvg file to exclude any file, file system, directory or patterns that you do not need in your backup. Use the -e flag with the `mksysb` command to use the exclude.rootvg file.
- /tmp is used as a work area by the `mksysb` command. It typically needs 8 - 12 MB of free space in /tmp. Use the -X flag with `mksysb` to automatically expand the /tmp file system, otherwise you will encounter an error similar to:
  - `0511-432 A write error occurred: There is not enough space in the file system.`

  and `mksysb` will fail.
- Use the -p flag (disable software packing of backup) only if you know that your tape drive does not do compression.

Figure 99 summarizes the methods used to back up system and user data.

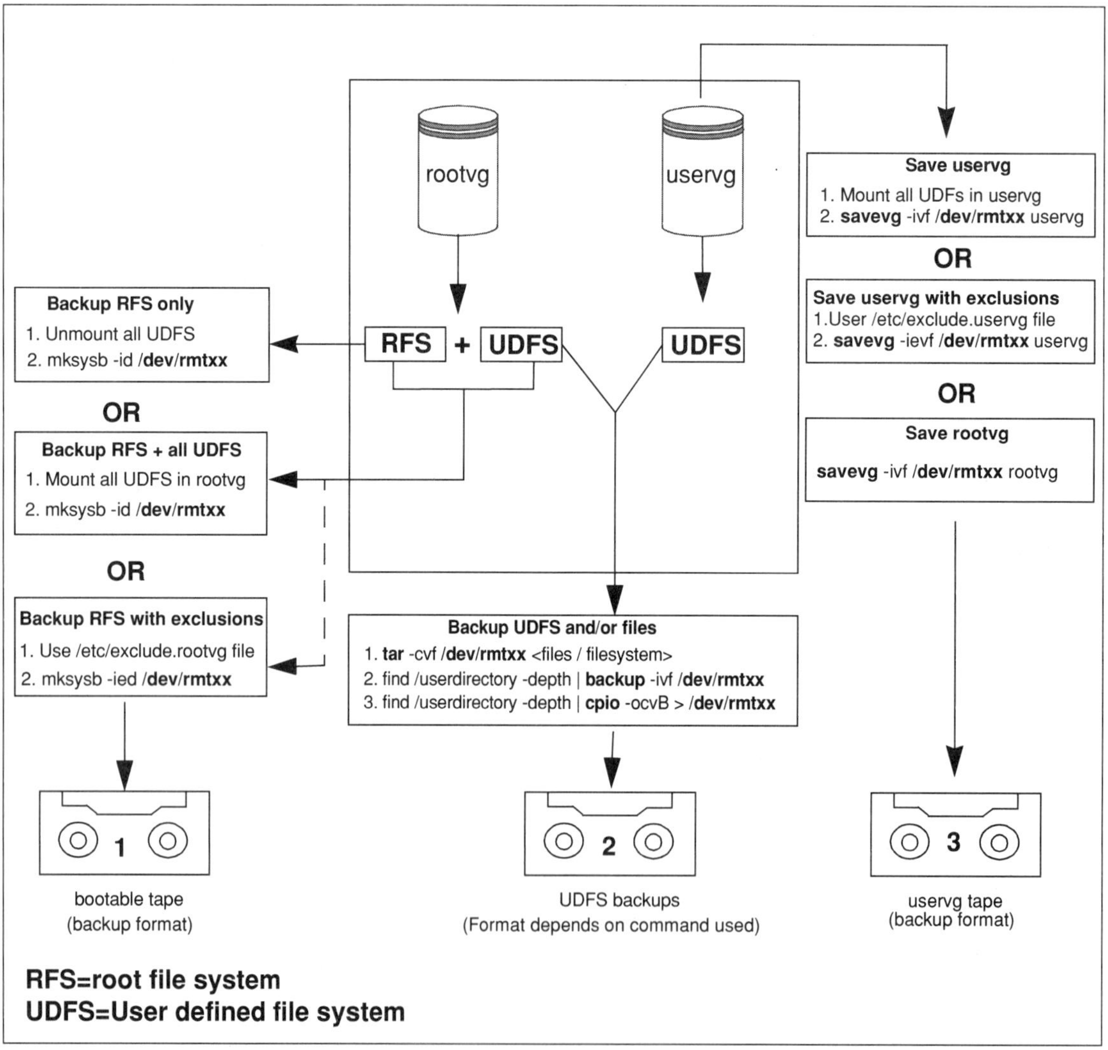

Figure 99. Saving Information

8.2 The Data Layout of a mksysb Tape

The contents of a mksysb tape are shown in Figure 100 on page 185.

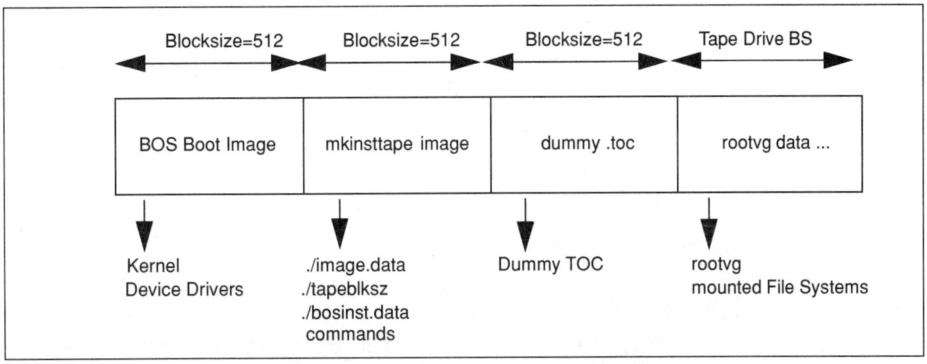

Figure 100. mksysb Tape Contents

8.2.1 BOS Boot Image

The BOS boot image contains a copy of the system's kernel and device drivers needed to boot from the tape. It is created with the `bosboot` command. You can also use the `bosboot` command to remake the boot image on a hard disk.

8.2.2 mkinsttape Image

This image contains the files described in the following sections:

8.2.2.1 ./image.data

This file, created by the `mkszfile` command, contains information describing the image installed during the BOS installation process. This information includes the sizes, names, maps, and mount points of logical volumes and file systems in the root volume group. It is not recommended to modify this file directly. Changing the value of one field without correctly modifying any related fields can result in a failed installation and a corrupted backup image. The only exception to this recommendation is the SHRINK field, which the user may modify to instruct the BOS installation routines to create the file systems (listed in image.data file) only as large as the actual contents. For example, if a file system is 20 MB with only 4 MB of space actually used by the file system, the SHRINK option will create a file system of only 4 MB in size.

8.2.2.2 ./tapeblksz

This file contains the block size the tape drive was set to when the backup was done. In order to find out what the block size was when the `mksysb` command was executed, run the following commands:

1. Rewind the tape using the command:

```
tctl -f /dev/rmtxx rewind
```

2. Change the block size of the tape to 512-bytes using the command:

```
chdev -l rmtxx -a block_size=512
```

3. Restore from the second image and extract the ./tapeblksz file using the command:

```
restore -s2 -xqvdf /dev/rmtxx.1 ./tapeblksz
```

8.2.2.3 ./bosinst.data

This file contains the customized BOS install procedures and dictates how the BOS install program will behave. You can customize this file before doing the `mksysb`.

8.2.3 Dummy TOC

This image is 512 bytes long and contains one file with DUMMY TOC in it. This image is used to make the mksysb tape contain the same number of images as a BOS install tape. If you want to view this file run the following commands:

1. Rewind the tape using the command:

```
tctl -f /dev/rmtxx rewind
```

2. Move the tape forward two file markers to stop at the beginning of third file marker using the command:

```
tctl -f /dev/rmtxx.1 fsf 2
```

3. Restore the third image from the tape using the command:

```
restore -xvdf /dev/rmtxx.1
```

8.2.4 User Data

This image contains all the user data that is to be stored on the tape. The `mksysb` command uses the image.data file to backup all the files.

8.3 Verifying System Backups

The only method to verify that the system backup will correctly restore with no problems is to actually restore all the files listed in the company's Disaster Recovery Plan. However, in order to minimize problems due to tape media damage, there are a number of ways you can verify whether your backup has been done properly or not:

- Using SMIT
- Using the `restore` command

> **Note**
>
> The only way to verify that the `mksysb` tape will successfully boot is to bring the machine down and boot from the tape. No data needs to be restored. Data verification can be done using the preceding techniques.
>
> However, caution must be taken if the PROMPT field in the bosinst.data file is set to NO, which will cause the system to begin a `mksysb` restore automatically.

8.3.1 Using SMIT to Verify a Tape

Generally, `mksysb` is an unattended activity, therefore you need to look for errors that might have occurred during the save operation and will render data unavailable once you try to restore it. It is always a good practice to look at your smit.log file after a `mksysb` is run from SMIT. It is recommended that you do not run `mksysb` directly from the command line in order to ensure that you do not miss errors generated during a save operation.

In order to verify the `mksysb` tape use the SMIT fast path:

```
smitty lsmksysb
```

A screen similar to Figure 101 will be shown.

```
                         List Files in a System Image

Type or select values in entry fields.
Press Enter AFTER making all desired changes.

                                                        [Entry Fields]
* DEVICE or FILE                                      [/dev/rmt0]            +/
  Number of BLOCKS to read in a single input          []                     #
     (Leave blank to use a system default)
  Verify BLOCK size if tape device?                    no                    +










F1=Help             F2=Refresh          F3=Cancel           F4=List
F5=Reset            F6=Command          F7=Edit             F8=Image
F9=Shell            F10=Exit            Enter=Do
```

Figure 101. List mksysb Tape Contents

4. Select your backup device name.
5. Select defaults for all other parameters and press **Enter=DO**. This will list the contents of your `mksysb` tape and log them in the smit.log as shown below:

```
New volume on /dev/rmt0.1:
Cluster size is 51200 bytes (100 blocks).
The volume number is 1.
The backup date is: Tue Nov 10 17:02:28 CST 1998
Files are backed up by name.
The user is root.
./bosinst.data
./image.data
./tmp/vgdata/rootvg/copied.map
./tmp/vgdata/rootvg/fslv00.map
./tmp/vgdata/rootvg/hd1.map
./tmp/vgdata/rootvg/hd2.map
...
```

Cross check the listing and verify that none of your important files are missing. This will ensure that data will be available to you once you need it. The listing that is generated as a result of executing this command is helpful in finding out the date this tape was generated, which might help you if you do a `mksysb` on a regular basis and do not rotate tapes. If your tape tags are accidently destroyed you can still find out the latest backup you have by using this method.

8.3.2 Using Restore to Verify a Tape

In order to verify a `mksysb` tape without using SMIT, you need to use the `restore` command since all the files with `mksysb` are backed up in backup file format using `backup` command.

Data on a `mksysb` tape is written from the fourth file marker onwards (see section 8.2, "The Data Layout of a mksysb Tape" on page 184 for details on `mksysb` tape format), therefore you need to control the tape manually to move to the correct segment of the tape. Use the `tctl` command to control the tape. The general syntax of the `tctl` command is as follows:

```
tctl [ -f Device ] [ eof | weof | fsf | bsf | fsr | bsr | rewind | offline
| rewoffl | erase | retension | reset | status ] [ Count ]
```

The `tctl` command gives subcommands to a streaming tape device. Subcommands most frequently used by `tctl` are listed in Table 14.

Table 14. tctl Subcommands

Subcommand	Description
rewind	Rewinds the tape.
status	Prints status information about the specified tape device.
fsf *Count*	Moves the tape forward the number of file marks specified by the Count parameter and positions it on the end-of-tape (EOT) side of the file mark.
bsf *Count*	Moves the tape backward the number of file marks specified by the Count parameter and positions it on the beginning-of-tape (BOT) side of the file mark. If the bsf subcommand moves the tape past the beginning, the tape rewinds, and the `tctl` command returns EIO.
offline or rewoffl	Rewinds the tape and takes the tape drive offline. This will unload the tape when appropriate. The tape must be reinserted before the device can be used again.

To see the contents of the `mksysb` tape use the following sequence of commands:

1. Rewind the tape using the command:

   ```
   tctl -f /dev/rmtxx rewind
   ```

2. Move to the fourth file marker, read the contents of the tape and redirect the output to a file using the command:

```
restore -s4 -Tvqf /dev/rmtxx.1 > /tmp/mksysb.log
```

This will generate a listing similar to the smit.log output shown in section 8.3.1, “Using SMIT to Verify a Tape” on page 187.

Note

You may encounter an error similar to:

```
0511-160 Cannot read backup media
/dev/rmtx.1 There is an input or output error.
```

If this happens, your tape block size has changed since your last backup, use the following command to reset the block size:

```
chdev -l rmtxx -a block_size=0
```

8.4 Saving User Data

User data in rootvg is stored with `mksysb` depending on what file systems you have mounted at the time of the execution of the command and the contents of the /etc/exclude.rootvg file. Alternatively, you can use the `tar`, `cpio`, `dd`, or `backup` commands to save user files, directories, and file system.

Since the `mksysb` command only backs up rootvg, in order to save user volume groups, use the `savevg` command. Refer to Figure 99 on page 184 to see the flow of the `savevg` command. The volume group you are trying to save must be varied-on, and the file systems must be mounted. All logical volume information in the volume group is archived and will be recreated. However, only JFS mounted file system data will be archived. Raw logical volume data will not be archived using the `savevg` command. In order to save a raw logical volume use the `dd` command and proceed with the following sequence of steps to save your raw logical volumes:

1. Check the block size of the tape using the `tctl` command:

```
tctl -f /dev/rmtxx status
```

2. Change the block size of the tape to your required block size using:

```
chdev -l rmtxx -a block_size=<tape block size>
```

3. Save the raw logical volume onto a tape device using:

```
dd if=/dev/lvname of=/dev/rmtxx ibs=512 obs=<tape block size>
```

This will create a back up of the raw logical volume on the tape.

If you use the `savevg` command to save a rootvg the only difference between a `mksysb` image and an `savevg` image is that the `mksysb` command creates the bos/install images and places them on the tape to create a bootable/installable tape. A `savevg` image is not capable of being installed directly.

8.4.1 Block Size Determination

Generally, the problems encountered during verification or restoration of data on your system are related to incompatibility of block sizes between your drive and tape. You can use several methods to determine the block size of the data that was written on a tape. Following are a few methods to find out the block size:

- Method 1

  Use `dd` command to read a single block from the device and find out what is the block size used for the archive:

  ```
  dd if=/dev/rmtxx bs=128k count=1 | wc -c
  ```

  This will return to you the size in bytes of the block being read. Assuming that your backup was made with the same physical block size, you can change your device to use this block size.

- Method 2

  Use `tcopy` command as follows to find out the block size.

  ```
  #tcopy /dev/rmtxx
  tcopy : Tape File: 1; Records: 1 to 7179 ; size:512
  tcopy : Tape File: 1; End of file after :7179 records; 3675648 bytes
  tcopy : Tape File: 2; Records: 1 to 2900 ; size:512
  tcopy : Tape File: 2; End of file after 2900 records, 76890 bytes
  ...
  ```

  This will give you a list of all the files found on the media with their byte count, the block size used and the total number of records for each individual file.

8.5 Restoring Information

Once you have a backup of your data you can restore it in a number of ways. The flow of the restore process is shown in Figure 102 on page 192.

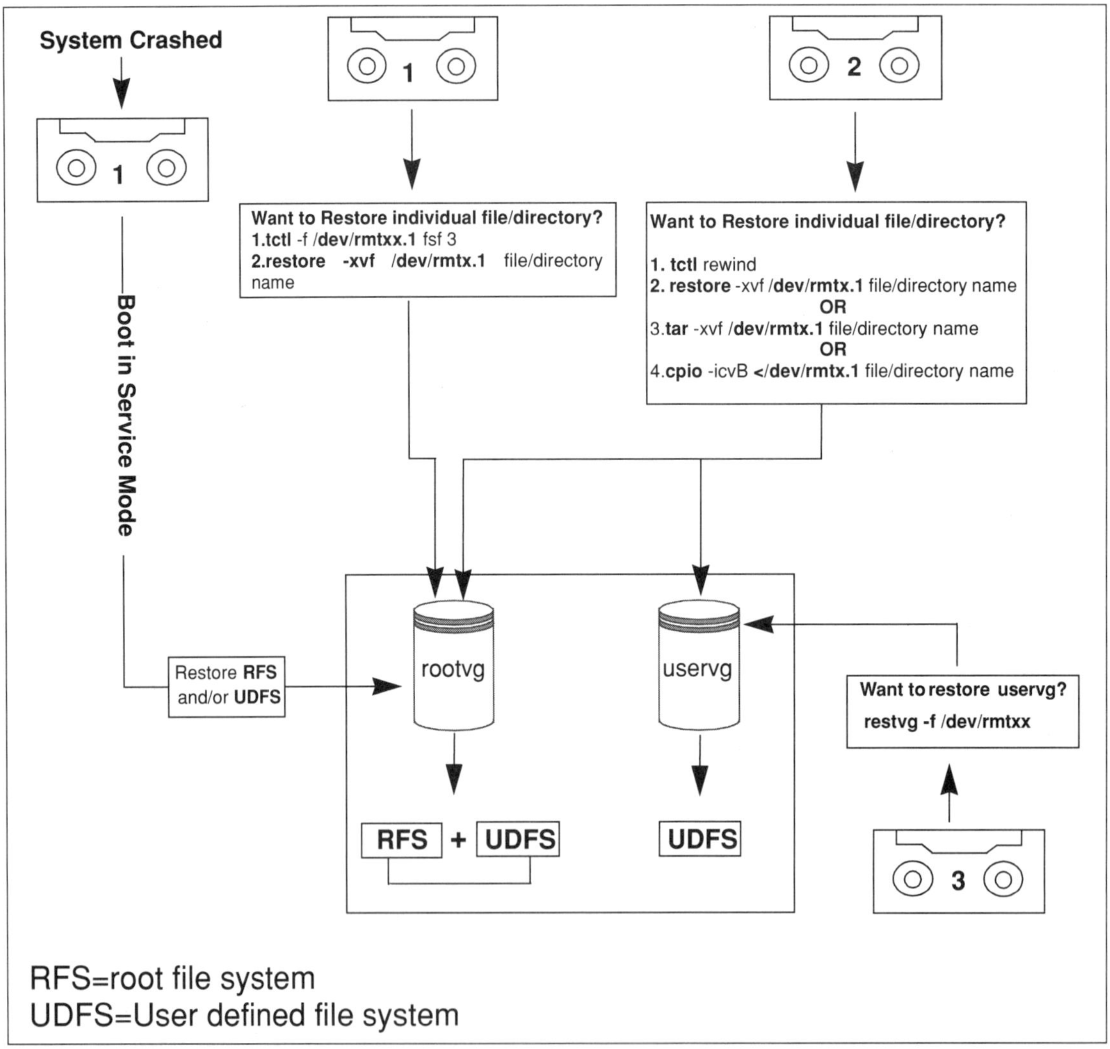

Figure 102. Restoring Information

There are a number of problems that you may encounter while you are restoring data back onto your system. Following is a short list of the problems that you may encounter while restoring data

1. The most general problem that you can face is the incorrect block size which results in a restore failure. See section 8.4.1, "Block Size Determination" on page 191 for how to recover from this problem.
2. Your storage media can be physically damaged. Media errors are recorded in the error log. If the media can be read successfully with the `dd` or the

tcopy command, a syntax or usage problem possibly exists. Syntax or usage problems could include:

- Incorrect archive utility was used.
- cpio backup was not written with ASCII headers and the command specifies ASCII headers (-c).
- tar command has calculated a checksum different from what is recorded on the tape indicating that the incorrect volume may be in the drive. (Use the -i flag to ignore checksums.)
- For tapes, the archive utility does not have enough buffer space to hold an entire block from the tape file.

3. During a restvg command execution (used for restoring user volume group), you may encounter a failure. Since it expects the savevg image to be the first image on the tape. This means that you cannot use a mksysb tape to restore the root volume group through the restvg command, therefore you can only restore a mksysb tape in the service mode.
4. You may run out of space on a file system restore if the new file system you created does not have enough space on it.

8.6 References

The following publications are suitable as a source for additional information.

- *Monitoring and Managing IBM SSA Disk Subsystems*, SG24-5251
- *AIX Version 4.3 Installation Guide*, SC23-4112
- *URL:* http://service.software.ibm.com/support
- *URL:* http://www.developer.ibm.com

8.7 Quiz

1. Which of the following files contains the logical volume and filesystem information that mksysb saves during a system backup?

   A. /fs.size

   B. /image.data

   C. /bosinst.data

   D. /install.data

2. A system administrator would like to have the system eject a backup tape each night after the system backup is complete to ensure that it is not

overwritten. Which of the following commands can be used to eject the tape?

A. `tctl`

B. `eject`

C. `rmdev`

D. `rmtape`

3. At the XYZ Company, the system administrator has implemented a daily backup schedule for the /home filesystem. The filesystem is stored on the 4 mm tape drive /dev/rmt1 using tar. What command can be used to verify the most recent tape has successfully stored the files in /home.

A. `tar -ivf /dev/rmt1`

B. `tar -tvf /dev/rmt1`

C. `tar -lvf /dev/rmt1.1`

D. `tar -ivf /dev/rmt1.1 /home`

4. At XYZ company, a nightly backup is performed to the tape drive using mksysb scheduled by cron. Where can the system administrator look to find the output of the `mksysb` command?

A. /smit.log

B. /var/adm/messages

C. /var/spool/mail/root

D. /var/spool/cron/cronlog

5. The system administrator at ABC calls to ask for assistance while backing up of the rootvg with the `mksysb` command. The `mksysb` command fails with the following error message:

```
0511-084 internal packing error
```

What should the system administrator do to resolve this error?

A. Use the -p flag with `mksysb`.

B. Run `fsck` on the rootvg file system.

C. Disable compression on the tape drive.

D. Specify an alternate density setting on the tape drive.

6. The system administrator of company ABC has been asked to restore some files from an old backup of the /home filesystem. The restore is failing because the block size of the tape drive is incorrect. The system administrator does not know to what block size the backup was written. What command can be used to determine the block size of the tape?

   A. `tar`

   B. `tctl`

   C. `cpio`

   D. `tcopy`

7. The intranet Web server for the ABC company experienced a disk drive failure and the system must be restored for the mksysb backup tape. With the backup tape in the tape drive, what is the first step the system administrator should use to initiate the mksysb restore?

   A. Boot the server in service mode.

   B. Issue the `boot -mksysb` command.

   C. Press the reset button when the C31 LED appears.

   D. Hold down the reset button when powering on the server.

8. A technical specialist working on an RS/6000 Model 397 running AIX 4.3.1 determines that the system needs to be reinstalled with the same version of the operating system. What is the best method to perform the reinstallation without erasing /home and /data, a file system used to store project data?

   A. Reinstall bos.rte from the installation media.

   B. Perform a preservation installation from a mksysb.

   C. Perform a migration installation from the installation media.

   D. Perform a preservation installation from the installation media.

8.7.1 Answers

1. B
2. A
3. B
4. C
5. A
6. D

7. A
8. D

8.8 Exercises

1. Perform a back up of your system using `mksysb`. Make sure that you exclude the /tmp file system from your backup. In addition to this you must backup all your user file system in your rootvg.
2. Check out your smit.log for any errors during your backup operation.
3. With the `mksysb` tape you have just made, perform the following tasks:
    - Create a listing of the contents of the tape.
    - Verify that your backup contains all the files.
    - Find out the block size of the tape when you took your backup.
    - Using your `mksysb` tape, find out the date when it was saved.
    - Verify that you can boot off this `mksysb` tape.
    - Restore /etc/hosts and /etc/filesystems file from your `mksysb` tape.
4. Save your rootvg using the `savevg` command and use a separate tape for backup.
5. Try restoring your rootvg from your mksysb tape using the `restvg` command.
6. Create a raw logical volume and save your raw logical volume using the `dd` command.
7. Use `backup`, `restore`, and `tar` commands to backup your user file systems.

Chapter 9. System Performance

This chapter discusses the two system performance monitoring tools, vmstat and iostat, used to capture the data required to identify the performance problems related to CPU, memory, and I/O subsystem. The fileset bos.acct contains these tools.

9.1 Using the vmstat Command Tool

The `vmstat` command reports statistics about processes, virtual memory, paging activity, faults, CPU activity, and disk transfers. A sample of `vmstat` output report is shown in Figure 103.

```
# vmstat hdisk0 hdisk1 4
kthr     memory             page                    faults        cpu       disk xfer
----- ----------- ------------------------ ------------ ----------- -----------
 r  b   avm   fre  re  pi  po  fr   sr  cy  in   sy   cs us sy id wa  1  2  3  4
 0  1 37184   156   0   0   0   1    7   0 171  582   58  4  3 93  1  1  0
 1  1 37184   156   0   0   0   0    0   0 555 5373 1600 12 15 73  0  0  0
 2  1 37189   162   0   0   2   4   12   0 523 5477 1377 30 24 45  0  2  0
 2  1 37189   162   0   0   0   0    0   0 508 5623 1312 39 28 34  0  0  0
 0  1 37189   161   0   0   0   0    0   0 545 5382 1521 17 17 65  0  0  0
 0  1 37189   161   0   0   0   0    0   0 553 5337 1575 16 14 70  0  0  0
 0  1 37189  3053   0   0   0   0    0   0 553 5284 1566 16 16 68  0  0  0
 0  1 37189  3049   0   0   0   0    0   0 568 5308 1511 15 15 64  6  7  0
 0  1 37189  2890   0  18   0   0    0   0 578 5321 1587 15 16 47 22 28  0
 0  2 37189  2549   0  41   0   0    0   0 641 5329 1620 18 19  0 63 71  0
 1  2 37346  1925   0  25   0   0    0   0 621 21626 1559 19 25  5 51 67  0
 0  1 37346  1925   0   0   0   0    0   0 551 5275 1567 14 14 72  0  0  0
 0  1 37346  1630   0   0   0   0    0   0 565 5303 1513 17 21 61  1 10  0
 4  1 37377   121   0   0  56  60  296   0 620 5324 1234 40 45 13  3 46  7
 0  1 37377   125   0   0  16 186 4856   0 550 5219 1345 20 45 24 10  5 17
 0  1 37346   160   0   0   0 116  927   0 571 5397 1454 21 30 45  4 12  7
 0  1 37346   160   0   0   0   0    0   0 548 5281 1552 12 16 72  0  0  0
 0  1 37346   160   0   0   0   0    0   0 548 5259 1545 14 14 72  0  0  0
^C#
```

Figure 103. vmstat Output Example with Disk Activity

The following sections will discuss some of the frequently referenced fields for analysis from the preceding example of the `vmstat` report.

9.1.1 Paging Activity Statistics

When processes on the system require more pages of memory than are available in RAM, working pages may be paged out to paging space and then paged in when they are needed again. Accessing a page from paging space is considerably slower than accessing a page directly from RAM. For this reason, constant paging activity can cause system performance degradation. The paging activity is determined by the following four fields.

pi Number of pages per second paged in from paging space.

po Number of pages per second paged out to paging space.

fr Number of pages that must be freed to replenish the free list or to accommodate an active process.

sr Number of pages that must be examined in order to free **fr** number of pages.

9.1.1.1 Data Analysis

The following conclusions can be drawn from the various filed values.

- A consistent nonzero value of pi and po means high paging activity that can slow down the system. This can be due to a memory bottleneck.
- A high fr:sr ratio indicates that the memory is overcommitted. An fr:sr ratio of 1:4 means for every one page freed, four pages must be examined. It is difficult to determine a memory constraint based on this ratio alone and what constitutes a high ratio is workload/application dependent.

9.1.2 CPU Statistics

The following fields of vmstat report determine the status of CPU usage.

id Percentage of time the CPU is idle (the run queue is empty).

wa Percentage of time the CPU is idle (with pending local disk I/O).

r Number of threads (smallest work unit) placed on the run queue per second.

b Number of threads (smallest work unit) placed on the wait queue per second (awaiting resource or completion of an I/O).

us Percentage of CPU time spent in user mode.

sy Percentage of CPU time spent in system mode.

9.1.2.1 Data Analysis

The values of various fields can lead you to the following conclusions:

- If the id value is consistently 0 percent, the CPU is being used 100% of the time.
- A key factor when evaluating CPU performance is the size of the run queue. As the run queue increases, the users will notice degradation (an increase) in response time.

- If us+sy time is below 90 percent, a single user system is not considered CPU constrained. However, if us+sy time on a multiuser system exceeds 80 percent, the processes may spend time waiting in the run queue and therefore the response time and throughput might suffer.
- A wa value of over 40 percent indicates that the disk subsystem is not balanced or the work load is disk-intensive.

9.1.3 Determine the I/O for Persistent Storage

The I/O for persistent storage is the I/O (disk reads and writes) initiated by VMM excluding paging space I/O. The following example shows how to calculate I/O for persistent storage using `vmstat` command with -s option.

```
# vmstat -s
    3983934 total address trans. faults
     384406 page ins
     218433 page outs
      16928 paging space page ins
      35468 paging space page outs
          0 total reclaims
    1738350 zero filled pages faults
      19584 executable filled pages faults
    2035457 pages examined by clock
        132 revolutions of the clock hand
     393739 pages freed by the clock
      57211 backtracks
          0 lock misses
        161 free frame waits
          0 extend XPT waits
     197637 pending I/O waits
     340980 start I/Os
     340980 iodones
   16706966 cpu context switches
   46963483 device interrupts
          0 software interrupts
          0 traps
  161793600 syscalls
```

There are 23 separate events reported by the `vmstat -s` output, but the following four are used to calculate the persistent storage I/O.

page ins This field is the count of systemwide pages read from disk (including pages read from paging space). When a page is read from disk to memory, this count is incremented. It is a count of VMM-initiated read operations and, with the page outs field, represents the real I/O (disk reads and writes) initiated by the VMM.

page outs — This field is the count of systemwide pages written on to the disk (including pages written to the paging space). The process of writing pages to the disk is count incremented. The page outs field value is a total count of VMM-initiated write operations and, with the page ins field, represents the total amount of real I/O initiated by the VMM.

paging space page ins — This field is the count of pages read from paging space.

paging space page outs — This field is the count of pages written to paging space.

If the value for paging space page ins is subtracted from the (systemwide) value for page ins, the result is the number of persistent pages (files) that were read from disk. Similarly, if the value for paging space page outs is subtracted from the (systemwide) value for page outs, the result is the number of persistent pages (files) that were written to disk.

The preceding example shows that 367478 (384406-16928) number of pages are read from disk and 182965 (218433-35468) number of pages are written to the disk.

These counts apply to the time since system initialization. If you need counts for a given time interval, execute `vmstat -s` at the time you want to start monitoring and again at the end of the interval. The deltas between like fields of successive reports will be the count for the interval.

9.2 Using the iostat Command Tool

The `iostat` command tool reports the following three types of statistics.

- Terminal statistics
- CPU statistics
- Disk statistics

This section discusses the `iostat` command to identify I/O-subsystem and CPU bottlenecks using CPU statistics and disk statistics. The following is a sample iostat output report.

```
# iostat

tty:       tin        tout   avg-cpu:  % user    % sys     % idle    % iowait
           0.1         9.0              7.7       6.8       85.0      0.5

Disks:         % tm_act     Kbps      tps    Kb_read   Kb_wrtn
hdisk1           0.1        0.7      0.0      39191    242113
hdisk0           0.8       11.1      0.8    3926601    822579
cd0              0.0        0.0      0.0        780         0
```

The following sections will discuss some of the frequently referenced fields from the preceding example.

9.2.1 CPU Statistics

The following fields of CPU statistics in the iostat report determine the CPU usage and the I/O status.

% user The % user column shows the percentage of CPU resource spent in user mode. A UNIX process can execute in user or system mode. When in user mode, a process executes within its own code and does not require kernel resources.

% sys The % sys column shows the percentage of CPU resource spent in system mode. This includes CPU resource consumed by kernel processes and others that need access to kernel resources. For example, the reading or writing of a file requires kernel resources to open the file, seek a specific location, and read or write data. A UNIX process accesses kernel resources by issuing system calls.

% idle The % idle column shows the percentage of CPU time spent idle, or waiting, without pending local disk I/O. If there are no processes on the run queue, the system dispatches a special kernel process called wait. On most AIX systems, the wait process ID (PID) is 516.

% iowait The % iowait column shows the percentage of time the CPU was idle with pending local disk I/O. The iowait state is different from the idle state in that at least one process is waiting for local disk I/O requests to complete. Unless the process is using asynchronous I/O, an I/O request to disk causes the calling process to block (or sleep) until the request is completed. Once a process's I/O request completes, it is placed on the run queue.

9.2.1.1 Data Analysis

The following conclusions can be drawn from the iostat reports.

- A system is CPU-bound if the sum of user and system time exceeds 90 percent of CPU resource on a single-user system or 80 percent on a multiuser system. This condition means that the CPU is the limiting factor in system performance.
- A high iowait percentage indicates the system has a memory shortage or an inefficient I/O subsystem configuration. Understanding the I/O bottleneck and improving the efficiency of the I/O subsystem requires more data than `iostat` command output can provide. However, typical solutions might include:
  - Limiting the number of active logical volumes and file systems placed on a particular physical disk (the idea is to balance file I/O evenly across all physical disk drives).
  - Spreading a logical volume across multiple physical disks (this is useful when a number of different files are being accessed).
  - Creating multiple JFS logs for a volume group and assigning them to specific file systems (this is beneficial for applications that create, delete, or modify a large number of files, particularly temporary files).
  - Backing up and restoring file systems to reduce fragmentation. (Fragmentation causes the drive to seek excessively and can be a large portion of overall response time).
  - Adding additional drives and rebalancing the existing I/O subsystem.
- On systems running a primary application, high I/O wait percentage may be related to workload. In this case, there may be no way to overcome the problem.
- On systems with many processes, some will be running while others wait for I/O. In this case, the iowait can be small or zero because running processes *hide* wait time. Although iowait is low, a bottleneck may still limit application performance.

To understand the I/O subsystem thoroughly, you need to examine the disk statistics of iostat report in the following section.

9.2.2 Disk Statistics

The disk statistics portion of the iostat output determines the I/O usage. This information is useful in determining whether a physical disk is the bottleneck for performance. The system maintains a history of disk activity by default. The history is disabled if you see the following message:

```
Disk history since boot not available.
```

Disk I/O history should be enabled since the CPU resource used in maintaining it is insignificant. History-keeping can be disabled or enabled by executing `smitty chgsys`, the SMIT fast path command that will display the screen as shown in Figure 104. Change the option `Continuously maintain DISK I/O history` to `TRUE` to enable the history keeping option..

```
              Change / Show Characteristics of Operating System

Type or select values in entry fields.
Press Enter AFTER making all desired changes.

                                                        [Entry Fields]
  Maximum number of PROCESSES allowed per user        [40]                +#
  Maximum number of pages in block I/O BUFFER CACHE   [20]                +#
  Maximum Kbytes of real memory allowed for MBUFS     [0]                 +#
  Automatically REBOOT system after a crash            false              +
  Continuously maintain DISK I/O history               true               +
  HIGH water mark for pending write I/Os per file     [0]                 +#
  LOW water mark for pending write I/Os per file      [0]                 +#
  Amount of usable physical memory in Kbytes           65536
  State of system keylock at boot time                 normal
  Enable full CORE dump                                false              +
  Use pre-430 style CORE dump                          false              +



F1=Help             F2=Refresh          F3=Cancel           F4=List
F5=Reset            F6=Command          F7=Edit             F8=Image
F9=Shell            F10=Exit            Enter=Do
```

Figure 104. Enabling the Disk I/O History

The following fields of the `iostat` report determine the physical disk I/O.

Disks The Disks column shows the names of the physical volumes. They are either hdisk or cd followed by a number. (hdisk0 and cd0 refer to the first physical disk drive and the first CD disk drive, respectively.)

% tm_act The % tm_act column shows the percentage of time the volume was active. This is the primary indicator of a bottleneck.

Kbps Kbps shows the amount of data read from and written to the drive in KBs per second. This is the sum of Kb_read plus Kb_wrtn, divided by the number of seconds in the reporting interval.

tps tps reports the number of transfers per second. A transfer is an I/O request at the device-driver level.

Kb_read Kb_read reports the total data (in KB) read from the physical volume during the measured interval.

Kb_wrtn Kb_wrtn shows the amount of data (in KB) written to the physical volume during the measured interval.

9.2.2.1 Data Analysis

There is no unacceptable value for any of the fields in the preceding section because statistics are too closely related to application characteristics, system configuration, and types of physical disk drives and adapters. Therefore, when evaluating data, you must look for patterns and relationships. The most common relationship is between disk utilization and data transfer rate.

To draw any valid conclusions from this data, you must understand the application's disk data access patterns (sequential, random, or a combination) and the type of physical disk drives and adapters on the system. For example, if an application reads and writes sequentially, you should expect a high disk-transfer rate when you have a high disk-busy rate. (Note: Kb_read and Kb_wrtn can confirm an understanding of an application's read and write behavior, but they provide no information on the data access patterns).

Generally you do not need to be concerned about a high disk-busy rate as long as the disk-transfer rate is also high. However, if you get a high disk-busy rate and a low data-transfer rate, you may have a fragmented logical volume, file system, or individual file.

What is a high data-transfer rate? That depends on the disk drive and the effective data-transfer rate for that drive. You should expect numbers between the effective sequential and effective random disk-transfer rates. The effective transfer rates for a few of the common SCSI-1 and SCSI-2 disk drives are shown in Table 15:

Table 15. Effective Transfer Rates (KB/sec)

Type of Access	Read Sequential	Read Random	Write Sequential	Write Random
400 MB DRIVE	1589	241	1185	327
670 MB DRIVE	1525	172	1108	275
857 MB DRIVE	2142	262	1588	367
1.2 GB DRIVE	2169	292	1464	362
1.37 GB DRIVE	2667	299	2189	491
1.2 GB S-2 DRIVE	2180	385	2156	405
1.37 GB S-2 DRIVE	3123	288	2357	549

You can also use the data captured by the `iostat` command to analyze the requirement of an additional SCSI adapter (if the one installed in your system is the I/O bottleneck) by tracking transfer rates, and finding the maximum data transfer rate for each disk.

The disk usage percentage (% tm_act) is directly proportional to resource contention and inversely proportional to performance. As disk use increases, performance decreases and response time increases. In general, when a disk's use exceeds 70 percent, processes are waiting longer than necessary for I/O to complete because most UNIX processes block (or sleep) while waiting for their I/O requests to complete.

To overcome I/O bottlenecks, you can perform the following actions:

- Look for busy versus idle drives. Moving data from more busy to less busy drives may help alleviate a disk bottleneck.
- Check for paging activity because paging to and from disk will also contribute to the I/O load. Move paging space from a more busy drive to a less busy drive to improve the performance.

9.3 Paging Space Management

Paging space requirements are unique for each system depending upon the kind of applications running and/or the number of active users.

9.3.1 Do You Need More Paging Space?

If any of the following messages appear on the console or in response to a command on any terminal, it indicates a low paging space.

```
"INIT: Paging space is low"

"ksh: cannot fork no swap space"

"Not enough memory"

"Fork function failed"

"fork () system call failed"

"Unable to fork, too many processes"

"Fork failure - not enough memory available"

"Fork function not allowed. Not enough memory available."

"Cannot fork: Not enough space"
```

9.3.2 Paging Space Tips

The following tips, in general, will help in creating or increasing the paging space.

- Do not allocate more than one paging space logical volume on a physical volume. All processes started during the boot process are allocated paging space on the default paging space logical volume (hd6). After the additional paging space logical volumes are activated, paging space is allocated in a round robin manner in 4 KB blocks. If you have paging space on multiple physical volumes and have more than one paging space on one physical volume, you are no longer spreading paging activity over multiple physical volumes.
- Avoid putting a paging space logical volume on a heavily active logical volume. For example a volume that is being used by a database. It is not necessary to put a paging space logical volume on each physical volume.
- Make each paging space logical volume roughly equal in size. If you have paging spaces of different sizes, and the smaller ones become full, you will no longer be spreading your paging activity across all of the physical volumes.
- Do not extend a paging space logical volume onto multiple physical volumes. If a paging space logical volume is spread over multiple physical volumes, you will not be spreading paging activity across all the physical volumes. If you want to allocate space for paging on a physical volume that does not already have a paging space logical volume, create a new paging space logical volume on that physical volume.
- For the best performance on a system having multiple disk controllers, allocate paging space logical volumes on physical volumes that are each attached to a different disk controller.

9.3.3 Managing Default Paging Space (hd6)

The AIX installation defaults to a paging logical volume (hd6) on drive hdisk0, that contains part or all of the busy / (root) and /usr file systems.

A special procedure is required for removing the default paging space (hd6). These paging spaces are activated during boot time by shell scripts that configure the system. To remove one of the default paging spaces, these scripts must be altered and a new boot image must be created.

9.3.3.1 Reducing the Size of hd6 Paging Space

The following example shows the steps involved in reducing the size of hd6 paging space from 160 MB to 120 MB.The steps in the following procedures are all necessary, even those not directly related to the hd6 paging space. The additional steps are needed because a paging space cannot be deactivated while the system is running

Note

- AIX Version 4.2.1 and later does not support reducing the size of hd6 below 32 MB or the system will not boot.
- If you decide to reduce hd6, you must leave enough space for the software in rootvg. A rule of thumb for reducing hd6 paging space is to leave enough space to match physical memory. To find out the amount of physical memory, use the following command:

```
lsattr -E -l sys0 -a realmem
```

1. Create a temporary paging space on rootvg by executing the following command:

   ```
   mkps -a -n -s 30 rootvg hdisk0
   ```

   This command outputs the name of the paging space (paging00 if no others exist).

2. Use the following command to deactivate the hd6 paging spaces in preparation for the reboot later in the procedure:

   ```
   chps -a n hd6
   ```

3. Change the paging space entry in the /sbin/rc.boot file from:

   ```
   swapon /dev/hd6
   ```

   to

   ```
   swapon /dev/paging00.
   ```

4. Execute the following command to check the primary dump device designation:

   ```
   # sysdumpdev -l
   primary              /dev/hd6
   secondary            /dev/sysdumpnull
   copy directory       /var/adm/ras
   forced copy flag     TRUE
   always allow dump    FALSE
   ```

5. If the primary dump device is hd6, change it to some other paging space. The following command shows how to change the primary dump device to paging00:

   ```
   # sysdumpdev -P -p /dev/paging00
   primary              /dev/paging00
   secondary            /dev/sysdumpnull
   ```

```
copy directory        /var/adm/ras
forced copy flag      TRUE
always allow dump     FALSE
```

6. Create a bootable image with the `bosboot` command for a hard disk image:

```
bosboot -d /dev/hdisk0 -a
```

7. Put the system key (if present) in the normal position and use the following command, which will both shutdown the operating system and reboot it:

```
shutdown -r
```

8. After the system reboots, remove the hd6 paging space:

```
rmps hd6
```

9. Create a new paging space logical volume of the size 120 MB for the hd6 paging space:

```
mklv -t paging -y hd6 rootvg 30
```

10. Change the primary dump device designation back to be the paging space hd6:

```
sysdumpdev -P -p /dev/hd6
```

11. Change the paging space entry in the /sbin/rc.boot file from

```
swapon /dev/paging00 to swapon /dev/hd6.
```

12. Create a bootable image with the `bosboot` command for a hard disk image;

```
bosboot -d /dev/hdisk0 -a
```

13. Execute the following command to make the new hd6 paging space automatically activated when the system reboots:

```
chps -a y hd6
```

14. Execute the following command to change the attribute of temporary paging space, paging00, so that it does not automatically activate after next reboot:

```
chps -a n paging00
```

15. Put the system key (if present) in the normal position and use the following command, to shutdown and reboot the system:

```
shutdown -r
```

16. After the system reboots, remove the temporary paging space:

```
rmps paging00
```

Use the `lsps -a` command to verify the reduced size of default paging space (hd6).

9.3.3.2 Moving the hd6 Paging Space to Another Volume Group

Moving a paging space with the name hd6 from rootvg to another volume group is not recommended because the name is hard-coded in several places.

Only the paging spaces in rootvg will be active during the second phase of the boot process, and having no paging space in rootvg could severely affect system boot performance. If you want the majority of paging space on other volume groups, it is better to make hd6 as small as possible (the same size as physical memory) and then create larger paging spaces on other volume groups.

9.3.3.3 Moving the hd6 Paging Space within the Same VG

Moving the default paging space from hdisk0 to a different disk within the same volume group does not require system reboot.

The following example shows the command used to move the default (hd6) paging space from hdisk0 to hdisk1:

```
migratepv -l hd6 hdisk0 hdisk1
```

This may take a few minutes depending upon the size of paging space.

9.3.4 References

The following publications contains more information about system performance tools.

- *AIX Version 3.2 & 4 Performance Tuning Guide*, SC23-2365
- *AIX Version 4.3 Messages Guide and Reference*, SC23-4129
- *URL:* `http://service.software.ibm.com/rs6k/techdocs`

9.4 Quiz

1. A client needs more disk space for another volume group and has decided to use hdisk12 from the uservg volume group. Theclient realizes that paging space, paging12, must first be removed from hdisk12. Which of the following is the correct sequence of events?

   A. `chps -an paging12, rmps paging12`

   B. `swapoff paging12, rmps paging12`

   C. `swapoff paging12, reboot, rmps paging12`

   D. `chps -an paging12, swapoff paging12, rmps paging12`

2. A customer would like to remove an unneeded, but active, paging space called paging00. What is proper sequence of steps to accomplish this?

   A. Remove the paging space with the `rmps` command and reboot the system.

   B. Disable the paging space with the `chps` command, reboot the system and remove the paging00 logical volume with the `rmps` command.

   C. Disable the paging space with the `chps` command, remove the paging00 logical volume with the `rmps` command, and reboot the system.

   D. Disable the paging space with the `chps` command, reboot the system and remove the paging00 logical volume with the `rmlv` command.

3. Company ABC has sent a technical specialist to a customer site in response to a complaint about slow system performance . The technical specialist verified unusually slow performance on the customer's system, and is attempting to find the source of the problem using the `vmstat` command. Given the output of the `vmstat` command below, what is the most likely cause of the performance problem?

```
kthr     memory             page              faults        cpu
----- ----------- ------------------------ ------------ -----------
 r  b   avm   fre  re  pi  po  fr   sr  cy  in   sy  cs us sy id wa
 0  0  5311 48642   0   0   0   0    0   0 102    4  11  0  0 99  0
 0  1 52197  1756   0   0   0   0    0   0 206  157  26 28 12  0 60
 0  1 51192  2751   0   0   0   0    0   0 204   24  22 22 12  0 66
```

   A. High user process activity

   B. Excessive system paging

   C. Poor disk drive I/O response time

   D. Excessive system CPU interrupts

4. A system administrator runs the `vmstat` command due to system performance problems. The output of `vmstat` is shown. What can be concluded from this output?

```
kthr     memory             page              faults        cpu
----- ----------- ------------------------ ------------ -----------
 r  b   avm   fre  re  pi  po  fr   sr  cy  in   sy  cs us sy id wa
 2  0  9200 11027   0   0   0   0    0   0 103   52  14 44 46  9  0
 2  1  9200 11027   0   0   0   0    0   0 207  251  29 45 45  9  0
 3  1  9200 11027   0   0   0   0    0   0 207  120  29 46 47  7  0
 5  1  9200 11027   0   0   0   0    0   0 206  120  29 43 55  2  0
 4  1  9200 11027   0   0   0   0    0   0 207  131  32 49 48  3  0
```

   A. The CPU is not sufficient for the load.

B. The machine needs a memory upgrade.

C. The machine needs a FDDI card installed.

D. A user program is causing unnecessary paging.

5. A system administrator is experiencing performance problems and runs the `vmstat` command. The output of vmstat is shown. What can be concluded from this output?

```
kthr     memory             page              faults        cpu
----- ----------- ------------------------ ------------ -----------
 r  b   avm   fre  re  pi  po  fr   sr  cy  in   sy  cs us sy id wa
 2  0  9200 11027   0   0   0   0    0   0 103   52  14 14 16  0 69
 2  1  9200 11027   0   0   0   0    0   0 207  251  29 12 11  0 67
 3  1  9200 11027   0   0   0   0    0   0 207  120  29  9 11  0 80
 5  1  9200 11027   0   0   0   0    0   0 206  120  29 13  5  0 79
 4  1  9200 11027   0   0   0   0    0   0 207  131  32  9  8  0 72
```

A. The machine is I/O bound.

B. The machine needs memory optimized.

C. The machine needs a FDDI card installed.

D. A user program is causing unnecessary paging.

6. The system administrator for Company XYZ is monitoring a system that has recently shown a decrease in performance. What is the best tool to identify where a performance bottleneck may exist?

A. `lsps`

B. `errpt`

C. `svmon`

D. `vmstat`

7. A system has a 128-port controller with 130 TTYs configured total for the system and the terminal input and output is slowing down. The console is exhibiting the same behavior. Systems support runs `netstat`, `vmstat` and `ps aux` commands. Based on the outputs of these commands, what needs to be done to remedy the problem?

```
# vmstat

kthr     memory             page              faults        cpu
----- ----------- ------------------------ ------------ -----------
 r  b   avm   fre  re  pi  po  fr   sr  cy  in   sy  cs us sy id wa
 0  0  9778  1262   0   0   0   0    0   0 161   72  32 10 15 75  0
 0  0  9778  1261   0   0   0   0    0   0 171  161  38 11 20 69  0
 0  0  9778  1261   0   0   0   0    0   0 162  119  32 11 20 69  0
 0  0  9778  1261   0   0   0   0    0   0 163  119  32 12 20 68  0
 0  0  9778  1261   0   0   0   0    0   0 164  120  33 11 20 69  0
```

```
# netstat

16 mbufs in use:
0 mbuf cluster pages in use
4 Kbytes allocated to mbufs
110 requests for mbufs denied
0 calls to protocol drain routines
0 sockets not created because sockthresh was reached

# ps aux

USER       PID %CPU %MEM   SZ  RSS    TTY STAT    STIME   TIME COMMAND
root       516 99.1  0.0    4    8      - A      Jul 27 2851:18 kproc
root     14474  1.1  1.0  980 1180      - A    08:01:48   1:09 /usr/dt/bin/dtter
root      1032  0.2  0.0  316  232      - A      Jul 27   6:51 kproc
root      2258  0.2  1.0  964 1148      - A    08:01:13   0:14 /usr/dt/bin/dtter
user1     2364  0.1  5.0 5468 4768      - A      Jul 27   2:02 /usr/lpp/X11/bin/
root      5676  0.0  0.0  116  184      - A      Jul 27   1:11 ./sapd
root      4154  0.0  0.0   84   96      - A      Jul 27   0:53 /usr/sbin/syncd 6
root         0  0.0  0.0    8   12      - A      Jul 27   0:31 swapper
root      4044  0.0  2.0 1808 2008      - A    08:00:43   0:01 dtwm
root         1  0.0  0.0  384  436      - A      Jul 27   0:07 /etc/init
root      7740  0.0  1.0  980 1132      - A      Jul 27   0:04 /usr/sbin/snmpd
root       774  0.0  0.0   12   16      - A      Jul 27   0:03 kproc
user2     3376  0.0  0.0  432  428      - A      Jul 27   0:02 /usr/dt/bin/dtlog
user2     8796  0.0  0.0  232  312      - A      Jul 27   0:01 /usr/sbin/cron
root      7998  0.0  0.0  272  260      - A      Jul 27   0:01 /usr/sbin/tftpd -
root      5196  0.0  1.0  456  532      - A      Jul 27   0:01 /usr/bin/cnsview
imnadm   12132  0.0  2.0 1756 1808      - A      Jul 27   0:00 /usr/IMNSearch/ht
```

A. Add another paging space.

B. Increase the value of the wall.

C. Increase the size of paging space.

D. Run `kill -9` on PID of kproc process.

8. A customer is experiencing performance problems and runs the `vmstat` command. The output of `vmstat` is shown. What can be concluded from this output?

```
kthr      memory              page                 faults        cpu
----- ----------- ------------------------ ------------ -----------
 r  b   avm   fre  re  pi  po  fr   sr  cy  in   sy  cs us sy id wa
 1  0  9200    27   0  87  89   0    0   0 103   52  14 10 15  9 65
 2  1  9200    22   0 136 122   0    0   0 207  251  29  9 12  8 71
 3  1  9200    19   0 112 107   0    0   0 207  120  29 11  9  7 73
 5  1  9200    17   0  99 122   0    0   0 206  120  29 12  8  8 72
```

A. The machine needs a CPU upgrade.

B. Another ATM card needs to be added.

C. The paging space needs to be optimized.

D. A user program is causing a system loop.

9. A customer is experiencing performance problems and runs the `iostat` command. The output of the `iostat` command is shown. What should be recommended?

```
tty:      tin         tout   avg-cpu:  % user    % sys     % idle    %
iowait
        0.0        170.2               7.1      12.1        0.8      80.0

Disks:         % tm_act     Kbps      tps    Kb_read   Kb_wrtn
hdisk0           0.0       0.0       0.0         0          0
hdisk1           0.0       0.0       0.0         0          0
cd0             55.9     622.4     155.6      1250          8

tty:      tin         tout   avg-cpu:  % user    % sys     % idle    %
iowait
        0.0        170.2               5.1      14.1        0.8      80.0

Disks:         % tm_act     Kbps      tps    Kb_read   Kb_wrtn
hdisk0           0.5       2.0       0.5         4          0
hdisk1           0.0       0.0       0.0         0          0
cd0             55.9     622.4     155.6      1270          0
```

A. A user program needs optimizing.

B. Another ATM card needs to be added.

C. The CD-ROM needs to be removed from the configuration.

D. Space permitting, the volume mounted on the CD-ROM should be moved to a disk.

9.4.1 Answers

1. A
2. B
3. C
4. A
5. A
6. D
7. B
8. C
9. D

9.5 Exercises

1. Execute the `iostat` command on the system and analyze the output for CPU statistics, and disk statistics.
2. Execute the `vmstat` command on the system and analyze the output for CPU statistics and paging activity.
3. Determine the I/O for persistent storage on your system using the `vmstat -s` command.
4. Increase the default paging space (hd6) on the system by 5 MB and then reduce the size of the default paging space by 5 MB. How many system reboots are required to accomplish this task?

Chapter 10. Networking

There are a few areas that should be learned as a starting point when diagnosing network problems such as access and performance problems, because some networking facilities have security implications. These topics are presented in this chapter.

10.1 The DISPLAY Environment Variable

X-Windows consists of three components: the server, client programs, and the communications channel. The server distributes user input to and accepts output requests from various client programs (applications) located either on the same machine or elsewhere on the network.

The display name or DISPLAY environment variable is a string with the following format:

`HostName:Number.Screen`

`HostName` Specifies the name of the host system where the display is physically attached. The host name should be followed by a : (colon).

`Number` Specifies the ID number of the display server on that host machine. The display number can be followed by a . (period).

`Screen` Specifies the number of the screen on that host server. Multiple screens can be connected to or controlled by a single X server.

By default, the DISPLAY environment variable is set to `:screen#`. When you log in to the graphic console, the DISPLAY environment variable is:

```
# echo $DISPLAY
:0.0
#
```

10.1.1 Failing to Start an X-Windows Application

By default, the DISPLAY environment variable is not set when you Telnet or rlogin to a remote host. An attempt to start an X-windows application will fail if:

- The DISPLAY environment variable is not set up.
- The X-windows server has not been started.
- The X-windows server access control has been enabled and your remote host is not on the access control list.

Each of these conditions is dicussed in the following sections.

10.1.1.1 The DISPLAY Environment Variable is Not Set

If you have not set your DISPLAY environment variable, you will see these messages:

```
# echo $DISPLAY

# aixterm
1363-008 aixterm: Cannot make a connection to X server .
        If the X server is not running, run the xinit command.
        If the X server is running, check the specified display number.
```

Note that the name of the X-windows server is empty. Rectify this by setting up your DISPLAY environment variable.

10.1.1.2 The X-Windows Server is Not Started

If you have not started the X-Windows server, you will see these messages:

```
# export DISPLAY='sv1166a:0'
# aixterm
1363-008 aixterm: Cannot make a connection to X server sv1166a:0.
        If the X server is not running, run the xinit command.
        If the X server is running, check the specified display number.
#
```

The hostname `sv1166a` is just an example. Replace it with the appropriate hostname. Rectify this by starting the X-windows server on your local host using the `xinit` command.

10.1.1.3 X-Windows Server Access Control List

If access control is enabled and the hostname `sv1166a` is not on the access control list, you will see these messages:

```
# echo $DISPLAY
sv1166a:0
# aixterm
Xlib: connection to "sv1166a:0.0" refused by server
Xlib: Client is not authorized to connect to Server
1363-008 aixterm: Cannot make a connection to X server sv1166a:0.
        If the X server is not running, run the xinit command.
        If the X server is running, check the specified display number.
#
```

For AIX, rectify this from the local console on the local host by using:

- The `xhost +` command:

```
# xhost +
access control disabled, clients can connect from any host
```

Do this only if it does not violate the security guideline of your company.

- The `xhost +sv1050a` command:

```
# xhost +sv1050a
sv1166a being added to access control list
# xhost
access control enabled, only authorized clients can connect
INET:sv1050a.itsc.austin.ibm.com
#
```

The hostname of the remote host sv1050a is an example. Replace it with the appropriate hostname of the remote host that you have a telnet session with. You may see other hostnames on the access control list.

10.1.2 Setting Up the DISPLAY Environment Variable

The display name or DISPLAY environment variable is a string with the following format:

```
HostName:Number.Screen
```

Instead of using the host name, you can also use the IP address in the DISPLAY environment variable.

10.1.2.1 Using the Host Name

Using the host name is more convenient. Use the `hostname` command on one of your local sessions to find out the host name to use:

```
# hostname
sv1166a
#
```

Go back to your Telnet session and set up your DISPLAY environment variable by entering:

```
export DISPLAY='sv1166a:0'
```

The screen number does not need to be specified if you have only one screen connected or controlled by the X-windows server.

10.1.2.2 Using the IP Address

You can use the IP address at any time. When the Domain Name Server is down or when you are using dynamic IP address, you will not be able to use the host name and using the IP address is the only possible alternative.

10.2 Security Consideration with System and TCP/IP Files

All of the $HOME/.netrc, $HOME/.forward, $HOME/.rhosts, and /etc/hosts.equiv files have security implications for their implementation.

10.2.1 The $HOME/.netrc File

The $HOME/.netrc file contains information used by the automatic login feature of the `rexec` and `ftp` commands. It is a hidden file in a user's home directory and must be owned either by the user executing the command or by the root user. If the .netrc file contains a login password, the file's permissions must be set to 600 (read and write by owner only). The login password is in plain text. Even with permissions set to 600, passwords for remote systems are vulnerable to being revealed to any user with root authority.

10.2.2 The $HOME/.forward File

When mail is sent to a local user, the `sendmail` command checks for the $HOME/.forward file. The $HOME/.forward file can contain one or more addresses or aliases. If the file exists, the message is not sent to the user. The message is sent to the addresses or aliases in the $HOME/.forward file. All messages, including confidential ones, will never reach the user if this is implemented.

10.2.3 The /etc/hosts.equiv File

The /etc/hosts.equiv file, along with any local $HOME/.rhosts files, defines the hosts (computers on a network) and user accounts that can invoke remote commands on a local host without supplying a password. The $HOME/.rhosts file is similar to the /etc/hosts.equiv file, except that it is maintained for individual users.

10.2.4 The $HOME/.rhosts File

The $HOME/.rhosts file defines which remote hosts (computers on a network) can invoke certain commands on the local host without supplying a password. This file is a hidden file in the local user's home directory and must be owned by the local user. Although you can set any permissions for this file, it is recommended that the permissions of the .rhosts file be set to 600 (read and write by owner only). Bypassing the need for a password may be a security concern, especially if you allow all users on a particular system \access without needing a password.

The permissions and the entries in the $HOME/.rhosts file will affect whether a user on a remote host can successfully establish an rsh session. Some examples are:

Table 16. $HOME/.rhosts Definitions

Local Host (sv1050a) User itsouser	Remote Host (aix4xdev) User itsouser
$ cat > $HOME/.rhosts aix4xdev **$ chmod 600 $HOME/.rhosts** $	**$ rsh sv050a -l itsouser ls -a** rshd: 0826-813 Permission is denied. $
$ cat > $HOME/.rhosts aix4xdev itsouser **$ chmod 600 $HOME/.rhosts** $	**$ rsh sv050a -l itsouser ls -a** . .. .profile .rhosts .sh_history $
$ cat > $HOME/.rhosts aix4xdev + **$ chmod 600 $HOME/.rhosts** $	**$ rsh sv050a -l itsouser ls -a** . .. .profile .rhosts .sh_history $
$ chmod 644 $HOME/.rhosts $	**$ rsh sv050a -l itsouser ls -a** . .. .profile .rhosts .sh_history $
$ chmod 666 $HOME/.rhosts $	**$ rsh sv050a -l itsouser ls -a** rshd: 0826-813 Permission is denied. $
$ chmod 777 $HOME/.rhosts $	**$ rsh sv050a -l itsouser ls -a** rshd: 0826-813 Permission is denied. $

10.3 Removing a Network Adapter

To remove a token-ring network adapter from the system, first ensure that there is no user on the system, and then perform the following steps:

1. Delete the network interface definition for the adapter:

```
# ifconfig tr0 detach
#
```

2. Delete the network interface driver for the adapter:

```
# rmdev -l tr0 -d
tr0 deleted
#
```

3. Delete the adapter device from the system:

```
# rmdev -l tok0 -d
tok0 deleted
#
```

4. Shutdown, power off the system, and remove the adapter physically.
5. Power on to reboot the system.

   If you do not physically remove the network adapter before powering on the system, the `cfgmgr` program will detect the network adapter during the system boot, unless it is an ISA adapter, and redefine the device tok0 in the Customized Devices object database.

10.4 Enabling IP Packets To Be Forwarded

To enable IP packets to be forwarded, the `ipforwarding` attribute of the network option must be enabled. `ipforwarding` is a runtime attribute. The default value of `0` (zero) prevents forwarding of IP packets when they are not for the local system. A value of `1` (one) enables forwarding. Enable IP forwarding using the command:

```
no -o ipforwarding=1
```

You are trying to allow pings over multiple subnets on two interface boxes:

1. The first that is on your subnet 9.3.1 with IP address 9.3.1.124 that interfaces with the subnet 192.168.1 with IP address 192.168.1.1.
2. The second in the 192.168.1 subnet with IP address 192.168.1.2 that interfaces with the subnet 192.168.2.

On both the machines with IP addresses 192.168.1.1 and 192.168.1.2, the value of the ipforwarding attribute should be set to 1 (one), such that IP packets are forwarded. Remember that ipforwarding is an attribute having a value of 0 (zero) or 1 (one); it is not a counter.

10.5 Changing the Primary Name Server

The presence of the /etc/resolv.conf file indicates to a host that it should go to a name server to resolve a name first. The sample `/etc/resolve.conf` shows that the primary name server to use is 9.3.1.74:

```
# cat /etc/resolv.conf
nameserver      9.3.1.74
domain  itsc.austin.ibm.com
#
```

Change the IP address of the nameserver entry in the /etc/resolv.conf file to that of the new domain name entry at address 9.3.1.121:

```
# cat /etc/resolv.conf
nameserver      9.3.1.121
domain  itsc.austin.ibm.com
#
```

10.6 When a Domain Name Server is Unreachable

When the domain name server is unreachable, a ping will hang for some time before returning an error message. The domain name server at 9.3.1.121 is currently not available, and it takes more than five minutes before the error message is returned:

```
# ping 9.3.1.121
PING 9.3.1.121: (9.3.1.121): 56 data bytes
^C
----9.3.1.121 PING Statistics----
3 packets transmitted, 0 packets received, 100% packet loss
# date +%H:%M:%S
16:20:10
# ping sv1166f
0821-062 ping: host name sv1166f NOT FOUND
# date +%H:%M:%S
16:25:16
```

10.7 The /etc/netsvc.conf File

The /etc/netsvc.conf file is used to specify the ordering of certain services in AIX, specifically, name resolution for sendmail, the gethostbyname, gethostaddr, and gethostent subroutines, in addition to alias resolution for sendmail.

AIX offers several services for resolving host names and aliases. The gethostbyname, gethostbyaddr, and gethostent subroutines use the services for resolving names. A default is set to determine the order in which these services are tried for resolving host names and Internet Protocol (IP) addresses.

The default order for resolving host names is:

1. BIND/DNS (named)
2. Network Information Service (NIS)
3. Local /etc/hosts file

This default order can be overwritten by creating the configuration file, /etc/netsvc.conf, and specifying the desired ordering. The environment variable NSORDER overrides the host settings in the /etc/netsvc.conf file.

If a particular machine in a subnet cannot resolve a hostname correctly, the default order may have been altered by the presence of the /etc/netsvc.conf file.

10.8 The NSORDER Environment Variable

When a process receives a symbolic host name and needs to resolve it into an address, it calls a resolver routine. By default, resolver routines attempt to resolve names using the above resources. BIND/DNS will be tried first. If the /etc/resolv.conf file does not exist or if BIND/DNS could not find the name, NIS is queried if it is running. If NIS is not running, then the local /etc/hosts file is searched. If none of these services could find the name then the resolver routines return with HOST_NOT_FOUND . If all of the services were unavailable, then the resolver routines return with SERVICE_UNAVAILABLE.

The NSORDER environment variable can be set to change the order the resolver routine takes to resolve a host name. If the NSORDER environment variable is set as:

```
NSORDER=local,bind
```

then the /etc/hosts file will be used for resolving the host names before the Domain Name Server is used.

If a particular machine in a subnet cannot resolve a hostname correctly, and the /etc/netsvc.conf file does not exist or is in order, the default order may have been altered by the setting of the NSORDER environment variable.

10.9 The ARP Cache

The Address Resolution Protocol (ARP) dynamically translates Internet addresses into the unique hardware addresses on local area networks. Nodes on the same segment of the same LAN use ARP to determine the hardware address of other nodes.

Unlike the routing table, you can only delete the ARP cache entries one host at a time:

```
# arp -a
  itsorusi.itsc.austin.ibm.com (9.3.1.74) at 10:0:5a:a8:42:14 [token ring]
  sv1166a.itsc.austin.ibm.com (9.3.1.25) at 0:6:29:f0:e2:77 [token ring]
  itsonv.itsc.austin.ibm.com (9.3.1.5) at 8:0:5a:48:4a:48 [token ring]
  netcomp.itsc.austin.ibm.com (9.3.1.232) at 10:0:5a:38:fb:3 [token ring]
  jc6003a.itsc.austin.ibm.com (9.3.1.111) at 0:6:29:f0:e1:2 [token ring]
# arp -d jc6003a
Entry jc6003a (9.3.1.111) was deleted from local arp table.
# arp -a
  itsorusi.itsc.austin.ibm.com (9.3.1.74) at 10:0:5a:a8:42:14 [token ring]
  sv1166a.itsc.austin.ibm.com (9.3.1.25) at 0:6:29:f0:e2:77 [token ring]
  itsonv.itsc.austin.ibm.com (9.3.1.5) at 8:0:5a:48:4a:48 [token ring]
  netcomp.itsc.austin.ibm.com (9.3.1.232) at 10:0:5a:38:fb:3 [token ring]
#
```

Entries in the ARP mapping table are deleted after 20 minutes; incomplete entries are deleted after three minutes. To make a permanent entry in the ARP mapping tables, use the `arp` command with the `pub` parameter:

Because the hardware address of the network adapter is used, moving a network adapter from one system to another may cause network traffic to be directed to the wrong system. You should either delete the ARP entry on every node in the segment, or ensure that at least 20 minutes have passed before you bring up the system receiving the network adapter.

10.10 Changing the State of the Token-Ring Network Interface

Changing the state of the token-ring network interface to up, down, and detach can have various effects on the output of the `netstat` command.

The output of the `netstat` command showing the configured interface and route table before the token-ring interface is changed from active to inactive is as follows:

```
# netstat -i
Name  Mtu   Network     Address             Ipkts Ierrs    Opkts Oerrs  Coll
```

```
lo0   16896 link#1                          340      0       341     0      0
lo0   16896 127         localhost           340      0       341     0      0
lo0   16896 ::1                             340      0       341     0      0
en0   1492  link#2      8.0.5a.f8.d6.cc      39      0         5     0      0
en0   1492  192.168.0   192.168.3.1          39      0         5     0      0
tr0   1492  link#3      0.4.ac.61.73.ee    6542      0       509     0      0
tr0   1492  9.3.1       sv1050a.itsc.aust  6542      0       509     0      0
# netstat -rn
Routing tables
Destination      Gateway           Flags   Refs     Use  If    PMTU  Exp  Groups

Route Tree for Protocol Family 2 (Internet):
default          9.3.1.74          UG         0        0 tr0      -    -
9.3.1/24         9.3.1.141         U          2       60 tr0      -    -
127/8            127.0.0.1         U          4      111 lo0      -    -
192.168.0/16     192.168.3.1       U          0        4 en0      -    -

Route Tree for Protocol Family 24 (Internet v6):
::1              ::1               UH         0        0 lo0 16896    -
#
```

Changing the state of the token-ring interface configuration from active to inactive does not have much effect on the `netstat` command output:

```
# ifconfig tr0 down
# netstat -i
Name  Mtu   Network     Address            Ipkts Ierrs    Opkts Oerrs  Coll
lo0   16896 link#1                          338      0       339     0      0
lo0   16896 127         loopback            338      0       339     0      0
lo0   16896 ::1                             338      0       339     0      0
en0   1492  link#2      8.0.5a.f8.d6.cc      39      0         5     0      0
en0   1492  192.168.0   192.168.3.1          39      0         5     0      0
tr0*  1492  link#3      0.4.ac.61.73.ee    5954      0       434     0      0
tr0*  1492  9.3.1       sv1050a            5954      0       434     0      0
Routing tables
Destination      Gateway           Flags   Refs     Use  If    PMTU  Exp  Groups
# netstat -rn
Route Tree for Protocol Family 2 (Internet):
default          9.3.1.74          UG         0        0 tr0      -    -
9.3.1/24         9.3.1.141         U          2      731 tr0      -    -
127/8            127.0.0.1         U          4      337 lo0      -    -
192.168.0/16     192.168.3.1       U          0        4 en0      -    -

Route Tree for Protocol Family 24 (Internet v6):
::1              ::1               UH         0        0 lo0 16896    -
#
```

However, if the token-ring interface is removed from the network interface list, the token-ring entries no longer exist in the interface configuration and route table of the `netstat` command output:

```
# ifconfig tr0 detach
# netstat -i
Name  Mtu   Network     Address            Ipkts Ierrs    Opkts Oerrs  Coll
lo0   16896 link#1                          789      0       790     0      0
lo0   16896 127         loopback            789      0       790     0      0
lo0   16896 ::1                             789      0       790     0      0
en0   1492  link#2      8.0.5a.f8.d6.cc      39      0         5     0      0
en0   1492  192.168.0   192.168.3.1          39      0         5     0      0
Routing tables
Destination      Gateway           Flags   Refs     Use  If    PMTU  Exp  Groups
```

```
# netstat -rn
Route Tree for Protocol Family 2 (Internet):
127/8            127.0.0.1        U         3      378  lo0      -   -
192.168.0/16     192.168.3.1      U         0        4  en0      -   -

Route Tree for Protocol Family 24 (Internet v6):
::1              ::1              UH        0        0  lo0 16896    -
#
```

Simply configuring the token-ring interface state to `up` is not enough to return the network back to the original status as the route for the default gateway needs to be defined also.

```
# ifconfig tr0 9.3.1.141 netmask 255.255.255.0 up
# netstat -i
Name  Mtu   Network     Address            Ipkts Ierrs    Opkts Oerrs  Coll
lo0   16896 link#1                          991     0      992     0     0
lo0   16896 127         localhost           991     0      992     0     0
lo0   16896 ::1                             991     0      992     0     0
en0   1492  link#2      8.0.5a.f8.d6.cc      39     0        5     0     0
en0   1492  192.168.0   192.168.3.1          39     0        5     0     0
tr0   1492  link#3      0.4.ac.61.73.ee      76     0       18     0     0
tr0   1492  9.3.1       sv1050a.itsc.aust    76     0       18     0     0
# netstat -rn
Routing tables
Destination      Gateway          Flags   Refs     Use  If    PMTU  Exp  Groups

Route Tree for Protocol Family 2 (Internet):
9.3.1/24         9.3.1.141        U         0       22  tr0      -   -
127/8            127.0.0.1        U         3      380  lo0      -   -
192.168.0/16     192.168.3.1      U         0        4  en0      -   -

Route Tree for Protocol Family 24 (Internet v6):
::1              ::1              UH        0        0  lo0 16896    -
# route add -net 0 9.3.1.74
9.3.1.74 net 0: gateway 9.3.1.74
# netstat -rn
Routing tables
Destination      Gateway          Flags   Refs     Use  If    PMTU  Exp  Groups

Route Tree for Protocol Family 2 (Internet):
default          9.3.1.74         UG        0        0  tr0      -   -
9.3.1/24         9.3.1.141        U         2      189  tr0      -   -
127/8            127.0.0.1        U         3      380  lo0      -   -
192.168.0/16     192.168.3.1      U         0        4  en0      -   -

Route Tree for Protocol Family 24 (Internet v6):
::1              ::1              UH        0        0  lo0 16896    -
#
```

10.11 The Default Route

Any packets sent to destinations not previously defined and not on a directly-connected network will go through the default gateway. Without the default gateway defined in the routing table, remote destinations are unreachable.

Consider a remote host with IP address 9.8.0.8. The `traceroute` command output shows the path used to get there starting from the default gateway:

```
# netstat -rn
Routing tables
Destination      Gateway            Flags   Refs     Use  If    PMTU  Exp  Groups

Route Tree for Protocol Family 2 (Internet):
default          9.3.1.74           UG        0        0  tr0      -   -
9.3.1/24         9.3.1.141          U        12     1501  tr0      -   -
127/8            127.0.0.1          U         2      382  lo0      -   -
192.168.0/16     192.168.3.1        U         0        4  en0      -   -

Route Tree for Protocol Family 24 (Internet v6):
::1              ::1                UH        0        0  lo0 16896    -
# ping 9.8.0.8
PING 9.8.0.8: (9.8.0.8): 56 data bytes
64 bytes from 9.8.0.8: icmp_seq=0 ttl=49 time=384 ms
64 bytes from 9.8.0.8: icmp_seq=1 ttl=50 time=354 ms
^C
----9.8.0.8 PING Statistics----
2 packets transmitted, 2 packets received, 0% packet loss
round-trip min/avg/max = 354/369/384 ms
# traceroute 9.8.0.8
trying to get source for 9.8.0.8
source should be 9.3.1.141
traceroute to 9.8.0.8 (9.8.0.8) from 9.3.1.141 (9.3.1.141), 30 hops max
outgoing MTU = 1492
 1 itso.austin.ibm.com (9.3.1.74)  11 ms  2 ms  2 ms
 2  9.444.33.129 (9.444.33.129)  4 ms  4 ms  4 ms
 3  9.444.33.129 (9.444.33.129)  4 ms  4 ms  4 ms
 4 site1.austin.ibm.com (9.3.90.200)  7 ms site2.south.ibm.com (9.3.200.20
2)  8 ms  7 ms
 5 site3.austin.ibm.com (199.4.213.125)  17 ms  19 ms  17 ms
 6  9.88.1.174 (9.88.1.174)  74 ms  80 ms  71 ms
 7  9.8.0.8 (9.8.0.8)  327 ms  329 ms  327 ms
#
```

Without the default gateway, only the directly attached hosts are accessible and the remote destination can no longer be reached:

```
# route -f
default              itsorusi.itsc.austin done
# netstat -rn
Routing tables
Destination      Gateway            Flags   Refs     Use  If    PMTU  Exp  Groups

Route Tree for Protocol Family 2 (Internet):
9.3.1/24         9.3.1.141          U        11     1265  tr0      -   -
127/8            127.0.0.1          U         2      382  lo0      -   -
192.168.0/16     192.168.3.1        U         0        4  en0      -   -

Route Tree for Protocol Family 24 (Internet v6):
::1              ::1                UH        0        0  lo0 16896    -
# ping 9.8.0.8
PING 9.8.0.8: (9.8.0.8): 56 data bytes
0821-069 ping: sendto: Cannot reach the destination network.
ping: wrote 9.8.0.8 64 chars, ret=-1
0821-069 ping: sendto: Cannot reach the destination network.
ping: wrote 9.8.0.8 64 chars, ret=-1
^C
----9.8.0.8 PING Statistics----
2 packets transmitted, 0 packets received, 100% packet loss
# traceroute 9.8.0.8
trying to get source for 9.8.0.8
source should be 9.3.1.141
```

```
traceroute to 9.8.0.8 (9.8.0.8) from 9.3.1.141 (9.3.1.141), 30 hops max
sendto: Cannot reach the destination network.
 1 traceroute: Partial write of -1 bytes
outgoing MTU = 32768
 *sendto: Cannot reach the destination network.
traceroute: Partial write of -1 bytes
 *sendto: Cannot reach the destination network.
traceroute: Partial write of -1 bytes
^C#
# ping 9.3.1.124
PING 9.3.1.124: (9.3.1.124): 56 data bytes
64 bytes from 9.3.1.124: icmp_seq=0 ttl=255 time=0 ms
64 bytes from 9.3.1.124: icmp_seq=1 ttl=255 time=0 ms
^C
----9.3.1.124 PING Statistics----
2 packets transmitted, 2 packets received, 0% packet loss
round-trip min/avg/max = 0/0/0 ms
#
```

10.12 Problem With Incorrect Subnet Mask

A standard Internet Protocol address field has two parts: a network address and a local address. Subnet addressing allows an autonomous system made up of multiple networks to share the same Internet address. To make subnets possible, the local address part of an Internet address is divided into a subnet number and a host number. The bits that identify the subnet are specified by a bit mask.

A machine with IP address 192.168.3.1 is communicating with another IP address, 192.168.1.2, both with netmask 255.255.0.0, such that they are both on network address 192.168.

The network definition of the first machine with IP address 192.168.3.1 is as follows:

```
# netstat -rn
Routing tables
Destination      Gateway           Flags    Refs       Use  If    PMTU  Exp
Groups

Route Tree for Protocol Family 2 (Internet):
default          9.3.1.74          UG          0         3  tr0      -    -
9.3.1/24         9.3.1.141         U          37     44175  tr0      -    -
127/8            127.0.0.1         U           3       332  lo0      -    -
192.168.0/16     192.168.3.1       U           0        17  en0      -    -

Route Tree for Protocol Family 24 (Internet v6):
::1              ::1               UH          0         0  lo0 16896    -
# ifconfig en0
```

```
en0:
flags=e080863<UP,BROADCAST,NOTRAILERS,RUNNING,SIMPLEX,MULTICAST,GROUPRT,64
B
IT>
        inet 192.168.3.1 netmask 0xffff0000 broadcast 192.168.255.255
# ping 192.168.1.2
PING 192.168.1.2: (192.168.1.2): 56 data bytes
64 bytes from 192.168.1.2: icmp_seq=0 ttl=255 time=1 ms
64 bytes from 192.168.1.2: icmp_seq=1 ttl=255 time=0 ms
^C
----192.168.1.2 PING Statistics----
2 packets transmitted, 2 packets received, 0% packet loss
round-trip min/avg/max = 0/0/1 ms
#
```

The network definition of the first machine with IP address 192.168.1.2 is as follows:

```
# netstat -rn
Routing tables
Destination      Gateway           Flags   Refs     Use  If   PMTU  Exp
Groups

Route Tree for Protocol Family 2 (Internet):
default          9.3.1.74          UG        0       13  tr0     -    -
9.3.1/24         9.3.1.124         U        33   784208  tr0     -    -
127/8            127.0.0.1         U         4      319  lo0     -    -
192.168.0/16     192.168.1.2       U         0        4  en0     -    -

Route Tree for Protocol Family 24 (Internet v6):
::1              ::1               UH        0        0  lo0 16896    -
# ifconfig en0
en0:
flags=e080863<UP,BROADCAST,NOTRAILERS,RUNNING,SIMPLEX,MULTICAST,GROUPRT,64
B
IT>
        inet 192.168.1.2 netmask 0xffff0000 broadcast 192.168.255.255
# ping 192.168.3.1
PING 192.168.3.1: (192.168.3.1): 56 data bytes
64 bytes from 192.168.3.1: icmp_seq=0 ttl=255 time=1 ms
64 bytes from 192.168.3.1: icmp_seq=1 ttl=255 time=0 ms
^C
----192.168.3.1 PING Statistics----
2 packets transmitted, 2 packets received, 0% packet loss
round-trip min/avg/max = 0/0/1 ms
#
```

If the netmask definition of the machine with IP address 192.168.1.2 is changed to 255.255.255.0 making the network address 192.168.1, then the two machines will no long communicate:

```
# netstat -rn
Routing tables
Destination      Gateway            Flags   Refs     Use  If    PMTU  Exp
Groups

Route Tree for Protocol Family 2 (Internet):
default          9.3.1.74           UG         0      13  tr0      -    -
9.3.1/24         9.3.1.124          U         34  822719  tr0      -    -
127/8            127.0.0.1          U          4     319  lo0      -    -
192.168.1/24     192.168.1.2        U          0       0  en0      -    -

Route Tree for Protocol Family 24 (Internet v6):
::1              ::1                UH         0       0  lo0 16896     -
# ifconfig en0
en0:
flags=e080863<UP,BROADCAST,NOTRAILERS,RUNNING,SIMPLEX,MULTICAST,GROUPRT,64
B
IT>
        inet 192.168.1.2 netmask 0xffffff00 broadcast 192.168.1.255
# ping 192.168.3.1
PING 192.168.3.1: (192.168.3.1): 56 data bytes
^C
----192.168.3.1 PING Statistics----
2 packets transmitted, 0 packets received, 100% packet loss
#
```

The network definition of the machine with IP address 192.168.3.1 is unchanged, but the `ping` command no longer works:

```
# netstat -rn
Routing tables
Destination      Gateway            Flags   Refs     Use  If    PMTU  Exp
Groups

Route Tree for Protocol Family 2 (Internet):
default          9.3.1.74           UG         0       3  tr0      -    -
9.3.1/24         9.3.1.141          U         37   44663  tr0      -    -
127/8            127.0.0.1          U          3     332  lo0      -    -
192.168.0/16     192.168.3.1        U          0      26  en0      -    -

Route Tree for Protocol Family 24 (Internet v6):
::1              ::1                UH         0       0  lo0 16896     -
# ifconfig en0
```

```
en0:
flags=e080863<UP,BROADCAST,NOTRAILERS,RUNNING,SIMPLEX,MULTICAST,GROUPRT,64
BIT>
        inet 192.168.3.1 netmask 0xffff0000 broadcast 192.168.255.255
# ping 192.168.1.2
PING 192.168.1.2: (192.168.1.2): 56 data bytes
^C
----192.168.1.2 PING Statistics----
4 packets transmitted, 0 packets received, 100% packet loss
#
```

10.13 Value of thewall on Network Traffic

To avoid fragmentation of kernel memory and the overhead of numerous calls to xmalloc(), common buffer pools are shared by the various layers of the communication subsystem. The mbuf management facility controls two pools of buffers: a pool of small buffers (256 bytes each), which are simply called mbufs, and a pool of large buffers (4096 bytes each), which are usually called mbuf clusters, or just clusters. The pools are created from system memory by making an allocation request to the Virtual Memory Manager (VMM). The pools consist of pinned pieces of virtual memory; this means that they always reside in physical memory and are never paged out. The result is that the real memory available for paging in application programs and data has been decreased by the amount that the mbuf pools have been increased. On the other hand, network problem will arise if there is not enough memory available for the buffer pools to satisfy network sessions.

The maximum amount of memory, in kilobytes, allocated to the mbuf pools is specified in the thewall parameter of the no command. The default values for thewall in various AIX versions are:

AIX Version 4.2.1. and earlier The default value is 1/8 of real memory or 65536 (64 megabytes), whichever is smaller.

AIX Version 4.3.0 The default value is 1/8 of real memory or 131072 (128 megabytes), whichever is smaller.

AIX Version 4.3.1 and later The default value is 1/2 of real memory or 131072 (128 megabytes), whichever is smaller.

When the `no` command is used to change parameters, the change is in effect only until the next system boot. At that point all parameters are initially reset to their defaults. To make the change permanent, you should put the appropriate `no` command in the /etc/rc.net file.

10.13.1 Setting the Value of thewall to Raise the Number of mbufs

The mbuf allocation mechanism in AIX Version 4 is substantially different. In AIX Version 4, you can set the maximum amount of memory that will be used by the network allocator in the same way you set this in AIX Version 3.2.5—with the `no` command and thewall parameter. All other tuning options that were available in AIX Version 3.2.5 have been removed from AIX Version 4 because the AIX Version 4 mbuf allocation mechanism is much more self-tuning.

While you will not be able to alter the lowclust and lowmbuf attributes as in AIX Version 3, you can increase the amount defined to thewall and observe from the kernel malloc statistics from the `netstat -m` command that the number of mbufs has been raised.

The initial default value of `thewall` and the output from `netstat -m` are:

```
# no -o thewall
thewall = 65488
# netstat -m
Kernel malloc statistics:

******* CPU 0 *******
By size       inuse     calls failed    free   hiwat   freed
32              163       313      0      93     640       0
64               88       158      0      40     320       0
128              71       316      0      25     160       0
256              99      2726      0      13     384       0
512              76       375      0       4      40       0
1024             32       104      0       4     100       0
2048              0         4      0       2     100       0
4096             35        68      0       3     120       0
16384             1         1      0      18      24       7
32768             1         1      0       0     511       0

By type       inuse     calls failed  memuse  memmax  mapb

Streams mblk statistic failures:
0 high priority mblk failures
0 medium priority mblk failures
0 low priority mblk failures
#
```

The value of `thewall` is then increased from 65488 to 98232:

```
# no -o thewall=98232
#
```

The change takes effect immediately for new connections. However, there will not be any change to the kernel malloc statistics until some network traffic has occurred. Perform an FTP session to transfer some files from another system. This updates the kernel malloc statistics. The `netstat -m` command output is:

```
# netstat -m
Kernel malloc statistics:

******* CPU 0 *******
By size        inuse     calls failed    free   hiwat   freed
32               163       321      0      93     640       0
64                88       160      0      40     320       0
128               71       355      0      25     160       0
256               99     16439      0      29     384       0
512               76       662      0       4      40       0
1024              32       120      0       4     100       0
2048               0      7858      0      12     100       0
4096              35        68      0       1     120       0
16384              1         1      0      18      24       7
32768              1         1      0       0     511       0

By type        inuse     calls failed  memuse  memmax  mapb

Streams mblk statistic failures:
0 high priority mblk failures
0 medium priority mblk failures
0 low priority mblk failures
#
```

The number of 256-byte mbufs has increased from 112 to 128. The number of 2048-byte mbufs has increased from 2 to 12. However, the number of 4096-byte mbufs has decreased from 38 to 36. Overall, there is an increase of mbufs available when the `thewall` value is raised. The decrease in the number of 4096-bye mbufs demonstrates the self-tuning function of the AIX Version 4 mbuf allocation mechanism.

10.13.2 Tuning Parameters for Buffer Pools and Others

The network tuning parameters available in AIX Version 4 are:

- thewall

  The thewall parameter of the network option provides an absolute upper bound on the amount of real memory that can be used by the communication subsystem. Change the value of thewall parameter in kilobytes, preferably in multiples of 4, using the `no -o thewall=` command. Usually, the size is increased during tuning.

- sockthresh

  In AIX Version 4.3.1 or later, the sockthresh parameter of the network option provides a way to prevent new sockets from being created when almost all the network memory is in use. The default is 85 percent of thewall. Change the value in the range of 1 to 100 percent of thewall using the `no -o sockthresh=` command. Usually, the percentage is decreased during tuning.

- sb_max

  The sb_max parameter of the network option provides an absolute upper bound on the size of TCP and UDP socket buffers. The default value is 65536. Change the value, preferably in multiples of 4096, using the `no -o sb_max=` command. Usually, the size is increased during tuning.

- rfc1323

  The rfc1323 parameter of the network option has a value of 1 to indicate that tcp_sendspace and tcp_recvspace can exceed 64 KB. The default value is 0 (zero). Change the value to 1 (one) using the command `no -o rfc1323=` command before attempting to set tcp_sendspace and tcp_recvspace to more than 64 KB.

- udp_sendspace

  The udp_sendspace parameter of the network option provides the default value for the size of the UDP socket send buffer. The value must not be greater than that of sb_max. The default value is 9216. Change the value in the range of 0 (zero) to 65536, preferably in multiples of 4096, using the `no -o udp_sendspace=` command. Usually, the size is increased during tuning.

- udp_recvspace

  The udp_recvspace parameter of the network option provides the default value of the size of the UDP socket receive buffer. The value must not be greater than that of sb_max. The default value is 41600. Change the value, preferably in multiples of 4096, using the `no -o udp_recvspace=` command. Usually, the size is increased during tuning.

- tcp_sendspace

  The tcp_sendspace parameter of the network option provides the default value of the size of the TCP socket send buffer. The default value is 16384. The allowed range is 0 to 64 KB if rfc1323=0, and 0 to 4 GB if rfc1323=1. The value must be less than or equal to sb_max and should be equal to tcp_recvspace and uniform on all frequently accessed AIX systems. Change the value, preferably in multiples of 4096, using the `no -o tcp_sendspace=` command. Usually, the size if increased during tuning to fix the poor-throughout problem.

- tcp_recvspace

  The tcp_recvspace parameter of the network option provides the default value of the size of the TCP socket receive buffer. The default value is 16384. The allowed range is 0 to 64 KB if rfc1323=0, and 0 to 4 GB if rfc1323=1. The value must be less than or equal to sb_max, and should be equal to tcp_sendspace and uniform on all frequently accessed AIX systems. Change the value, preferably in multiple of 4096, using the `no -o tcp_recvspace=` command. Usually, the size is increased during tuning to fix the poor-throughout problem.

- ipqmaxlen

  The ipqmaxlen parameter of the network option specifies the maximum number of entries on the IP input queue. The default value is 50. Change the value using the `no -o ipqmaxlen=` command. Usually, the size is increased during tuning.

- xmt_que_size

  The xmt_que_size parameter specifies the maximum number of send buffers that can be queued up for the device. The default value is 30. The allowed range is 20 to 150. To display the value of the first token-ring adapter on the system, use the `lsattr -E -l tok0 -a xmt_que_size` command. To change the value, you must first remove the network interface configuration, change the device xmt_que_size value, and then activate the network interface configuration:

  ```
  ifconfig tr0 detach
  chdev -I tok0 -a xmt_que_size=newvalue
  ifconfig tr0 hostname up
  ```

  The change is effective across system boot. Usually, the size is increased during tuning. It should be set to 150 as a matter of course on network-oriented systems, especially servers.

- rec_que_size

  This is only tunable in AIX Version 3. The rec_que_size specifies the maximum number of receive buffers that can be queued up for the interface. The default value is 30. The allowed range is 20 to 150. To display the value of the first token ring adapter in the system, us the `lsattr -E -l tok0 -a rec_que_size` command. To change the value, you must first remove the network interface configuration, change the device xmt_que_size value, and then activate the network interface configuration:

```
ifconfig tr0 detach
chdev -I tok0 -a rec_que_size=newvalue
ifconfig tr0 hostname up
```

The change is effective across system boot. Usually, the size is increased during tuning. It should be set to 150 as a matter of course on network-oriented systems, especially servers.

- MTU

  The maximum transmission unit (MTU) limits the size of packets that are transmitted on the network.The default value for 16 Mb token-ring adapters is 1492, and for Ethernet adapters it is 1500. Use the `lsattr -E -l tr0` command to display the MTU of the first token ring adapter in the system. Use the `chdev -l tr0 -a mtu=NewValue` command to change the MTU size of the first token-ring adapter on the system.

Note

The MTU size cannot be changed while the interface is in use. Because all systems on a LAN must have the same MTU, they must all change simultaneously.

Apart from token-ring and loopback definition on AIX Version 3, the default should be kept for other interfaces. Usually, the size is increased during tuning. Change is effective across system boots.

10.14 Errors when inetd is Not Started

TCP is a peer-to-peer, connection-oriented protocol. There are no master/slave relations. The applications, however, use a client/server model for communications.

Taking out the rc.tcpip entry in /etc/inittab during IPL means that you are not starting any server applications.

Note

If you have a graphic console, make sure you also take out the rc.dt entry in the inittab, together with rc.tcpip in the /etc/inittab file. Otherwise, your console will hang when you login. Unless you have an ASCII terminal connected to the serial port, there is no way you can recover as you will not be able to communicate with the machine through the `telnet` or `rlogin` commands with no TCP/IP server application started.

Without the server applications started, you will not be able to Telnet or FTP to this machine from another host.

However, as long as you have not brought down the network interface, you can still utilize the client network services. You can still ping other hosts, you can still Telnet to other hosts, and you can still FTP to other hosts.

The `ping` command sends an Internet Control Message Protocol (ICMP) ECHO_REQUEST to obtain an ICMP ECHO_RESPONSE from a host and does not need any server application. Therefore, even without starting any server application, the machine will still response to a ping request from other hosts.

10.15 Network Hardware Configuration Problems

Even though all the TCP/IP configuration parameters have been defined correctly, there are still cases when you may not be able to connect to the network. You should then check the hardware configuration again for your network adapter.

For token-ring network adapters, make sure that it is set to the right ring speed (4 MB to 16 MB).

For Ethernet network adapters, make sure that the connecter type is defined correctly (bnc or dix).

10.16 References

The following publications contain more information about networking:

- *AIX Versions 3.2 and 4 Performance Tuning Guide*, SC23-2365
- *AIX Version 4.3 Commands Reference, Volume 4*, SC23-4118
- *AIX Version 4.3 Problem Solving Guide and Reference*, SC23-4123

10.17 Quiz

1. Which of the following must be performed in order to change the primary name server a system is pointing to?

   A. Run `ypwhich`

   B. Edit the /etc/hosts file

   C. Edit the /etc/resolv.conf file

   D. Run `no -o name_server=<new_server>`

2. A system administrator has just moved an Ethernet adapter to another slot, removed the old definition and added the IP address and subnet mask just as before. The `netstat` and `ifconfig` commands show the interface just as before, but the system administrator still cannot communicate with any other servers. Which of the following could cause this problem?

   A. The connecter type has changed to BNC.

   B. The adapter speed has changed to 10 Mbps.

   C. The adapter should be removed and reseated.

   D. The drivers were not reloaded after moving the adapter.

3. A system administrator is able to log in to system A's console and other systems can ping system A, but the system administrator is unable to Telnet or rlogin to system A from any other system on the network. Which of the following is the most likely cause of this problem?

   A. The inetd is not running on system A.

   B. The routed is not running on system A.

   C. The routing table on system A is corrupted.

   D. The domain name server is not functioning correctly.

4. User X on machine AAA is trying to rsh to machine BBB. The user is prompted for a password, even though a /u/X/.rhosts file is configured on machine BBB. The user discovers this is a permission problem with the .rhosts file. Which of the following are the correct permissions of a .rhosts file?

   A. 400

   B. 440

   C. 600

   D. 660

5. A system administrator is logged onto the local system, Carolina, and Telnets to a remote system, Florida, to remotely start any application. The following error message is displayed:

   ```
   cannot open DISPLAY:
   ```

   The system administrator proceeds to enter the following command in response to the error message:

   ```
   export DISPLAY=corolina.domain0001.com:0.0
   ```

   The system administrator re starts the application and receives the same error message:

   ```
   cannot open DISPLAY
   ```

   The system administrator echoes the DISPLAY variable, determines that it is set to carolina.domain001.com, nd performs an nslookup of Carolina, which returns a good TCP/IP address of 9.90.90.9, as expected. The system administrator loaded both servers and knows that the graphics subsystem is properly installed on both systems and is started at boot time.

   The system administrator exports the DISPLAY variable from Florida to Carolina, and still cannot connect. What should be the next logical step?

   A. Issue the `netstat -i` command to check the network.

   B. From Carolina, issue the `lshost` command to see if Florida is allowed host access.

   C. From Carolina, issue the `xhost list` command to see if Florida is allowed host access and if not, issue the `xhost add Florida` command.

   D. From Carolina, issue the `xhost` command to see if Florida is allowed host access and if not, from Carolina, issue the `xhost + Florida` command.

10.17.1 Answers

1. C
2. A
3. A
4. C
5. D

10.18 Exercises

1. Use rlogin to another system and run an X application. Set the DISPLAY variable using both hostname and IP address to prevent the unable to open DISPLAY error message. Compare the error message with that caused by xhost error.
2. Experiment with the `xhost` command to allow and disallow an X-windows application client to connect to the host.
3. Explain the security implication for the .rhost, .netrc, .forward, and hosts.equiv files.
4. Experiment with the content and permission bits of the $HOME/.rhosts file to show the effect on an rsh session from another host.
5. Using a test system that does not affect any user, remove a network adapter.
6. Set the value of the IP forwarding attribute of the network option to something other than 0 (zero) and 1 (one) to show that IP forwarding is enabled if the value of the parameter is set to other than 0 (zero).
7. If possible, test the value of the ipfowarding parameter of the network option to allow pings over multiple subnets on two interface boxes.
8. On a test system that does not affect any user, change the reference to the primary name server by editing the /etc/resolv.conf file. Observe the result when you try to access other hosts by hostname and by IP addresses.
9. On a test system that does not affect any user, change the name resolution default order by editing the /etc/netsvc.conf file, such that /etc/hosts file will be used before the domain name server. Add an entry to the /etc/hosts file, such that the hostname of a system has a different IP address and then try to access that hostname.
10. Set the value of the NSORDER environment value to override the /etc/netsv.conf file.
11. Use the `arp` command to display, delete, and add entries in the ARP cache
12. On a test system that does not affect any user, change the state of the network interface from active to inactive and observe the results. Remove the network interface and observe the result.
13. Add the network interface back in and make it active again. Perform additional tasks to bring the network back into operation.
14. On a test system that does not affect any user, flush the routing table and try to access hosts on the same and different subnet.

15.On a test system that does not affect any user, change the subnet mask to different values and check if it can still communicate with other hosts.

16.On a test system that does not affect any user, change the thewall value and observe the effect on the buffer pools over a period of time.

17.On a test system that does not affect any user, set the value of various tunable parameters of the network option and observe the result over a period of time.

18.On a test system that does not affect any user, stop the inetd daemon and Telnet to other systems. Ping this test system from another host and try to Telnet to it. Observe the result.

19.On a test system that does not affect any user, change the token ring speed of a token-ring network adapter, or change the connecter type of an Ethernet network adapter and observe the result.

Chapter 11. Printers

This chapter covers printing and common support procedures involved in ensuring an AIX printer, whether remotely or locally, remains operational. You are guided through problem determination and troubleshooting of printer problems.

11.1 The Printer Colon Files

Printer and printer data stream attributes reside in colon files. Colon files reside in the /usr/lib/lpd/pio/predef and /var/spool/lpd/pio/@local/custom/* directories. The /usr/lib/lpd/pio/predef directory contains the predefined database and the /var/spool/lpd/pio/@local/custom/* directory contains the customized database.

11.2 Remote Printing

Remote printing allows different computers to share printers. To use remote printing facilities, the computers must be connected using the Transmission Control Protocol/Internet Protocol (TCP/IP) protocol and must support the required TCP/IP applications, such as the lpd daemon.

Figure 105 on page 242 shows the logic flow of a remote printer request:

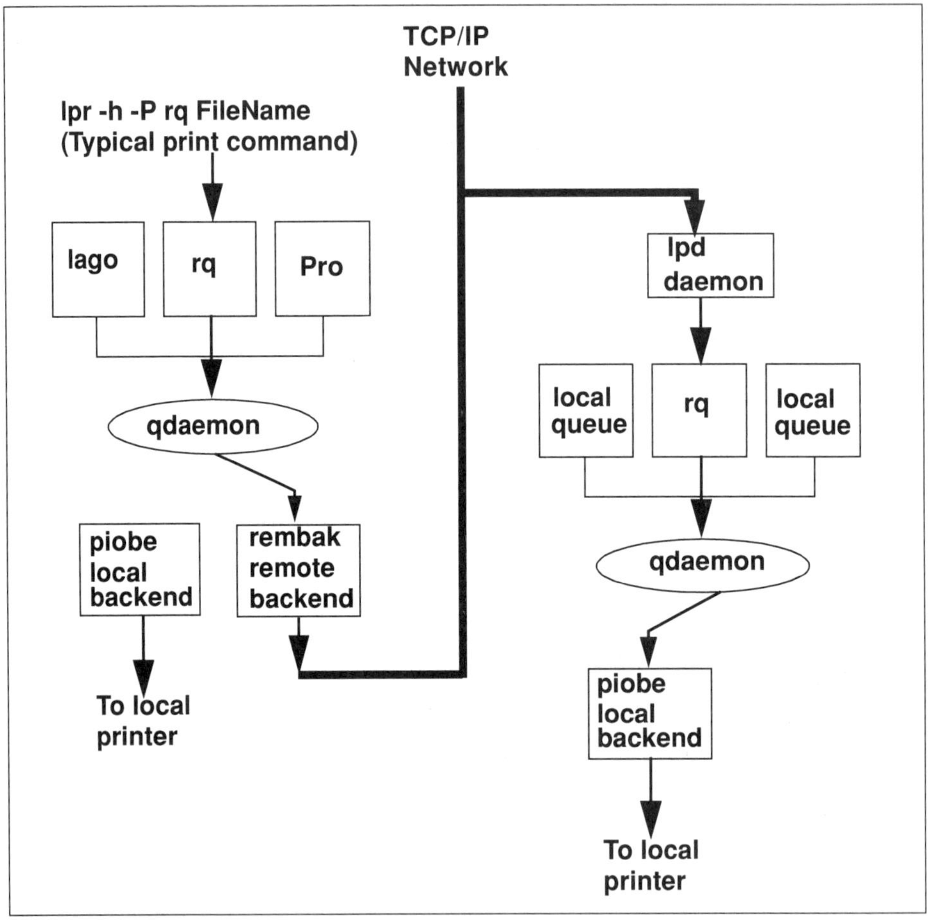

Figure 105. Remote Print Request

The /etc/hosts.lpd file, one of the important files in remote printing, is discussed in the following section.

11.2.1 The /etc/hosts.lpd File

The /etc/hosts.lpd file defines which remote systems are permitted to print on the local system. The remote systems listed in this file do not have the full privileges given to files listed in the /etc/hosts.equiv file.

The hosts.lpd file supports the following host name entries:

+	Signifies that any host on the network can print using the local host.

HostName The name of a remote host and signifies that HostName can print, using the local host.

-HostName Signifies the host is not allowed to print using the local host.

+@NetGroup Signifies all hosts in the netgroup are allowed to print using the local host.

-@NetGroup Signifies that no hosts in the netgroup are allowed to print using the local host.

Entries in this file can be made using the System Management Interface Tool (SMIT) or the `ruser` command.

> **Note**
>
> Comments must be entered on separate lines in the hosts.lpd file. Comments should not be entered on lines containing host names.

To implement hosts.lpd file changes without restarting the system, use the System Resource Controller (SRC) `refresh` command.

11.2.2 The /etc/hosts.equiv File

The /etc/hosts.equiv file, along with any local $HOME/.rhosts files, defines the hosts (computers on a network) and user accounts that can invoke remote commands on a local host without supplying a password. A user or host that is not required to supply a password is considered trusted.

When a local host receives a remote command request, the appropriate local daemon first checks the /etc/hosts.equiv file to determine if the request originates with a trusted user or host. For example, if the local host receives a remote login request, the rlogind daemon checks for the existence of a hosts.equiv file on the local host. If the file exists but does not define the host or user, the system checks the appropriate $HOME/.rhosts file. This file is similar to the /etc/hosts.equiv file, except that it is maintained for individual users.

Both files, hosts.equiv and .rhosts must have permissions denying write access to group and other. If either group or other have write access to a file, that file is ignored.

Do not give write permission to the /etc/hosts.equiv file to group and other. Permissions of the /etc/hosts.equiv file should be set to 600 (read and write by owner only).

If a remote command request is made by the root user, the /etc/hosts.equiv file is ignored and only the /.rhosts file is read.

Note

Be careful when establishing trusted relationships. Networks that use trusted facilities can be less secure than those that do not.

11.2.3 Controlling the lpd Daemon

Controlling the lpd daemon includes starting and stopping the lpd subsystem and changing the characteristics of the lpd subsystem. Use the SMIT or System Resource Controller (SRC) commands to control the lpd daemon.

There are three ways to start the lpd daemon. If it is not currently running, you can start the daemon at any time. You also have the option of having the lpd daemon start at system restart or to have it start both at the current time and at system restart. The same options are available to stop the lpd daemon: stop now, stop at system restart, or stop both now and at system restart. You can run the lpd daemon with DEBUG, SYSLOG, both DEBUG and SYSLOG, or with neither.

To control the lpd daemon with SMIT, type `smitty lpd`, then select the desired options from the SMIT menus. To control the lpd daemon with the SRC, use the following SRC commands:

startsrc Starts a subsystem, group of subsystems, or a subserver.

stopsrc Stops a subsystem, group of subsystems, or a subserver.

lssrc Gets the status of a subsystem, group of subsystems, or a subserver.

refresh Causes the subsystem or group of subsystems to reread the appropriate configuration file.

traceson Enables tracing of a subsystem, group of subsystems, or a subserver.

tracesoff Disables tracing of a subsystem, group of subsystems, or a subserver.

11.3 Virtual Printers

Virtual printers are unique to AIX, but have a heritage in UNIX called *printcap files*. They basically add commands to setup a printer to perform certain operations and then provide simple formatting for ASCII text. They are not an

API. They are a set of attributes that control what gets sent to the printer as setup commands before and after the print job. Virtual printers also do simple text formatting like adding carriage returns to line feeds.

11.3.1 Files Used with Virtual Printers

The following files are important when looking at virtual printers:

/usr/sbin/mkvirprt Contains the `mkvirprt` command.

/etc/qconfig Contains configuration files.

/usr/lib/lpd/pio/predef/* Contains predefined printer attribute files.

/var/spool/lpd/pio/@local/custom/* Contains customized virtual printer attribute files.

/usr/lib/lpd/pio/etc/*.attach Contains attachment type files.

/usr/lib/lpd/pio/etc/*.config Contains the configuration file for the printer.

/var/spool/lpd/pio/@local/ddi* Contains digested virtual printer attribute files.

11.3.2 Key Commands

Some of the virtual printer commands are:

`smitty mkpq` Command to add a virtual printer. Also adds printer device.

`smitty chpq` Command to change a virtual printer.

`smitty rmpq` Command to remove a virtual printer.

`lsvirprt` Command to change individual attributes of virtual printer. Also used to list all attributes of a virtual printer.

`smitty chvirprt` Change a virtual printer attribute.

> **Note**
>
> Virtual Printers do not support graphics except to pass it through to a printer.

A virtual printer is actually a fairly simple interface to a printer. It basically performs these functions:

1. Initializes the printer.
2. Provides a hook or interface to filters.

3. Formats ASCII data.
4. Translates from the input code page to the output printer symbol set. (ASCII only)
5. Resets the printer to a predefined condition.
6. Calls the program to send the header and trailer pages.
7. Sends a form feed at the end of job.

Virtual Printers do not:

1. Generate any printer language commands such as PostScript or PCL, other than the initialization and reset sequences.
2. Test for correctness of the format of data.
3. Automatically recognize the type of data except for very simple sniffing of the first couple of characters if set up properly.

So basically the virtual printer does almost nothing for any formatted PCL, formatted PPDS, graphics, or PostScript data except tell the printer what language is coming at it.

11.3.3 Creating a Virtual Printer

A virtual printer can be created using the `mkvirprt` command in AIX 3.2.5 or using the System Management Interface Tools (SMIT) fast path `smitty mkpq` in AIX Version 4. For this discussion, AIX Version 4 commands are used.

11.3.3.1 Using the smitty mkpq Command

The command `smitty mkpq` produces a screen similar to that shown in Figure 106 on page 247.

```
                              Add a Print Queue

Move cursor to desired item and press Enter. Use arrow keys to scroll.

  # ATTACHMENT TYPE      DESCRIPTION
    local                Printer Attached to Local Host
    remote               Printer Attached to Remote Host
    xstation             Printer Attached to Xstation
    ascii                Printer Attached to ASCII Terminal
    hpJetDirect          Network Printer (HP JetDirect)
    file                 File (in /dev directory)
    ibmNetPrinter        IBM Network Printer
    ibmNetColor          IBM Network Color Printer
    other                User Defined Backend

F1=Help                 F2=Refresh              F3=Cancel
F8=Image                F10=Exit                Enter=Do
/=Find                  n=Find Next
```

Figure 106. SMIT mkpq Command Screen

Perform the following steps:

1. Select `attachment type` **remote**, as not highlighted in Figure 106.
2. Select your preferred **Type of Remote Printing**. For this illustration it is **Standard processing**.
3. Fill in the characteristics for the virtual printer being created as shown in Figure 107 on page 248 and press the **Enter** key. After the `Command: OK` returns, exit SMIT and complete the process.

```
                        Add a Standard Remote Print Queue

Type or select values in entry fields.
Press Enter AFTER making all desired changes.

                                                         [Entry Fields]
* Name of QUEUE to add                                 [virprt1]
* HOSTNAME of remote server                            [sv1166f]
* Name of QUEUE on remote server                       [final]
  Type of print spooler on remote server                AIX Version 3 or 4      +
  Backend TIME OUT period (minutes)                    []                       #
  Send control file first?                              no                      +
  To turn on debugging, specify output                 []
      file pathname
  DESCRIPTION of printer on remote server              []





F1=Help             F2=Refresh          F3=Cancel           F4=List
F5=Reset            F6=Command          F7=Edit             F8=Image
F9=Shell            F10=Exit            Enter=Do
```

Figure 107. Adding a Standard Remote Print Queue

You will now use the `lsvirprt` command to list the virtual printers on the system. The command `lsvirprt` without flags produces a menu as in Figure 108, from which you can view and change the attributes of the virtual printer.

```
No. Queue               Device    Description
 1   virprt1            @sv1166f  Remote Printer

Enter number from list above (press Enter to terminate):  ->
```

Figure 108. lsvirprt Command Output Screen

Using the `smitty chvirprt` command, change attributes of the virtual printer. This command produces the screen in Figure 109 on page 250. From this screen you can supply the virtual printer queue, in this case `virprt1`, and then proceed to change the desired attributes for the virtual printer.

```
                        Print Queue to Change / Show

Type or select a value for the entry field.
Press Enter AFTER making all desired changes.

                                                    [Entry Fields]
  PRINT QUEUE name                                [virprt1]            +







F1=Help             F2=Refresh          F3=Cancel           F4=List
F5=Reset            F6=Command          F7=Edit             F8=Image
F9=Shell            F10=Exit            Enter=Do
```

Figure 109. SMIT chvirprt Command Screen

11.4 Troubleshooting Remote Printing Problems

Trying to find out why print jobs from a remote client get lost on the way to a server can be a frustrating problem. In this section, some common errors, as well as how to trace a job sent by a remote client using the iptrace facility, is discussed.

11.4.1 0781-374 Error Message

If you attempt to send a print job to a remote print server whose lpd daemon is down, you will receive the following message:

```
0781-374 Connection to server timed out after retrying
rembak:errno=79: A remote host refused an attempted connect operation
```

To correct this problem start the `lpd` daemon on the remote system using

```
startsrc -s lpd
```

11.4.2 0781-202 Error Message

If you have a queue, finprt or fin2, on a client system, sv1051c, and the host name for that client is not in the /etc/hosts.lpd or the /etc/hosts.equiv file then you will receive a 0781-202 error message when the lpstat command is run. See Figure 110 for an example of the command output. This problem is also seen with name server and routing problems.

```
# lpstat
Queue   Dev   Status    Job Files              User         PP %   Blks  Cp Rnk
------- ----- --------- --- ------------------ ---------- ---- -- ----- --- ---
finprt  @sv11 READY
finprt: 0781-202 your host does not have line printer access.
lpforu  lp0   READY
fin2    @sv11 READY
fin2: 0781-202 your host does not have line printer access.
#
```

Figure 110. 0781-202 Error Message

To correct this problem, you need to edit the /etc/hosts.lpd file on the server and enter the host name of the client system as in Figure 111.

```
# -host                     denies access to all users on host
# +@group                   allows access to all users on hosts in group
# -@group                   denies access to all users on hosts in group
sv1051c
~
~
~
~
~
~
~
~
~
~
~
~
~
~
~
~
~
~
~
~
~
~
"/etc/hosts.lpd" 61 lines, 1914 characters
```

Figure 111. Content of /etc/hosts.lpd

11.4.3 How to Run a Remote Trace

The question, "What is getting sent to the remote system when I print?" can be answered by using remote trace.

11.4.3.1 What an iptrace Can Tell You

The following list shows what an iptrace can tell you:

- Characters actually sent over the network, even binary control characters.
- Responses that come from the LPD.
- Content of the control file.
- Which side terminated the conversation.
- Status information being sent back by the LPD.
- If the entire file gets sent to the LPD.
- If the control files follow the RFC-1179 standard.

11.4.3.2 Using the iptrace Facility

The iptrace facility can easily show what is being sent to the remote system using the following command:

1. `iptrace -p printer -a -b -s source_host -d dest_host /tmp/trace.out`

Table 17 provides the `iptrace` command flags.

Table 17. Flags for the iptrace Command

Flag	Description
-p printer	Use the word printer or a number such as 515 that means look at port 515 only. This will not get logon traffic.
-a	Suppress ARP packets.
-i en0	Interface. Only use if multiple network cards are in the system.
-b	Change the -d and -s to bidirectional mode. Get data in both directions.
-s	Source hostname, or ipaddress where the print command is issued.
-d	Destination hostname, or ipaddress where the printer resides.
/tmp/trace.out	This can be any file name. It is created with 11 bytes and then will get filled with data. It is a binary file that must later be formatted with the `ipreport` command.

2. Print the job to the remote queue using the following command:

   `enq -Pqueue_name filename`

   or use:

   `lpstat -vqueue_name`

3. Check to see if the file has grown using `ls -l /tmp/trace.out`.

```
# ls -l /tmp/trace.out
-rw-r--r--   1 root     system      4538 Nov 09 11:17 /tmp/trace.out
```

4. If it is still 11 bytes, then you have made an error in the command. Use the `kill` command and end the process, then start again. Get the job ID using the command:

```
# ps -ef |grep ipt
root 30984     1   0 11:17:47      -  0:00 iptrace -p printer -a -b -s
sv1051c -d sv1166f /tmp/trace.out
root 31234 26556   1 11:20:46 pts/10  0:00 grep ipt
```

5. Kill the trace command using the command:

```
kill -9 job_id
```

6. Format the output into a text file:

```
ipreport /tmp/trace.out > /tmp/report.out
```

The report contains three or four parts for each packet of data. These are:

- MAC header
- IP header
- TCP header
- b>data (If to/from application layer, that is, if FLAG=PUSH)

11.4.3.3 How to Interpret the Trace

The MAC header does not supply much information useful to debugging printing.

The IP header gives the direction of the data flow and the number of bytes in the packet, but direction is also given in the TCP packet.

The TCP packet gives the:

- Direction of packet source port.
- Handshaking and purpose of packet flags.
- Source port number. This is important because of the multi-tasking environment. Packets from a status can be interspersed with packets from a print job, but for a single job the source port will remain the same.
- Packet identification. Use th_seq and th_ack to make sure the packets are in order, and to see which packet an ACK is responding to.
- Window size th_win. The data packet shows the actual data that is sent back and forth.

The data packets contain queue names, command information, actual data to be printed, print flags, and error messages back from the remote system lpd. It often simplifies the reading of the data to extract the data from the other packets. This is usually quite easy to do because all data lines of importance begin with at least four zeros. However when you do this, you corrupt the information about who sent individual packets.

```
grep 0000 /tmp/report.out > /tmp/datasent.out
```

The size of this file will largely depend upon the size of the data file being printed. For this reason, start with a small file. A useful command is:

```
echo "AAAAA" | qprt -Pqueue_name
```

This will show in the `grep` output as:

```
...
00000000     41414141 410a                           |AAAAA.          |
...
```

You will notice that the data is divided into three columns. These are:

- Column 1, a character count, prior to the current line
- Column 2, the data in HEX
- Column 3, the data in ASCII, with periods for non-printable characters

A PostScript output might look something like this:

```
!data        hex equivalent of the characters         ASCII equiv. of
!byte in     sent to the remote host                  the characters.
!packet
00000000     020405ac                                 |....            |
00000000     020405ac                                 |....            |
00000000     0266696e 616c0a                          |.final.         |
00000000     00                                       |.               |
00000000     03313033 20646641 31303137 73763130      |.103 dfA1017sv10|
00000010     3531630a                                 |51c.            |
00000000     00                                       |.               |
00000000     53746172 74207465 7374696e 670a5468      |Start testing.Th|
00000010     69732069 73206120 74657374 20707269      |is is a test pri|
00000020     6e74206a 6f622e0a 4920616d 20757369      |nt job..I am usi|
00000030     6e672069 70747261 63652074 6f207472      |ng iptrace to tr|
00000040     61636520 72656d6f 74652070 72696e74      |ace remote print|
00000050     206a6f62 732e0a46 696e6973 68207465      | jobs..Finish te|
00000060     7374696e 672e0a                          |sting..         |
00000000     00                                       |.               |
00000000     00                                       |.               |
```

```
00000000    02313038 20636641 31303137 73763130    |.108 cfA1017sv10|
00000010    3531630a                               |51c.            |
00000000    00                                     |.               |
00000000    48737631 30353163 0a50726f 6f740a66    |Hsv1051c.Proot.f|
00000010    64664131 30313773 76313035 31630a55    |dfA1017sv1051c.U|
00000020    64664131 30313773 76313035 31630a4e    |dfA1017sv1051c.N|
00000030    53544449 4e2e3237 3535300a 2d4e310a    |STDIN.27550.-N1.|
00000040    2d5a726f 6f744073 76313035 31630a2d    |-Zroot@sv1051c.-|
00000050    74726f6f 74407376 31303531 630a2d54    |troot@sv1051c.-T|
00000060    53544449 4e2e3237 3535300a             |STDIN.27550.    |
00000000    00                                     |.               |
00000000    00                                     |.               |
...
```

The information gained from this output includes:

- The remote queue name is final.
- The data file contains 103 bytes.
- The job number is 1017.
- The local host name is sv1051c.

Some of the things to look for in the output are:

There is always an initial handshake protocol that seems to look like:

```
00000000    020405ac                               |....
00000000    020405ac                               |....
```

The middle column always starts with 02 for the handshake part. The rest is identification information and doesn't matter in this discussion.

In general, lines like the following indicate a positive acknowledgment:

```
00000000    00                                     |.               |
```

One of the first lines in the file is the queue name:

```
00000000    0266696e 616c0a                        |.final.         |
```

Notice in the middle column that this begins with 02. This is a flag to indicate that this is the start of a print request. The name on the end of the line is the queue name.

Command Identifiers for LPD defined in RFC

A status request for a queue would start with an 03.The following binary identifiers are defined in the rfc.

01 Print any waiting jobs. Not supported by AIX rembak.

02 Receive a printer job. Standard command for printing.

03 Send queue state (short). Default status with `qchk`, `lpstat`, `enq -A`.

04 Send queue state (long).

05 Remove jobs.

A short distance down the file a line will contain the temporary file name:

```
00000000    03313033 20646641 31303137 73763130    |.103 dfA1017sv10|
00000010    3531630a                               |51c.            |
```

In this case it begins with `03` in the middle column for data file. This is a subcommand of the receive a printer job command.

The receive printer job subcommands are as follows:

01 Abort job.

02 Receive control file.

| 02 | Count | SP | Name | LF |

03 Receive data file.

| 03 | Count | SP | Name | LF |

The preceding example line shows a receive data file subcommand with the following information:

- The `103` in the 3rd column indicates the number of bytes in the file.
- The file name starts with df for data file.
- The job number is the next part of the data file, in this example it is 1017.
- The last part of the file name is the sending host name sv1051c.

The next packet of data from the client to the server is the data file itself. Check this file for extraneous characters, line feeds, spaces, tabs, and other things that might affect the format. The data in the right-hand column should be exactly what was on the client. As shown in the following example:

```
00000000    53746172 74207465 7374696e 670a5468    |Start testing.Th|
00000010    69732069 73206120 74657374 20707269    |is is a test pri|
00000020    6e74206a 6f622e0a 4920616d 20757369    |nt job..I am usi|
00000030    6e672069 70747261 63652074 6f207472    |ng iptrace to tr|
00000040    61636520 72656d6f 74652070 72696e74    |ace remote print|
00000050    206a6f62 732e0a46 696e6973 68207465    | jobs..Finish te|
00000060    7374696e 672e0a                        |sting..         |
```

The next packet from the client is usually the control file name, as shown in the following example:

```
00000000      02313038 20636641 31303137 73763130      |.108 cfA1017sv10|
00000010      3531630a                                 |51c.            |
```

The subcommand for control file begins with `02` in the middle column. The information from the receive control file is:

- `02` is a control-file descriptor.
- There is 108 bytes of control file information.
- The control file name starts with cfA.
- The job number 1017 was from host sv1051c.

A sample control file excerpt follows:

```
00000000      48737631 30353163 0a50726f 6f740a66      |Hsv1051c.Proot.f|
00000010      64664131 30313773 76313035 31630a55      |dfA1017sv1051c.U|
00000020      64664131 30313773 76313035 31630a4e      |dfA1017sv1051c.N|
00000030      53544449 4e2e3237 3535300a 2d4e310a      |STDIN.27550.-N1.|
00000040      2d5a726f 6f744073 76313035 31630a2d      |-Zroot@sv1051c.-|
00000050      74726f6f 74407376 31303531 630a2d54      |troot@sv1051c.-T|
00000060      53544449 4e2e3237 3535300a               |STDIN.27550.    |
```

The meaning of the control file format is shown in Table 18.

Table 18. Control File Format

Flag	Description
Hsv1051c	Shows the host name of the client
Proot	Shows the user identification
fdfA1017sv1051c	Shows the file to print
Udf1017sv1051c	Unlink (delete) file when done
NSTDIN.27550	Origin of the file
-N1	Make one copy
-Zroot@sv1051c	AIX originator of remote job flag
-troot@sv1051	AIX delivery flag
-TSTDIN.27550	AIX Title flag

11.5 Filters

Filters in UNIX are generally programs that read from standard in (stdin), and write to standard out (stdout), and somewhere in the middle modify the data in some way. Filters can be run directly from the command line, from a shell script, or from within a virtual printer. This section will cover how to use a filter from a virtual printer, and some of the details on filters available with AIX.

In AIX Version 4 Info Explorer there is a sample C filter for adding carriage returns to line feeds.

11.5.1 AIX Filters

The filters that are part of AIX are shown in Table 19.

Table 19. AIX Filters

Filters	Description
pr	A filter that formats ASCII data into pages, adds page numbers, and can provide print rotation and page numbers. Very similar to piobe formatting.
asa or fpr	This filter interprets the carriage-control characters in column one, sometimes known as FORTRAN formatting. Although this filter goes by two names, there is only one filter.
nroff, troff, psroff, hplj, psc, tbl, pic, eqn, grap	Filters for formatting xroff data to or from ditroff format. These filters allow a tagged file to create a formatted document that supports multiple fonts, tables, pictures, equations, and so forth.
enscript	Filter to convert ASCII TEXT data to PostScript

Filters are generally setup in a virtual printer to run before the data goes to the formatting pipeline. You can implement a filter even when the virtual printer is set in pass through mode and when it does not use either the ci (initialization) or cr (reset) sequences.

Filters are the first programs in the input data stream processing pipeline set up by piobe that have an opportunity to selectively manipulate the data stream. A particular filter can be selected from the command line on a per-job basis, or permanently selected by modifying the virtual printer definition.

The `qprt` command uses the -f flag to select a particular filter on a per-job basis. The argument to the -f flag is the second letter of the two letters that name the filter attribute in the virtual printer definition. For instance, to select the pr filter for a job on an ASCII queue named asc on an IBM 4029 LaserPrinter, you could issue the command:

```
qprt -Pasc -fp /etc/motd
```

The filter attribute that selects the pr filter is named fp, so the argument to the -f flag is just p, the second letter.

To permanently select the pr filter, use `lsvirprt` to edit the virtual printer definition and set the value of the _f attribute to p. The _f attribute selects a filter that will be used to pre-process any job submitted to the queue associated with this virtual printer definition.

Since the `lp`, `lpr`, and `qprt` commands are all just front ends to the `enq` command, the true entry point to the spooler, you would assume that `enq` must support the `-f` flag. If you issue the `enq` command with the `-f` flag, however, you will receive an error message as follows:

```
# enq -f
enq: Not a recognized flag: f
```

This is a situation where the previously described technique of mounting /bin/echo over /bin/enq proves useful.

The root user can issue the following commands from a shell prompt:

1. `mount /bin/echo /bin/enq`
2. `# qprt -Pasc -fp /etc/motd`

   `-P asc -o -f -o p /etc/motd`
3. `umount /bin/enq`

After the second command is issued the element defined by your TERM environment variable is displayed, as shown in step 2, above.

These are the arguments `qprt` tried to pass to `enq`. You get to see them because `qprt` found echo instead of `enq`. The following command is equivalent to the command shown in step 2 previously:

```
enq -P asc -o -f -o p /etc/motd
```

The `-o` option specifies that flags specific to the backend should be passed to the backend. The `-o` option can be thought of as a free pass through the syntax checking that occurs before the `enq` command builds a job description file and notifies the qdaemon of the existence of a new job.

11.5.1.1 Using Filters

In this section you will look at an example of a filter that maps linefeeds to carriage returns and linefeeds.

Many users have written or purchased applications that prepare data streams to fill in the blanks on pre-printed checks, invoices, bills-of-lading, or other forms. Printing these data streams requires precise control of the physical printer. It is often the case that the job processing pipeline created by piobe inserts or deletes enough data from the original data stream that the output data no longer falls at the proper position on the pre-printed form.

The root user can frequently use `lsvirprt` to set the value of the _d attribute in the virtual printer definition top. On an ASCII queue on an IBM 4029 Laser Printer, this would cause piobe to select the IP pipeline to process the job. The IP pipeline is for passthrough printing, which means that the formatter filters use the passthru() routine to simply pass the input data stream through to the printer without modification.

This frequently removes all the printer control problems that existed, but adds one new one. When the formatter filter operates in passthrough mode, the mapping of linefeeds to carriage returns and linefeeds is disabled. The forms still do not print correctly.

Supposing that the application does not allow the insertion of carriage returns into the data stream, you can fix this problem with a simple filter, as follows:

```
#include <stdio.h>
main(int argc, char **argv)
{
int ch;
while (EOF != (ch = fgetc(stdin)))
 {
  switch (ch)
   {
    case 10: fputc(ch,stdout);
             fputc(0x0D,stdout);
             break;
    default: fputc(ch,stdout);
             break;
   }
 }
}
```

Compile this and name it cr_mapper and install it somewhere accessible, such as /usr/lib/lpd. Assign it ownership of root.printq and permissions 555.

Assuming you have an ASCII queue named asc on an IBM 4029 Laser Printer, in AIX 4 you can use `lsvirprt` to select the asc queue and then format the `f1` filter attribute. You should see something like the following:

```
User defined filter 1
f1 =
```

As the `f1` attribute has a null default value, the definition is sparse.

Edit the `f1` attribute so its definition appears as follows:

```
User defined filter 1
f1 =
 '/usr/lib/lpd/cr_mapper'
```

When you save the new definition of `f1`, you can again format it with `lsvirprt`. you should see something like the following:

```
User defined filter 1
f1 = /usr/lib/lpd/cr_mapper
 '/usr/lib/lpd/cr_mapper'
```

The `f1` filter can now be used from the command line by using commands such as:

```
qprt -Pasc -f1 filename
enq -Pasc -o -f -o 1 filename
```

If the _d attribute was not set to p, the -dp flag and argument would have to be added to the commands as follows:

```
qprt -Pasc -dp -f1 filename
enq -Pasc -o -d -o p -o -f -o 1 filename
```

The cr_mapper program reads characters from stdin and writes them to stdout. Whenever it reads and writes a line feed (a hex A, or decimal 10), it writes out a carriage return (a hex D).

11.6 Clearing and Preventing Queue Hangs in AIX

In the AIX printing subsystem the file that defines queues is /etc/qconfig. This file is translated into a binary form called /etc/qconfig.bin. When the qdaemon is printing, this file is loaded into memory and used by the associated printing programs. When a change is made to /etc/qconfig, the current print jobs using the memory version of the file must complete printing before the new qconfig.bin can be loaded into memory for the new jobs to print. Thus, the current printing jobs must all finish before any jobs on the new or modified queue can print. When small jobs are printing, this is not a problem since the individual jobs finish quickly, and printing continues. But, when a large job is printing, or when a queue is in a DEV_WAIT state, all new or modified queues will appear hung until this condition is cleared and the printing finishes.

In order to correct a hung queue follow this procedure:

1. Run the `lpstat` command to get the status of the queue as follows:

```
# lpstat
Queue   Dev   Status    Job Files              User         PP %   Blks  Cp Rnk
------- ----- --------- --- ------------------ ---------- ---- -- ----- --- ---
lpforu  lp0   DEV_WAIT    5 /etc/hosts         root                    2   1   1
              QUEUED      6 /etc/hosts         root                    2   1   2
              QUEUED      7 /etc/hosts         root                    2   1   3
              QUEUED      8 /etc/hosts         root                    2   1   4
```

2. Stop the qdaemon before making any changes to a queue. This is easily done with the following command:

```
# stopsrc -c -s qdaemon
0513-044 The stop of the qdaemon Subsystem was completed successfully.
```

3. Make sure the qdaemon has stopped completely by checking with:

```
# lssrc -s qdaemon
Subsystem         Group            PID      Status
 qdaemon          spooler                   inoperative
```

4. Use `lpstat` or `enq -sA` to look for any DEV_WAIT conditions. Wait until all RUNNING jobs are completed, but do not worry about jobs that are QUEUED at this time with a NEW job number in AIX 3. You will not see any of these jobs in AIX 4.

5. Clear any DEV_WAIT conditions or cancel the jobs on those queues. Wait until any RUNNING jobs are finished. For details on clearing jobs, see section 11.7, "Flushing a Print Job" on page 263.

6. If any of these conditions persist and you are unable to cancel the jobs, look in the /var/spool/lpd/stat directory for files that begin with a "p." This indicate active jobs that need to finish or be cleared. The file contains the pid (process ID) for the qd fork or other associated backend printer program. Often these programs can be cleared out manually as follows.

   For example, if the file is /var/spool/lpd/stat/p.lpforu.lp0, then run the following command:

   ```
   cat /var/spool/lpd/stat/p.lpforu.lp0
   ```

   This returns the value:

   ```
   28080
   ```

   Verifying that `28080` is the pid for the qd fork process, run:

   ```
   # ps -ef|grep 28080
       root 28080 35258   0 10:52:13       -  0:00 qd fork
       root 35720 28570   2 10:56:54   pts/3  0:00 grep 28080
   ```

   To kill this process run the command:

```
kill -9 28080
```

To check if the process has stopped run:

```
# ps -ef | grep 28080
root 28084 28570   1 10:59:25  pts/3  0:00 grep 28080
```

Note

Some commands may require root user or system group authority.

Once the system has been cleared, printer jams fixed, paper trays filled, and the queues show READY, the qdaemon can be restarted and the printing subsystem should be in working order again.

This is the time to add new queues. Make changes to the queue, and then start the qdaemon back up with:

```
startsrc -s qdaemon
```

11.7 Flushing a Print Job

If you discovered that the first job you printed was the incorrect one, you printed the correct one but now want to delete the obsolete job. The following describes how to flush a print job.

Check the status of the print queue:

```
# lpstat -vlpforu
Queue  Dev  Status   Job  Files            User     PP %  Blks Cp Rnk
------ ---- -------- ---  ---------------- -------- ---- -- ---- -- ---
lpforu lp0  RUNNING       3  /etc/passwd      root        1 100   1  1    1
```

Print the /etc/hosts file to the default printer:

```
lpr -dlpforu /etc/hosts
```

Check the status of the print queue.

```
# lpstat -vlpforu
Queue  Dev  Status   Job  Files            User     PP %  Blks Cp Rnk
------ ---- -------- ---  ---------------- -------- ---- -- ---- -- ---
lpforu lp0  RUNNING    3  /etc/passwd      root        1 100   1  1   1
            QUEUED     4  /etc/hosts       root        1 100   2  1   2
```

Cancel the print job for /etc/passwd:

```
qcan -Plpforu -x3
```

Check the print queue using the `qchk` command:

```
# qchk -P lpforu
Queue  Dev  Status   Job Files            User       PP %  Blks Cp Rnk
------ ---- -------- --- ---------------- -------- ---- -- ---- -- ---
lpforu lp0  RUNNING    4 /etc/hosts       root         1 100    2  1   2
```

Another option for cancelling a print job is to use the `cancel` command with the job number, for example:

```
cancel 3
```

This will do the same as `qcan -Plpforu -x3`.

11.7.1 Summary

The previous procedure can be summarized as follows:

- Never change the queues or add queues while jobs are printing.
- Prevent new jobs submitted from interfering by stopping the qdaemon.
- Clear all paper jams or disable queues with problems before making any changes.
- Restart the qdaemon after making changes.

11.7.2 qdaemon Will Not Start

This is usually because of:

1. Bad lines or stanzas in /etc/qconfig caused
    - After manual editing of the file.
    - When removing queues while jobs still queued.
2. Incompatible qdaemon, enq, and digest after upgrade.

11.7.3 Cannot Add Printer Queue

If you attempt to add a new printer queue and receive the following error:

```
Not enough space in the /tmp directory
```

Since the /tmp file system is a mount point for a directory that contains system-generated temporary files, space will be required for those generated during the creation of the print queue. As such, these files cannot be written to /tmp and hence the previous error message. Troubleshoot this problem by increasing the size of /tmp or removing any unnecessary files in the /tmp.

11.8 Setting Default Printers

An administrator can set a print queue as the default print queue. There are two methods to set a default printer: using the `smitty qdefault` fast path and using the LPDEST environment variable.

11.8.0.1 Using smitty qdefault Fast Path

To define a default printer:

1. Enter the command `smitty qdefault`. The screen in Figure 112 is produced.

```
                        Set System's Default Print Queue

Type or select values in entry fields.
Press Enter AFTER making all desired changes.

                                                        [Entry Fields]
* System DEFAULT QUEUE name                           [virprt1]            +









F1=Help            F2=Refresh          F3=Cancel          F4=List
F5=Reset           F6=Command          F7=Edit            F8=Image
F9=Shell           F10=Exit            Enter=Do
```

Figure 112. Setting System Default Print Queue

2. Specify the queue name for the print queue you wish to be the default.
3. Press the **Enter** Key and wait until the `Command: Ok` screen displays, then exit SMIT to complete the process.

11.8.0.2 The LPDEST Environment Variable

The LPDEST environment variable specifies the default print queue once it has been set. A number of print commands, such as `enq`, `lprm`, `lpr`, `qstatus`, `pac`, and many more, use this environment variable as the default if it is set and if a printer is not specified. For some commands, it overrides the printer variable value.

Using the `printenv` command to look at a system before the LPDEST environment variable is set will produce the following output:

```
# printenv
_=/usr/bin/printenv
LANG=en_US
LOGIN=root
NLSPATH=/usr/lib/nls/msg/%L/%N:/usr/lib/nls/msg/%L/%N.cat
PATH=/usr/bin:/etc:/usr/sbin:/usr/ucb:/usr/bin/X11:/sbin
LC__FASTMSG=true
LOGNAME=root
MAIL=/usr/spool/mail/root
LOCPATH=/usr/lib/nls/loc
USER=root
AUTHSTATE=compat
SHELL=/bin/ksh
ODMDIR=/etc/objrepos
HOME=/
TERM=vt100
MAILMSG=[YOU HAVE NEW MAIL]
PWD=/
TZ=CST6CDT
A__z=! LOGNAME
```

To set the default queue using the LPDEST environment variable do the following:

1. Change the value of the LPDEST environment variable in one of the following ways:

   If you are in the sh (Bourne) shell, enter the following command:

   ```
   LPDEST=NewValue; export LPDEST
   ```

   If you are in csh (C) shell, enter the following command:

   ```
   setenv LPDEST=NewValue
   ```

   If you are in ksh (Korn) shell, enter the following command:

   ```
   export LPDEST=NewValue
   ```

2. To verify the current value of the LPDEST environment variable, use the following commands:

   ```
   # echo $LPDEST
   virprt1
   ```

3. Using the `printenv` command after setting the variable will produce the following output:

```
# printenv
_=/usr/bin/printenv
LANG=en_US
LOGIN=root
NLSPATH=/usr/lib/nls/msg/%L/%N:/usr/lib/nls/msg/%L/%N.cat
PATH=/usr/bin:/etc:/usr/sbin:/usr/ucb:/usr/bin/X11:/sbin
LC__FASTMSG=true
LOGNAME=root
MAIL=/usr/spool/mail/root
LOCPATH=/usr/lib/nls/loc
USER=root
AUTHSTATE=compat
SHELL=/bin/ksh
ODMDIR=/etc/objrepos
HOME=/
TERM=vt100
MAILMSG=[YOU HAVE NEW MAIL]
PWD=/
TZ=CST6CDT
LPDEST=virprt1
A__z=! LOGNAME
```

Note that the LPDEST environment variable is now set to virprt1 as highlighted in the preceding example.

11.9 References

The following provides additional information:

- *AIX Version 4.3 Guide to Printers and Printing, SC23-4130.*

11.10 Quiz

1. The system administrator is logged into host plainview.texas.com. The system administrator adds a remote print queue from plainview to host beaumont.texas.com and then runs the lpstat command to confirm the queues are ready to print. The results of the lpstat command are shown below.

```
Queue   Dev   Status    Job Files              User         PP %   Blks  Cp Rnk
------- ----- --------- --- ------------------ ---------- ---- -- ----- --- ---
lp0     lp0   STOPPED    1 /tmp/report        root               7911   1   1
rq0     @beau READY
rq0     rq0   HOST_DOWN
```

The lpstat output in the exhibit indicates that plainview cannot communicate with beaumont. The system administrator runs a `ping` command from plainview to beaumont and receives ping packets back. Which of the following actions can be performed so plainview can print to beaumont?

A. Execute `enq -d` on plainview.

B. Start the lpd daemon on beaumont.

C. Start the lpd daemon on plainview.

D. Add the beaumont host name to plainview's /etc/hosts.lpd file.

2. A system administrator is logged into host plainview.texas.com and executes `lpstat` as root. The system administrator adds a remote print queue from plainview to host beaumont.texas.com, re-executes `lpstat` to confirm the queues are ready to print, and gets the following results shown in the exhibit.

```
Queue   Dev   Status    Job Files              User        PP %   Blks  Cp Rnk
------- ----- --------- --- ------------------ ---------- ---- -- ----- --- ---
lp0     lp0   STOPPED    1 /tmp/report         root              7911   1   1
rq0     @beau READY
rq0     rq0   HOST_DOWN
```

Which of the following commands should be run to get the queued job in lp0 to begin printing?

```
qchk -q

enq -X lp0

stopsrc -s lpd;startsrc -s lpd

stopsrc -cs qdaemon;startsrc -s qdaemon
```

11.10.1 Answers

1. B
2. D

11.11 Exercises

1. Create a virtual printer with the name vprinter on a local system for the remote queue, qremote. If the remote queue does not exist on the remote system then create the remote queue.

2. Create a text file containing your name, address and telephone number on individual lines.
3. Start a trace for this virtual printer, vprinter.
4. Print the text file created in step 2 on the vprinter.
5. Using the results of the trace output determine:
    a. The remote queue name
    b. The number of bytes in the data file
    c. The job number
    d. The local host name
6. Stop the lpd daemon on the remote server.
7. Repeats steps 3 to 5.
8. Restart the lpd daemon.

Chapter 12. Asynchronous Point-to-Point Protocol

The asynchronous Point-to-Point Protocol (PPP) subsystem provides an alternative to SLIP. PPP provides a standard method for transporting multiprotocol datagrams over point-to-point media. PPP is comprised of three main layers:

- A method for encapsulating multiprotocol datagrams. AIX PPP supports the TCP/IP network layer protocols.
- A Link Control Protocol (LCP) for establishing, configuring, and testing the data-link connection. AIX PPP implements this through the streams kernel extensions.
- A family of Network Control Protocols (NCPs) for establishing and configuring different network layer protocols. AIX PPP supports Internet Protocol Control Protocol (IPCP) for negotiating a TCP/IP connection.

AIX PPP differentiates between client and server. An AIX system can act as both a client and a server. The distinction is made to simplify configuration. PPP servers tend to allocate a pool of IP addresses among the connections that are being made. There is some correlation between the media devices and AIX PPP breaks this correlation. All server PPP connections are allocated on a first-available basis. This facilitates the separation of PPP from the media. The attachment process must request to be linked to the proper type of link.

The Asynchronous Point-to-Point Protocol on AIX utilizes three user-level processes:

1. A control daemon, pppcontrold, executed by root under the system resource controller (`startsrc -s pppcontrold`). The control daemon's function encompasses loading and configuring all kernel extensions associated with the subsystem. It remains running as long as PPP function is required by the operating system.
2. An attachment process, pppattachd that binds a TTY stream to an instance of the Link Control Protocol, Network Control Protocol, and a datagram protocol. An instance of pppattachd exists for each active PPP connection in the system. Any user of the attachment process must belong to the uucp group and contain /usr/sbin within their PATH environment variable.
3. A dialer process, pppdial that establishes an outgoing connection. The dialer is intended to be executed by pppattachd as the connector program. Its purpose is to interact over the asynchronous device prior to PPP

negotiation. This interaction is defined similarly to the UUCP chat dialog format. The dialer capability is provided to assist in establishing a connection with a remote system. The actual session establishment is out of the scope of PPP.

12.1 Configuring Asynchronous PPP Server

Before configuration, ensure that the following fileset are installed on your AIX system:

- bos.net.ppp

Setting up the PPP Server basically requires six steps:

1. Setting up the PPP link control configuration
2. Assigning the PPP IP addresses
3. Setting up the special PPP dial-in ID
4. Adding the TTY port
5. Configuring the modem
6. Starting PPP

Details for the these steps are discussed in the following sections.

12.2 Setting Up the PPP Control Link

The following terms are used in this section for discussion:

PPP Subsystem Name A unique name to identify the PPP server.

Max Server Connections The greatest number of clients that may be served at any one time. Typically, this is the number of dial-in modems on the system.

Max Client Connections The greatest number of outgoing connections at any one time. Typically this is the number of dial-out modems on the system

Max Demand Interfaces The greatest number of peer connections allowed at any one time. These connections are established on demand, meaning they are triggered by an event.

	For example, a ping to the remote PPP host.
Max IP Interfaces	The total of the PPP interfaces for the system that is the sum of max server connections, max client connections and max demand connections.
Max Async HDLC Attachments	The number of concurrently active PPP sessions allowed. Typically equal to the Max IP Interface.

The following settings are examples used in this section, for configuring the control PPP daemon:

PPP Subsystem Name	mickey
Max Server Connections	1
Max Client Connections	0
Max Demand Interface	0
Max IP Interface	1
Max Async HDLC Attachments	1

Note

- Normally all other options on the SMIT screen are left at their default values.
- You must be root to start PPP and to have access to most files.

The following procedure guides you through creating the PPP Control Link.

1. On server mickey, add the link through SMIT by entering the command:

```
smitty ppp
```

2. Choose the option, **Link Control Configuration.**
3. Choose the option, **Add A Link Configuration.**
4. Fill in the accented fields, as follows, with the values specified previously:

```
                              LINK Configuration

Type or select values in entry fields.
Press Enter AFTER making all desired changes.

[TOP]                                                 [Entry Fields]
  PPP subsystem name                                [mickey]
  max server connections                            [1]                #
  max client connections                            [0]                #
  max demand connections                            [0]                #
  max ip interfaces                                 [1]                #
  max async hdlc attachments                        [1]                #
  mru                                               []                 #
  async character map                               []                 X
  transmit async character map                      []                 X
  negotiate MRU                                      yes               +
  negotiate magic number                             yes               +
  negotiate async map                                yes               +
  negotiate protocol compression                     yes               +
[MORE...8]

F1=Help             F2=Refresh          F3=Cancel           F4=List
Esc+5=Reset         Esc+6=Command       Esc+7=Edit          Esc+8=Image
Esc+9=Shell         Esc+0=Exit          Enter=Do
```

Figure 113. Link Configuration Screen

5. Press **Enter** to add the Link.

This process created a file /etc/ppp/lcp_config. You can examine this file as follows:

```
# cat /etc/ppp/lcp_config
server_name pppserver
lcp_server 1
lcp_client 0
lcp_demand 0
num_if 1
num_hdlc 1
```

12.3 Assigning the PPP IP Addresses

The following information is needed for this procedure: the IP address, gateway, and netmask for the host.

To get this information do the following:

- Enter smitty tcpip
- Select **Minimum Configuration & Startup**.
- Choose the Available Network Interface, such as en0 or tr0.

- Make note of the information required.

For the purposes of this discussion, the settings you will use are:

Hostname mickey

Internet Address 9.3.1.45

Network Mask 255.255.255.0

Nameserver 9.3.1.74

DOMAIN Name itsc.austin.ibm.com

GATEWAY Address 9.3.1.74

You will need to do the following:

1. Choose an unused address in the same domain: **9.3.1.46**.
2. Add an entry in the /etc/hosts file with the new address and hostname for the PPP client.
3. Add the PPP addresses by entering the command `smitty ppp`.
4. Choose the option **PPP IP Interfaces**.
5. Choose the option **Add a Server Interface**.
6. Fill in the fields, shown in Figure 114, with information provided previously.

```
                              PPP IP Configuration

Type or select values in entry fields.
Press Enter AFTER making all desired changes.

                                                        [Entry Fields]
  Local IP address                                   [9.3.1.45]
  Starting Remote IP address                         [9.3.1.46]
  Number of addresses                                [1]                 #
  Netmask                                            [255.255.255.0]










F1=Help              F2=Refresh           F3=Cancel            F4=List
F5=Reset             F6=Command           F7=Edit              F8=Image
F9=Shell             F10=Exit             Enter=Do
```

Figure 114. PPP IP Configuration

7. Press **Enter** to add the IP Server configuration. This creates a file entry in /etc/ppp/if_conf. The file can be viewed using the following:

```
# cat /etc/ppp/if_conf
interface
server
local_ip 9.3.1.45
remote_ip 9.3.1.46
netmask 255.255.255.0
```

8. Make sure ipforwarding is on. By default in AIX 4, ipforwarding is turned off. If you want your server to act as a router, you need to turn ipforwarding on. Check the value of ipforwarding with:

```
# no -a |grep ipf
               ipfragttl = 60
            ipforwarding = 0
```

If ipforwarding is 0, change it to 1 with:

```
no -o ipforwarding=1
```

9. Because you are adding the client to the same subnet as the server, you will want the server to respond to arp requests from other hosts in the network, so that all traffic to the client will get routed through the hosts. You can do this with a proxy arp.

Find the hardware address of the local adapter for the client using:

```
# netstat -i
Name  Mtu   Network    Address            Ipkts Ierrs    Opkts Oerrs  Coll
lo0   16896 link#1                         203625     0   203773     0     0
lo0   16896 127        loopback            203625     0   203773     0     0
lo0   16896 ::1                            203625     0   203773     0     0
en0   1500  link#2     2.60.8c.2f.47.42    712193     0   712606     0     0
en0   1500  9.3.5      goofy_en0           712193     0   712606     0     0
tr0   1492  link#3     10.0.5a.a8.3b.fa   1088842     0   769364     0     0
tr0   1492  9.3.1      goofy              1088842     0   769364     0     0
tr1   1492  link#4     10.0.5a.a8.d1.f3   1076155     0   726539     0     0
tr1   1492  9.3.4      goofy_stby         1076155     0   726539     0     0
```

Add an arp entry for the remote host using:

```
arp -s type hostname hardware address pub
```

where:

type	The type of your network adapter. Valid types are: ether, 802.3, fddi, 802.5 (token ring).
hostname	Hostname of the client.
hardware address	From `netstat -i`. Use colon separators.
pub	Indicates public and permanent.

The token ring (tr0) hardware address is used for this example.

For server mickey, this command is:

```
arp -s 802.5 goofy 10:0:5a:8c:3b:fa pub
```

10. Verify the arp entries with an `arp -a` command, the output is as follows:

```
goofy (9.3.1.46) at 10:0:5a:8c:3b:fa [token ring] permanent published
```

12.4 Adding a PPP Login User

When setting up a PPP server, the answering pppattachd daemon is started from the profile script of a special PPP user. The security of this user is dependent on the type of Internet server you are using and who will know the password of the server. In many cases, you will want this special user ID only available while starting a PPP session. This is especially true if you are setting up a server for outside users to dial into.

Special tasks specific to the PPP user include:

1. Make this user a member of the uucp group.
2. Do not allow other users to `su` to this user.
3. Do not allow a remote login to the user. (telnet, rlogin).
4. Disable ftp to the user.
5. Modify the .profile to start the pppahachd.

In this section you will create a PPP user through SMIT.

You will use the command `smitty user` fastpath as follows:

1. Enter the command `smitty user`.
2. Choose the option **Add a User**.
3. Fill in the screen ensuring that the following is set:

User Name	pppuser
Primary Group	uucp
Group Set	uucp
Administrative Groups	uucp
Another user can su to user	false (for security)
Su Groups	Nogroup
Home directory	/home/pppuser
Initial Program	/usr/bin/ksh

User can Login? true

User can Login Remotely? false

Press **Enter** to create user. Press **F3** to go to previous menu.

4. Select **Change a User's Password**. Give the user ID a password.

5. Edit the user .profile using:

   ```
   vi /home/pppuser/.profile
   ```

   Insert the first line:

   ```
   exec /usr/sbin/pppattachd server 2>/dev/null
   ```

6. At the initial login, the new user is prompted to change the assigned password. However, the chat script cannot do this and the connection will not be successful. Therefore, enter the following command to switch off this prompt:

   ```
   pwdadm -f NOCHECK USER_ID
   ```

   For this example, the command is:

   ```
   pwdadm -f NOCHECK pppuser
   ```

7. Put the PPP user name in the /etc/ftpusers file.

   Create the file if it does not exist.

The user is ready for PPP login.

12.4.1 Adding the TTY Port

In this section you will add a TTY port with login capability.

12.4.1.1 Add the TTY Device

The procedure adds a tty device:

1. Enter the command `smitty tty`.
2. Choose the option **Add a TTY**.
3. Choose your tty type from the resulting list.
4. Choose your parent adapter from the resulting script.
5. Make the following changes:
   - Set your port number.
   - Enable login.
   - Set baud rate to the baud rate of the modem.
   - Set flow control as rts.

6. Press **Enter** to add the tty.

12.4.1.2 Add TTY to /etc/uucp/Devices File

For the `cu` command to configure the modem and for PPP to work, you will need an entry in the /etc/uucp/Devices file for this tty. Add this as follows:

1. Enter the command `cd /etc/uucp`.
2. Enter the command `vi Devices`.
3. Add a line at the following line at the bottom of the Devices file:

   ```
   Direct tty# - baud-rate direct
   ```

   For this example it is:

   ```
   Direct tty0 - 9600 direct
   ```

4. Save and exit the file.

12.4.2 Configure the Dial-In Modem

The setup of a modem will be different for different types of modems, and will also be different for the client or the server. Since the server is answering the call, you will need to make sure that the modem is set to answer a call. Modem setup strings vary, but a frequently-used generic setup string is as follows: AT&F&C1&D2S0=1Q2&W. A different string may be required by your modem. Some modems allow you to configure them directly, and that clears up the need to do any of these configuration from the software level. See the installation manual for your modem for details.

To setup the modem, do the following:

1. Disable the login with `pdisable tty0`.
2. Connect to the modem with `cu -ml tty0`. The modem should respond with Connected.

   If an entry is not made for `tty0` in the /etc/uucp/Devices, file then the following error is displayed when the command `cu -ml tty0` is executed:

   ```
   # cu -ml tty0
   cu: 0835-028 The connection failed. NO DEVICES AVAILABLE.
   ```

Note

The command `cu -dml tty#` provides you with debug information for the `cu` command. If there is no response from the `cu -ml tty#` command, then execute the command with the `-d` flag and troubleshoot the problem from the information supplied in the output.

3. Type `AT` and press **Enter**. The modem should respond with `OK`.
4. Set the modem to answer after one ring with `ATS0=1`.
5. Enter the generic setup string or use the specific setup string for your modem.
6. Exit the cu session with ~. That is the tilda character followed by a dot.
7. Press **Enter**. This should return Disconnected.
8. Enable the login with `penable tty0`.

12.4.2.1 Capturing Diagnostic Output

Before dialing out, provide for diagnostic information to use in case of failure to establish a connection. Do the following:

1. In the /etc/syslogd.conf file, add the line: *.debug /tmp/ppp.
2. Create the file /tmp/ppp and set the permissions so it can be written to.
3. Tell syslogd that /etc/syslogd.conf has been updated. Enter the command: `refresh -s syslogd`.
4. pppcontrold can be set to provide more detailed output by sending it signal 30. Enter the following commands:
   - `lssrc -s pppcontrold` (Note the process ID (PID))
   - `kill -30 pppcontrold_PID` where pppcontrold_PID is the PID number of pppcontrold returned by the previous command.

   This will append a note to /tmp/ppp with a message indicating that debugging has been activated. This diagnostic output can be switched off using `kill -31 pppcontrold_PID`.

12.4.3 Start the PPP Control Daemon

Once the link and IP addresses are configured, you can start the control daemon pppcontrold. It is recommended that you do this from SMIT following the same procedure used for the server.

1. Return to the PPP main Panel that is using `smitty ppp`.

2. Select option **Start PPP**.
3. Select the type of startup you want.
4. At this point if you exit SMIT you can do the following to verify that the PPP subsystem is active on this system.

```
#lssrc -s pppcontrold

Subsystem          Group              PID      Status
pppcontrold        uucp               18914    active
```

This should show as active.

```
#ps -ef | grep ppp
root 18914  4456   0   Apr 18       -  0:00 /usr/sbin/pppcontrold
```

There should be a pppcontrold process running.

If there is a problem, look at the syslog daemon file /tmp/ppp you setup in section 12.4.2.1, "Capturing Diagnostic Output" on page 280.

12.5 AIX PPP Client

Now that the server (mickey) is up and operational, you will configure a client (goofy) and test the connection between mickey and goofy.

12.5.1 Configuring an AIX PPP Client

You will configuring the PPP client through SMIT with the following procedure:

1. On Goofy, enter the command, `smitty ppp`.
2. Select the option **Link Control Configuration**.
3. Select the option **Add a Link Configuration**.
4. Fill in the fields as follows:

PPP Subsystem Name	goofy
Max Server Connections	0
Max Client Connections	1
Max IP Interfaces	1
Max Async HDLC Attachments	1

   You are configuring a client, therefore, you do not need more than one client connection, no server connections, and only one IP interface and async HDLC Attachments. You will only be dialing out to one server.

   Take the defaults for everything else.

5. Press **Enter** to add the link.
6. The file /etc/ppp/lcp_config was created. A look at this file shows the following configuration for the client.

```
#cat /etc/ppp/lcp_config
server_name goofy
lcp_server 0
lcp_client 1
lcp_demand 0
num_if 1
num_hdlc 1
```

7. Add a TTY as shown in section 12.4.1, "Adding the TTY Port" on page 278. Ensure that **Enable LOGIN=disable** is set when configuring the TTY.
8. Configure the dial-out modem using the method in section 12.4.2, "Configure the Dial-In Modem" on page 279.

12.5.1.1 Start the PPP Control Daemon

Once the link is configured, you can start the control daemon pppcontrold. It is recommended that you do this from SMIT by following the same procedure as in section 12.4.3, "Start the PPP Control Daemon" on page 280.

Verify that the PPP interface is working by using the following command:

```
#ifconfig pp0
pp0: flags=6000030<POINTOPOINT,NOTRAILERS,GROUPRT,64BIT>
        inet 0.0.0.0 --> 0.0.0.0 netmask 0xff000000
```

The interface should display with Addresses of 0.0.0.0 set.

12.5.2 Create the Chat Dialog

A chat script is a file containing expect-send pairs separated by spaces or newline. These expect-send sequences instruct pppdial in how to dial-up and log into a remote PPP server. An example of a simple chat script follows:

```
''
AT
OK
ATDT4444444
CONNECT
''
ogin:
pppuser
ssword:
pppuser
```

Line by line, this script can be translated to mean:

- Expect nothing
- Send the command `AT` to the modem
- Expect `OK` to come back
- Send the modem `ATDT4444444` (to make the modem dial this number)
- Expect the **CONNECT** response from the modem
- Send a null string.
- Expect the string `ogin:` from the remote system
- Send the ppp ID `goofy`
- Expect a prompt (`ssword:`) for the password.
- Send the ppp ID password that is `goofy`.

This is only an example and, as such, before you establish a PPP connection, dial out to the remote system and see what is required to log in and start PPP.

You should now be able to use the command: `/usr/sbin/pppattachd tty0 client connect "/usr/sbin/pppdial -v -f chat_script_file"` to connect to the remote server.

A sample chat script (dial_out.example) can be found in the /etc/ppp directory. You can edit this script to reflect your requirements and use it to invoke the ppp connection.

If there are any problems with the connection, see the /tmp/ppp file created in section 12.4.2.1, “Capturing Diagnostic Output” on page 280 for diagnostic information to assist in troubleshooting the problem.

12.6 References

The following publications are suitable sources for additional information.

- *Dallas Systems Center PPP Tips,* `http://tesch.aix.dfw.ibm.com/ppptips/index.html`.
- *IBM Public Information and Services,* `http://w3.viewblue.ibm.com` (IBM Internal Users Only).

12.7 Quiz

1. What filesets need to be installed to support PPP?

A. bos.net.ppp, bos.uucp.net

B. bos.net.ppp, bos.net.uucp

C. bos.net.ppp

D. bos.net

2. Given the following command and output:

```
# cat /etc/ppp/lcp_config
server_name pppserver
lcp_server 1
lcp_client 0
lcp_demand 0
num_if 1
num_hdlc 1
```

Is this a server or client PPP system? How many server connections and client connects can this system make respectively.

A. Client, 2, 0

B. Client, 1, 0

C. Server, 0, 1

D. Server, 1, 0

12.7.1 Answers

1. C
2. D

12.8 Exercises

1. Create a link configuration for a PPP server with zero maximum client connections, three maximum server connections, no maximum demand, and maximum IP interface.
2. Add a TTY and use the `cu` command to configure and test your dial-in modem.
3. Use the lcp_config file to verify the configuration in 1.
4. Configure a PPP client to connect to this server with zero maximum server connections. Verify configuration using the lcp_config file.

Chapter 13. Network Installation Management

Network Installation Management (NIM) is used to manage remote sites on a network. The types of machines you can manage are *stand-alone*, *diskless*, and *dataless*. A *stand-alone* machine is one that can boot (start up) by itself. *Diskless* and *dataless* systems cannot boot by themselves; they must use remote resources to boot. *Diskless* systems have no disk drive. *Dataless* systems have a local disk drive but they cannot boot from it.

Using NIM, you can install a group of machines with a common configuration or customize an installation for the specific needs of a given machine. The number of machines you can install simultaneously depends on the throughput of your network, the disk access throughput of the installation servers, and the platform type of your servers.

The NIM environment comprises client and server machines. A server provides resources (for example, files and programs required for installation) to another machine. A machine that is dependent on a server to provide resources is known as a client. In this guide and reference, any machine that receives NIM resources is a client, although the same machine can also be a server in the overall network environment.

13.1 Debugging NIM Boot Images

If a client machine is unable to network boot from its boot server, there may be a problem in one or more of the following stages of the network boot:

- Establishing network communication between the client and server
- Obtaining the boot image from the server
- Running the boot image on the client

13.1.1 Establishing Network Communication

The following steps may be used to establish network communication:

1. Before initiating the network boot on the client, perform a ping test from the client bootp menus.
2. If the ping test fails, verify that the client, server, and gateway addresses are specified correctly.
3. If the addresses are correct, try to ping the server from a different machine in the client's subnet.

4. If the server can be pinged from another machine, the network adapter on the boot client may be faulty.

5. If the server cannot be pinged from another machine in the client's subnet, there may be routing problems between the client and the server, or else network communications on the server may be faulty. Perform network debugging procedures to determine the source of the problem.

13.1.2 Obtaining the Boot Image from the Server

The following steps may be used to obtain a boot image from the server.

1. If the ping test is successful, perform a network boot of the client. When a network boot is initiated on a client, a bootp request packet is sent from the client to the server.

   The server then replies with a packet to the client. The client machine displays the number of packets sent and received for the bootp request. If a packet is sent from the client, but none is received, another packet will be sent.

2. If bootp packets continue to be sent but not received, the boot server may not be responding to the request.

3. From the bootp server, view the /etc/bootptab file on the server. It should contain an entry for the client machine with the following information:

```
<hostname of client>
bf=<boot file>
ip=<client ip address>
ht=<network type>
sa=<boot server address>
sm=<client subnet mask>
ha=<network adapter hardware address> (required only if bootp requests
are sent by broadcasting)
```

   If an entry does not exist, either the `NIM` command used to set up the current operation failed, or the machine was reset before the boot operation could occur.

   Rerun the NIM bos_inst, diag, or maint_boot operation to prepare the server for the client boot request.

   If the entry exists in /etc/bootptab, verify that the specified data is correct. If a field contains incorrect data, the information that was used to define the machine or network in the NIM database was probably wrong. Correct this problem by resetting the client machine, correcting the incorrect data in the client or network definition, retrying the NIM operation, and rebooting the client.

4. If the /etc/bootptab file is correct, verify that the inetd daemon is running. If it is not running, start it and retry the network boot from the client. If the inetd daemon is running, it should automatically start the bootpd daemon when the bootp request is received at the server.
5. If the bootpd daemon is not started, verify that the bootps entry in the /etc/inetd.conf file is not commented out. If it is commented out, uncomment it and restart inetd with the `refresh -s inetd` command. Retry the network boot from the client.
6. If a bootp reply is still not received at the client, manually start the bootpd daemon in debug mode:
   - Comment out the bootps entry from the /etc/bootptab file on the server.
   - Stop all running bootpd processes.
   - Restart inetd using the `refresh -s inetd` command.
   - Start bootpd from the command line using the `/usr/sbin/bootpd -s -d -d -d` command.
7. Retry to network boot from the client. If no output is displayed from the running `bootpd` command, the client bootp request is not reaching the server. Verify that the addresses specified in the bootp menus are correct. If they are correct, perform network debugging procedures to determine why the packet is not reaching the server.
8. If the server receives the client bootp request, then running the `bootpd` command displays output matching the client data in the /etc/bootptab file. Verify that the specified addresses are correct. This information is sent back to the client in the bootp reply.
9. If the client is still not receiving the bootp reply, perform network debugging procedures to determine why the reply packet is not reaching the client.
10. After the client receives the bootp reply, it will use tftp to transfer the boot image from the server.
11. The number of tftp packets transferred to the client will be displayed at the client machine.
12. The boot image has been successfully retrieved at the client machine when the LED shows 299 on rs6k-platform machines or when the bottom third of the screen turns gray on other platforms.
13. If the tftp transfer of the boot image does not complete successfully, the client may be trying to get the wrong boot image. Verify that the client definition in the NIM database shows the correct platform and kernel type.

If the data is incorrect, correct it, reset the client machine, rerun the NIM operation, and reboot the client over the network.

14. Verify that the /tftpboot directory on the boot server contains a link with the client name to the correct boot image. If the link does not exist, reset the client machine, rerun the NIM operation, and reboot the client over the network.

15. If the link with the client name is pointing to the correct boot image and the tftp transfer of the boot image does not complete successfully, the boot image may be corrupted.

    Recreate the boot image by performing a NIM check operation with the force flag on the SPOT. If the client is not an rs6k-platform machine, also make sure the client has the latest version of the firmware installed.

13.1.3 Running the Boot Image on the Client

After the client machine has successfully received the boot image from the server, the most common errors encountered are hangs with the LED showing 608, 611, or 613. Some machines may not have LED displays. Debugging such problems on these machines will require using debug-enabled boot images.

13.1.3.1 Error 608

Attempting to retrieve the client.info file with tftp. Note that a flashing 608 indicates multiple attempt(s) to retrieve the client_info file are occurring.

13.1.3.2 Error 611

The /etc/exports file either does not have the correct permissions for the client to mount /usr or does not have any entry for /usr.

13.1.3.3 Error 613

The system is unable to set up the routing tables.

13.2 Error 611 - Network Error

If you get an error 611 during boot, the problem is that the /etc/exports file either does not have the correct permissions for the client to mount /usr or does not have any entry for /usr.

To rectify this problem type the following command:

```
exportfs
```

Using the `exportfs` command, verify that each entry is filled in correctly.

If you receive the following error message when adding the network boot client:

```
Configuring network boot for client thumper.aix.dfw.ibm.com
/usr/ro,root=thumper.aix.dfw.ibm.com
Starting NFS and BOOTP services..
exports: /usr: sub-directory (/usr/lpp) already exported
/usr not found in etc/exports
```

the client has been configured, but you must correct the problem with the export before booting the client.

Execute the `exportfs` command.

If you continue to have problems trying to export a /usr parent directory, check the /etc/exports file, and look for an existing /usr subdirectory that is not a filesystem. If you have a /usr subdirectory that is not a filesystem you will not be allowed to export /usr until you remove it from the /etc/exports/file.

An example would be:

```
/usr/sys/inst.images -rw
/usr/lpp             -root=mars,access=mars
```

In the above example the /usr/sys/inst.images is its own filesystem, but /usr/lpp is still part of the /usr filesystem.

Execute the following command to remove /usr/lpp from the /etc/exports file.

```
/usr/sbin/rmnfsexp -d /usr/lpp -B
```

Re-add the network boot client by running the `smitty sysback` command. Verify by executing the `exportfs` command.

13.3 The NIM Command

The `nim` command performs an operation on a NIM object. The type of operation performed is dependent on the type of object specified by the *ObjectName* parameter. Possible operations include initializing environments and managing resources. You can use the `lsnim` command to display the list of supported operations.

The `NIM` command syntax

```
nim {-o Operation} [ -F ] [ -t Type ] [ -a Attribute=Value . . . ]
{ObjectName}
```

Table 20 provides a list of the flags and their descriptions, the most important functions are the flag sub functions.

Table 20. Flags and Descriptions of nim Command

Flag	Flag Description
-a *Attribute* = *Value* . . .	Assigns the specified value to the specified attribute. Use the `lsnim` -q *Operation* `-t` *Type* command to get a list of valid attributes for a specific operation.
-F	Overrides some safety checks.

Flag	Flag Description
-o *Operation*	Specifies an operation to perform on a NIM object. The possible operations are: **allocate** Allocates a resource for use. **bos_inst** Performs a BOS installation. **change** Changes an object's attributes. **check** Checks the status of a NIM object. **cust** Performs software customization. **deallocate** Deallocates a resource. **define** Defines an object. **diag** Allows a machine to boot a diag image. **dkls_init** Initializes a diskless machine's env. **dtls_init** Initializes a dataless machine's env. **fix_query** Lists the fix info. for a given APAR or keyword. **lppchk** Verifies installed filesets on NIM machines and SPOTs. **lslpp** Lists licensed program information about an object. **maint** Performs software maintenance. **remove** Removes an object. **reset** Resets an object's NIM state. **sync_roots** Synchronizes root directories for diskless and dataless clients for a specific SPOT. **unconfig** Unconfigures the NIM master fileset. **maint_boot** Lets machine boot in maintenance mode. **showlog** Displays a client's install, boot or custom log, or a SPOT's install log from the NIM master. **showres** Displays the contents of a resource. **alt_disk_install** Performs an alternate disk installation.

Flag	Flag Description
-t *Type*	Specifies the type of the NIM object for define operations. The possible types are: **resource types:** **bosinst_data** Config file used during base system installation. **dump** Parent directory for client dump files. **fix_bundle** Fix (keyword) input file for the cust or fix_query operation. **home** Parent directory for client /home directories. **image_data** Config file used during base system installation. **installp_bundle** Installp bundle file. **lpp_source** Source device for optional product images. **mksysb** AIX mksysb image. **paging** Parent directory for client paging files. **root** Parent directory for client / directories. **script** Executable file that is run on a client. **shared_home** /home directory shared by clients. **spot** Shared Product Object Tree - equivalent to /usr file system. **tmp** Parent directory for client /tmp directory. **exclude_files** Files excluded from a mksysb image. **resolv_conf** Name-server configuration file. **machine types:** **diskless** All file systems and resources remote. **dataless** Local paging,dump; remote /,/usr; others remote or local. **standalone** Local file systems and resources. **master** Machine that controls the NIM environment. **network types:** **tok** Token-Ring network. **ent** Ethernet network. **fddi** FDDI network. **generic** Other TCP/IP networks. **group types:** **mac_group** Group of machines. **res_group** Group of resources.

The following are examples of using the `nim` command:

To define a resource that is a directory containing installable images that is located on server altoid and has a path name of `/usr/sys/inst.images`, and name that resource images, enter:

```
nim -o define -t lpp_source -a server=altoid \
     -a location=/usr/sys/inst.images images
```

To remove a resource named dump_files, enter:

```
nim -o remove dump_files
```

Machines on the BLDG905 network use the gateway905 gateway to reach the OZ network. Machines on the OZ network use the gatewayOZ gateway to reach the BLDG905 network. To add a route between two networks named BLDG905 and OZ, enter:

```
nim -o change -a routing1="OZ gateway905 gatewayOZ" BLDG905
```

To have NIM check on the usability of a SPOT named myspot, enter:

```
nim -o check myspot
```

To allocate resources to a diskless workstation with the name of syzygy and SPOT attribute value of spot1 ,enter:

```
nim -o allocate -a spot=spot1 syzygy
```

To deallocate an `lpp_source` named `images` from the standalone machine `client1`, enter:

```
nim -o deallocate -a lpp_source=images client1
```

To install the machine bluefish, using the resources `spot1`, `images1`, `bosinst_data1`, and `rconf1`, first allocate the resources by entering:

```
nim -o allocate -a spot=spot1 -a lpp_source=images1 \
-a bosinst_data=bosinst_data1 -a resolv_conf=rconf1 bluefish
```

Then, perform the BOS installation by entering:

```
nim -o bos_inst bluefish
```

To install a software product into a spot, `spot1`, such that the image for the installable option, `adt`, resides in the `lpp_source`, `images`, enter:

```
nim -o cust -a lpp_source=images -a filesets=adt spot1
```

To uninstall the software products `bos.INed` and `adt` from a spot, `spot1`, enter:

```
nim -o maint -a installp_flags="-u" -a filesets="bos.INed adt" spot1
```

To initialize the environment for a diskless workstation with the name of syzygy, using the resources spot1, root1, dump1, and paging1, first allocate the resources by entering:

```
nim -o allocate -a spot=spot1 -a root=root1 -a dump=dump1 \
-a paging=paging1 syzygy
```

Then initialize the resources for the client machine by entering:

```
nim -o dkls_init syzygy
```

To initialize the environment for a dataless workstation with the name of syzygy, using the resources spot1, root1, and dump1, first allocate the resources by entering:

```
nim -o allocate -a spot=spot1 -a root=root1 -a dump=dump1 syzygy
```

Then initialize the resources for the client machine by entering:

```
nim -o dtls_init syzygy
```

To list information about fixes installed on client Standalone1 for 20 APAR numbers, create the file /tmp/apar.list with one APAR number per line, as shown:

```
IX123435
IX54321
IX99999
...
```

then enter:

```
nim -o define -t fix_bundle -alocation=/tmp/apar.list \
   -aserver=master fix_bun
nim -o allocate -a fix_bundle=fix_bun Standalone1
nim -o fix_query Standalone1
```

To allocate all resources applicable to standalone machines from the NIM resource group res_grp1, to the machine mac1, enter:

```
nim -o allocate -a group=res_grp1 mac1
```

To install the machine bluefish while allocating the resources spot1, images1, bosinst_data1, and rconf1 automatically when the bos_inst operation starts, enter:

```
nim -o bos_inst -a spot=spot1 -a lpp_source=images1 \
-a bosinst_data=bosinst_data1 -a resolv_conf=rconf1 bluefish
```

To define default routes for the networks net1 and net2 that use default gateways gw1 and gw2 respectively, enter the following two commands:

```
nim -o change -a routing1="default gw1" net1
nim -o change -a routing1="default gw2" net2
```

To install the machine `catfish` with the contents of the `installp_bundle` `bundle1`, while allocating this resource and the `lpp_source` `images1` when the cust operation runs, enter:

```
nim -o cust -a installp_bundle=bundle1 -a lpp_source=images1 catfish
```

To define a machine group named DisklsMacs1 with members that are NIM diskless machines named `diskls1`, `diskls2`, and `diskls3`, enter:

```
nim -o define -t mac_group -a add_member=diskls1 \
-a add_member=diskls2 -a add_member=diskls3 DisklsMacs1
```

To initialize the group of diskless machines defined by the machine group `dtgrp1`, while allocating the required and optional resources defined by the resource group `dk_resgrp1`, when the `dkls_init` operation runs, enter:

```
nim -o dkls_init -a group=dtgrp1 dk_resgrp1
```

To exclude the member named `dataless1` from operations on the machine group `DatalsMacs1`, and then initialize the remaining members while allocating the dataless resources defined by the resource group named `DatalsRes1`, enter the following two commands:

```
nim -o select -a exclude=datals2 DatalsMacs1
nim -o dtls_init -a group=DatalsMacs1 DatalsRes1
```

To verify the file checksums for all packages beginning with the name `bos` on NIM targets in the group of standalone machines `macgrp1`, and displaying detailed error information and updating the software database to match the actual file checksum when inconsistencies are found, enter:

```
nim -o lppchk -a lppchk_flags='-c -m3 -u' -a filesets='bos*' macgrp1
```

Since the `lppchk` operation runs in the background on group members by default, to view the output from the `lppchk` operation enter:

```
nim -o showlog -a log_type=lppchk macgrp1
```

From the master, to uninstall the software products bos.INed and adt from a standalone machine, `stand1`, such that `installp_bundle`, `bundle2`, contains the names of the installable options, enter:

```
nim -o maint -a installp_flags="-u" -a installp_bundle=bundle2 stand1
```

To enable the NIM standalone client, `stand1`, to boot in maintenance mode, enter:

```
nim -o maint_boot stand1
```

To view the boot logs of the machines defined by the group DisklsMacs1, enter:

```
nim -o showlog -a log_type=boot DisklsMacs1
```

To list all problems fixed by software on the lpp_source lpp_source1, use:

```
nim -o showres -a instfix_flags="T" lpp_source1
```

To clone a rootvg on client austin to hdisk2, but only run phase1 and phase2 (leaving the /alt_inst file systems mounted), enter:

```
nim -o alt_disk_install -a source=rootvg -a disk='hdisk2'\
-a phase=12 austin
```

13.4 The showmount Command

The `showmount` command displays a list of all clients that have remotely mounted a file system from a specified machine in the `Host` parameter. This information is maintained by the mountd daemon on the `Host` parameter. This information is saved in the /etc/rmtab file in case the server abnormally terminates. The default value for the `Host` parameter is the value returned by the hostname command.

The `showmount` command syntax:

```
showmount [ -a ] [ -d ] [ -e ] [ Host ]
```

The Flags for the `showmount` command are described in Table 21.

Table 21. Flags for the showmount Command

Flag	Description
-a	Prints all remote mounts in the format *HostName:Directory*, in which *HostName* is the name of the client and *Directory* is a directory pathname that has been remotely mounted.
-d	Lists only directories that have been remotely mounted by clients.
-e	Prints the list of exported directories.

To check which filesystems are allowed to be exported type:

```
# lsfs
Name            Nodename   Mount Pt               VFS   Size     Options   Auto
Accounting
/dev/hd4        --         /                      jfs   24576    --        yes
no
/dev/hd1        --         /home                  jfs   360448   --        yes
no
/dev/hd2        --         /usr                   jfs   663552   --        yes
no
/dev/hd9var     --         /var                   jfs   401408   --        yes
no
/dev/hd3        --         /tmp                   jfs   65536    --        yes
no
/dev/lv00       --         /export/lpp_source     jfs   884736   rw        yes
no
/dev/lv01       --         /export/spot           jfs   442368   rw        yes
no
```

Run the `showmount` command to display a list of all clients that have remotely mounted a file system.

```
# showmount
raven.itsc.austin.ibm.com
```

Run `showmount -a` to see which directories have been remotely mounted with the host details.

```
# showmount -a
raven.itsc.austin.ibm.com:/export/spot/aix432spot/usr
```

The `showmount -d` command is similar to the `showmount -a` command except it does not show the host details.

```
# showmount -d
/export/spot/aix432spot/usr
```

The `showmount -e` command displays a list of exported directories:

```
# showmount -e
export list for aix4xdev:
/richfs           raven.itsc.austin.ibm.com
/export/redbooks (everyone)
```

The `showmount -e raven` command displays a list of exported directories on the remote host.

```
# showmount -e raven
export list for raven:
/elaine (everyone)
```

13.5 Quiz

1. Company ABC recently ordered 30 new model F50 systems, which they are custom installing with AIX 4.3.1 as branch office servers. The system administrator decided to use NIM to install the new servers with the base operating system and all of the applications the systems will need. The install type is spot, using a non /usr spot named 431spot. The installation of the first system is hanging at 611 LED, but all the filesystems appear to be properly exported from the NIM server. Which of the following commands will build debug boot images?

   A. `nim -o check -a debug=yes 431spot`

   B. `nimclient -o check -a debug=yes 431spot`

   C. `nim -o debug 431spot`

   D. `lsnim -a debug=yes 431spot`

2. Company ABC is migrating all of the plant servers from AIX 4.2.1 to AIX 4.3.1 using NIM. The 240 server in the customer services department is hanging during the install, and the LED is at 611, indicating a failure mounting a network file system from the NIM server. What can the system administrator do to determine which file system the NIM client is unable to mount.

   A. Unmount the NFS file systems exported from the server to the client.

   B. Put the tftp daemon on the server in debug mode.

   C. Restart the install using NIM debug boot images.

   D. Restart the NFS services on the NIM server.

13.5.1 Answers

1. A
2. C

13.6 Exercises

1. How do you debug a NIM install? Which command would you use?
2. Debug NIM error code 611.
3. Determine if the NIM spot and lpp_source are exported. What command would you use?

Chapter 14. The cron Daemon and crontab

The cron daemon runs shell commands at specified dates and times. The AIX cron daemon is similar to the System V Release 2 cron daemon. An entry in the /etc/inittab file starts the cron daemon at system initialization.

Regularly scheduled commands can be specified according to instructions contained in the crontab files. You can submit your crontab file with the `crontab` command. Use the `at` command to submit commands that are to be run only once. You can also use the `batch` command that is a shell script invoking the `at` command.

14.1 The at Command

The `at` command reads from standard input the names of commands to be run at a later time and allows you to specify when the commands should be run. The `at` command mails you all output from standard output and standard error for the scheduled commands, unless you redirect that output. It also writes the job number and the scheduled time to standard error.

Submit a job to be run at a later time using the format:

```
at -f filename -t CCYYMMDDhhmmSS Increment
```

where the values of the -t and -f flags are:

CC Specifies the first two digits of the year (the century). If this is not specified, the default value is 19 if the value of YY is between 70 and 99. The default value is 20 if the value of YY is between 00 and 37.

YY Specifies the second two digits of the year.

MM Specifies the month of the year (01 through 12).

DD Specifies the day of the month (01 through 31).

hh Specifies the hour of the day (00 through 23).

mm Specifies the minute of the hour (00 through 59).

SS Specifies the second of the minute (00 through 59). The default value is 00 is it is not specified.

filename Specifies the command file to be run at a later time.

The optional Increment parameter can be one of the following:

- A + (plus sign) followed by a number and one of the following words:

    - minute[s]
    - hour[s]
    - day[s]
    - week[s]
    - month[s]
    - year[s]
- The special word is followed by one of these words:
    - minute[s]
    - hour[s]
    - day[s]
    - week[s]
    - month[s]
    - year[s]

Instead of the -t flag, you can also use the following keywords:

- noon
- midnight
- now

Other flags and values can be found in the AIX product documentation.

14.1.1 Location of the Spool Area Directory for the at Command

The spool area directory for the `at` command is /var/spool/cron/atjobs. After a job is scheduled to run, a file exists in the /var/spool/cron/atjobs directory and the `atq` command shows:

```
# ls /var/spool/cron/atjobs
root.915213600.a
# atq
root.915213600.a        Fri Jan  1 12:00:00 CST 1999
```

After the job is deleted, the /var/spool/cron/atjobs directory is empty and the `atq` command no longer shows anything:

```
# at -r root.915213600.a
The root.915213600.a at file is deleted.
# ls /var/spool/cron/atjobs
# atq
```

14.2 Location of crontab Files

The crontab files are kept in the /var/spool/cron/crontabs directory. Each user has a crontab file with the user name as the file name in the /var/spool/cron/crontabs directory. The content of a sample /var/spool/cron/crontabs directory is shown in Figure 115:

```
# ls -l /var/spool/cron/crontabs
total 12
-rw-r--r--   1 adm      cron         2031 Sep 18 1997  adm
-rw-------   1 root     cron         1130 Nov 05 09:48 root
-rw-r--r--   1 sys      cron          864 Sep 18 1997  sys
-rw-r--r--   1 root     cron         1133 Jul 31 10:31 uucp
# █
```

Figure 115. Sample /var/spool/cron/crontabs Directory Content

A sample of the /var/spool/cron/crontabs/root file is shown in Figure 116 on page 302:

```
# crontab -l
# @(#)08        1.15.1.3  src/bos/usr/sbin/cron/root, cmdcntl, bos430, 9737A_430
 2/11/94 17:19:47
# IBM_PROLOG_BEGIN_TAG
# This is an automatically generated prolog.
#
# bos430 src/bos/usr/sbin/cron/root 1.15.1.3
#
# Licensed Materials - Property of IBM
#
# (C) COPYRIGHT International Business Machines Corp. 1989,1994
# All Rights Reserved
#
# US Government Users Restricted Rights - Use, duplication or
# disclosure restricted by GSA ADP Schedule Contract with IBM Corp.
#
# IBM_PROLOG_END_TAG
#
# COMPONENT_NAME: (CMDCNTL) commands needed for basic system needs
#
# FUNCTIONS:
#
# ORIGINS: 27
#
# (C) COPYRIGHT International Business Machines Corp. 1989,1994
# All Rights Reserved
# Licensed Materials - Property of IBM
#
# US Government Users Restricted Rights - Use, duplication or
# disclosure restricted by GSA ADP Schedule Contract with IBM Corp.
#
#0 3 * * * /usr/sbin/skulker
#45 2 * * 0 /usr/lib/spell/compress
#45 23 * * * ulimit 5000; /usr/lib/smdemon.cleanu > /dev/null
0 11 * * * /usr/bin/errclear -d S,O 30
0 12 * * * /usr/bin/errclear -d H 90
0 4 * * * /usr/bin/rmxcred -d 4 1>/dev/null 2>/dev/null
# █
```

Figure 116. A Sample /var/spool/cron/crontabs/root File

14.3 Verifying Job Runs

You can examine each file in the /var/spool/cron/crontabs directory to verify what cron jobs are scheduled to run at a certain time. Together with the `atq` command, you can determine whether some jobs need to be rescheduled to better utilize the system resources. Both the users root and deploy have scheduled a job to run using the `at` command as shown by the `atq` command in Figure 117 on page 303:

```
# atq
deploy.910389157.a      Fri Nov  6 15:52:37 CST 1998
root.910389186.a        Fri Nov  6 15:53:06 CST 1998
# ▌
```

Figure 117. Sample Output of the atq Command

14.4 Crontab File Record Format

A crontab file contains entries for each cron job. Entries are separated by newline characters. Each crontab file entry contains six fields separated by spaces or tabs in the following form:

```
minute  hour  day_of_month  month  weekday  command
```

These fields accept the following values:

minute	0 through 59
hour	0 through 23
day_of_month	1 through 31
month	1 through 12
weekday	0 through 6 for Sunday through Saturday
command	A shell command

You must specify a value for each field. Except for the command field, these fields can contain the following:

- A number in the specified range. To run a command in May, specify 5 in the month field.
- Two numbers separated by a dash to indicate an inclusive range. To run a cron job on Tuesday through Friday, place 2-5 in the weekday field.
- A list of numbers separated by commas. To run a command on the first and last day of January, you would specify 1,31 in the day_of_month field.
- An * (asterisk), meaning all allowed values. To run a job every hour, specify an asterisk in the hour field.

14.5 Scheduling Run

Consider the following script called program in the /appl directory:

```
#!/usr/bin/ksh
print program executed at 'date +%H:%M' >> /data/output
```

Some examples of the crontab entries for scheduling this /appl/program to run are shown in Table 22:

Table 22. Sample crontab Entries for Scheduling a Running of a Program

Program Run Time	crontab Entry
Every Tuesday at 02:00	`0 2 * * 2 /appl/program`
Every night at 02:00	`0 2 * * * /appl/program`
Every night at midnight	`0 0 * * * /appl/program`
On the 7th, 14th, and 21st day at 4:20 pm	`20 16 7,14,21 * * /appl/program`
Monday through Friday at 4:20 pm	`20 16 * * 1-5 /appl/program`
1st January, 1st July, and 1st December at 4:20 pm	`20 16 1 1,7,12 * /appl/program`

To schedule /appl/program to run every five minutes, you can either use the `crontab` command or the `at` command.

Technically, you can define all the values in the hour in five minute intervals starting at 0, 1, 2, 3, or 4, as one of the following crontab entries:

```
0,5,10,15,20,25,30,35,40,45,50,55 * * * * /appl/program
1,6,11,16,21,26,31,36,41,46,51,56 * * * * /appl/program
2,7,12,17,22,27,32,37,42,47,52,57 * * * * /appl/program
3,8,13,18,23,28,33,38,43,48,53,58 * * * * /appl/program
4,9,14,19,24,29,34,39,44,49,54,59 * * * * /appl/program
```

Alternatively, you can use the `at` command. For scheduling the /appl/program to run every five minutes, or some short intervals repeatedly, modify the /appl/program file by adding the `at` command as follows:

```
#!/usr/bin/ksh
at now + 5 minutes -f /appl/program > /dev/null 2>&1
print program executed at 'date +%H:%M' >> /data/output
```

Start the first job with the command:

```
at now -f appl/program > /dev/null 2>&1
```

When the /appl/program runs for the first time, it schedules the next run five minutes later. This process repeats itself until you stop it by entering the `atq` command to get the scheduled job name and then the `at -r` command to remove the scheduled job.

14.6 Allowing Users to Use the crontab Command

The /var/adm/cron/cron.allow and /var/adm/cron/cron.deny files control which users can use the `crontab` command. A root user can create, edit, or delete these files. Entries in these files are user login names with one name per line. A user cannot use the `crontab` command if one of the following is true:

- The cron.allow file and the cron.deny file do not exist (allows root user only).
- The cron.allow file exists, but the user's login name is not listed in it.
- The cron.deny file exists and the user's login name is listed in it.

If neither the cron.allow nor the cron.deny file exists, only someone with root user authority can submit a job with the `crontab` command.

The empty /var/adm/cron/cron.deny file has been deleted for security reasons. To allow the people in charge of application deployment to schedule applications to be run, a /var/adm/cron/cron.allow file is created as in Figure 118:

```
# cat > /var/adm/cron/cron.allow
root
deploy
# █
```

Figure 118. Creating the cron.allow File

There are also the /var/adm/cron/at.allow and /var/adm/cron/at.deny files that control which users can use the `at` command using the same rules as the /var/adm/cron/cron.allow and /var/adm/cron/cron.deny files.

14.7 Creating and Updating the Crontab File

The user deploy uses the `crontab -e` command to create and update the crontab file. The `crontab` command invokes the editor. If the EDITOR environment variable exists, the command invokes the editor it specifies. Otherwise, the `crontab` command uses the vi editor. On saving and exiting from the editor, a message indicating the change is sent to the cron daemon.

The content of the /var/spool/cron/crontabs directory and the content of the crontab file created by the user deploy is show in Figure 119 on page 306:

```
# ls -l /var/spool/cron/crontabs
total 13
-rw-r--r--   1 adm      cron        2031 Sep 18 1997  adm
-rw-------   1 root     cron          26 Nov 05 13:07 deploy
-rw-------   1 root     cron        1130 Nov 05 09:48 root
-rw-r--r--   1 sys      cron         864 Sep 18 1997  sys
-rw-r--r--   1 root     cron        1133 Jul 31 10:31 uucp
# cat /var/spool/cron/crontabs/deploy
30 13 * * * /appl/program
#
```

Figure 119. crontab Entry Created by the User Deploy

The user deploy is scheduling to run /appl/program at 1:30 p.m. everyday.

14.8 Verifying Job Schedules

As a general user without root authority, the user deploy is not authorized to list the content of the /var/spool/cron/crontabs/deploy file. However, the user can still verify his job schedules by using the `crontab -l` command as shown in Figure 120:

```
$ whoami
deploy
$ set -o vi
$ whoami
deploy
$ cat /var/spool/cron/crontabs/deploy
cat: 0652-050 Cannot open /var/spool/cron/crontabs/deploy.
$ crontab -l
30 13 * * * /appl/program
$
```

Figure 120. Using the crontab -l Command

14.9 Checking the Time of the Crontab File

Merely verifying the job schedule is not enough to prove that Cron will schedule the command to run at that time. If you have submitted your crontab file past the time the command is scheduled to run, nothing would have been scheduled. Use the `crontab -v` command to check the crontab submission time as shown in Figure 121 on page 307:

```
$ crontab -l
30 13 * * * /appl/program
$ crontab -v
Crontab file: deploy     Submission time: Thu Nov  5 13:07:50 CST 1998
$ date
Thu Nov  5 13:57:55 CST 1998
$ cat /data/output
program executed at 13:30
$ █
```

Figure 121. The crontab -v Command

The /appl/program is scheduled to run at 1:30 p.m. everyday. The crontab file is submitted at 1:07 p.m. The time now is 1:57 p.m. The command should have been scheduled to run. Checking the /data/output file confirms that the /appl/program has been run.

14.10 Removing the Crontab File

The responsibility for scheduling jobs to run is now moved from the application deployment group to the operations group. The user name deploy in the /var/adm/cron.allow file has been replaced by another user name from operations. The user deploy then removes the /var/spool/cron/crontabs/deploy file with the `crontab -r` command. The /var/spool/cron/crontabs/deploy is simply deleted without any message. Until the operations people create their crontab file, the content of the /var/spool/cron/crontabs directory is reverted back to the state as shown in Figure 115 on page 301.

Note

Avoid running `crontab -r` when you are logged in as root. It removes the /var/spool/cron/crontabs/root file. This file usually contains the scheduling of housekeeping jobs like diagnostics of hardware errors. You will have to restore the file from your backup.

14.11 Using Crontab to Append a User's Cron File

The operations group has been given a user name ops. They do not want to start from scratch for scheduling jobs. Instead, they just want to reschedule the time of run for the jobs that the application deployment people run. The application deployment group has actually saved up a backup copy of their crontab file as shown in Figure 122 on page 308:

```
$ crontab -l > deploy.schedule
$ cat deploy.schedule
30 13 * * * /appl/program
$ █
```

Figure 122. A Saved Copy of the crontab File

The operations people are given access to this deploy.schedule file. They can then create their crontab file using the `crontab file` command as shown in Figure 123:

```
$ whoami
ops
$ crontab -l
0481-103 Cannot open a file in the /var/spool/cron/crontabs directory.
A file or directory in the path name does not exist.
$ crontab ~deploy/deploy.schedule
$ crontab -l
30 13 * * * /appl/program
$ █
```

Figure 123. Creating the crontab File Using an Existing File

After that, they will use the `crontab -e` command to edit the time to schedule the command to be run at a different time.

14.12 References

The following publications contain more information about cron:

- *AIX Version 4.3 System Management Guide: Operating System and Devices*, SC23-4126
- *AIX Version 4.3 Commands Reference, Volume 1*, SC23-4115

14.13 Quiz

1. The system administrator of Company ABC needs to automatically run the script /usr/local/bin/system.backup every Sunday morning at 1:00am. What line should be added to the crontab of the root user to accomplish this task?

   A: 0 1 * * 0 /usr/local/bin/system.backup

   B. 1 0 * * 0 /usr/local/bin/system.backup

   C. 0 1 * * 1 /usr/local/bin/system.backup

   D. 1 0 * * 1 /usr/local/bin/system.backup

2. The system administrator at XYZ Company has noticed peaks in system activity occurring in the early evening on the development server. It is suspected that this activity is being caused by users scheduling jobs to be run via the `at` command. How can the system administrator find all jobs currently scheduled to run via the `at` command?

   A. `lsat -l`

   B. `at -l ALL`

   C. Browse the files in the /var/spool/at/atjobs directory

   D. Browse the files in the /var/spool/cron/atjobs directory

3. If a user runs the command `crontab /tmp/mycron`, what would be the result of this command?

   A. The user's crontab file would be replaced with the contents of /tmp/mycron.

   B. The entries contained in /tmp/mycron would be appended to the user's crontab file.

   C. The current contents of the user's crontab file would be written to the file /tmp/mycron.

   D. An error message would be generated. This is not valid syntax for the crontab.

14.13.1 Answers

1. A
2. D
3. A

14.14 Exercises

1. Add entries to crontab to run at specific times.
2. Reschedule jobs to run at a later time.
3. Check the existence of the crontab files and note their location.
4. Check the existence of the `at` jobs files.
5. Use various `crontab` command flags to list, edit, verify, and delete crontab entries.
6. Use various `at` command flags to schedule, report, and remove job.

Chapter 15. Editing and Viewing Files and Strings

In this chapter you will be given a basic overview of how to use the vi editor to edit ASCII files. You will also learn how to view a file using various commands and the differences between these commands.

15.1 The vi File Editor

The vi editor is a full-screen file editor that was developed from the ex editor. It is also common to all versions of UNIX. The `vedit` command starts a version of the vi editor intended for beginners. In the vedit editor, the report option is set to 1, the showmode option is set, and the novice option is set, making it a line editor.

15.1.1 vi Editor Limitations

The following list provides the maximum limits of the vi editor. These counts assume single-byte characters.

- {LINE_MAX} characters per line
- 256 characters per global command list
- 128 characters in the previously inserted and deleted text
- 128 characters in a shell escape command
- 128 characters in a string-valued option
- 30 characters in a tag name
- 128 map macros with 2048 characters total
- 1,048,560 lines of {LINE_MAX} characters per line silently enforced

Note

Running the vi editor on a file larger than 64 MB may cause the following error message to display:

```
0602-103 file too large to place in /tmp
```

15.1.2 vi Editing Modes

The vi editor operates in the following modes:

command mode When you start the vi editor, it is in command mode. You can enter any subcommand except those designated for use only in the text input mode. The vi editor returns to command mode when subcommands and other modes end. Press the **Esc** key to cancel a subcommand.

text-input mode You use the vi editor in this mode to add text. Enter text input mode with any of the following subcommands: `a`, `A`, `i`, `I`, `o`, `O`, `cx` (where the `x` represents the scope of the subcommand), `C`, `s`, `S`, and `R`. After entering one of these subcommands, you can enter text into the editing buffer. To return to command mode, press the **Esc** key for normal exit or press Interrupt (the Ctrl-C key sequence) to end abnormally.

last-line mode Subcommands with the prefix `:` (colon), `/` (slash), `?` (question mark), `!` (exclamation point), or `!!` (two exclamation points) read input on a line displayed at the bottom of the screen. When you enter the initial character, the vi editor places the cursor at the bottom of the screen, where you enter the remaining characters of the command. Press the **Enter** key to run the subcommand, or press Interrupt (the Ctrl-C key sequence) to cancel it. When the `!!` prefix is used, the cursor moves only after both exclamation points are entered. When you use the `:` prefix to enter the last-line mode, the vi editor gives special meaning to the following characters when they are used before commands that specify counts:

`%` All lines regardless of cursor position

`$` Last line

`.` Current line

15.1.3 The vi Command Flags

Table 23 shows the flags that can be used with the `vi` command.

Table 23. The vi Editor Flags

Flag	Flag Description
-c*Subcommand*	Carries out the `ex` editor subcommand before viewing with `vi` begins. The cursor moves to the line affected by the last subcommand to be carried out.
-l	Enters the vi editor in LISP mode. In this mode, the vi editor creates indents appropriate for LISP code, and the **(**, **)**, **{**, **}**, **[[**, and **]]** subcommands are modified to act appropriately for LISP.

Flag	Flag Description
-r*[File]*	Recovers a file after a vi editor or system malfunction. If you do not specify the File variable, the vi editor displays a list of all saved files.
-R	Sets the read-only option to protect the file against overwriting.
-t*Tag*	Edits the file containing the *Tag* variable and positions the vi editor at its definition. To use this flag, you must first create a database of function names and their locations using the `ctags` command.
-v	Enters the vi editor in the verbose mode.
-w*Number*	Sets the default window size to the value specified by the Number variable. This flag is useful when you use the vi editor over a low-speed line.
-y*Number*	Overrides the maximum line setting of 1,048,560 with any value greater than 1024. You should request twice the number of lines that you require because the vi editor uses the extra lines for buffer manipulation.
+*[Subcommand]*	Carries out the ex editor subcommand before editing begins. If you do not specify the Subcommand variable, the cursor is placed on the first line of the file. This + flag is incompatible with the -c flag. Do not specify both flags at the same time.

15.1.4 vi Editor Subcommands

The list of subcommands is very extensive, so you are only going to learn some of the more common subcommands used. You would use the subcommands to perform these kinds of actions:

- Moving the cursor
- Editing text
- Manipulating files
- Other actions

Enter the following subcommands in command mode. You can cancel an incomplete command by pressing the **Esc** key.

15.1.4.1 Moving the Cursor

Use subcommands to move the cursor within a file in these ways:

- Moving within a line

Left Arrow or **h** or **Ctrl-H**	Moves the cursor one character to the left.
Down Arrow or **j** or **Ctrl-J** or **Ctrl-N**	Moves the cursor down one line (it remains in the same column).
Up Arrow or **k** or **Ctrl-P**	Moves the cursor up one line (it remains in the same column).
Right Arrow or **l**	Moves the cursor one character to the right.

- Moving within a line by character position

^	Moves the cursor to the first nonblank character.
0	Moves the cursor to the beginning of the line.
$	Moves the cursor to the end of the line.
fx	Moves the cursor to the next x character.
Fx	Moves the cursor to the last x character.
tx	Moves the cursor to one column before the next x character.
Tx	Moves the cursor to one column after the last x character.
;	Repeats the last f, F, t, or T subcommand.
,	Repeats the last f, F, t, or T subcommand in the opposite direction.

- Moving to words

w	Moves the cursor to the next small word.
b	Moves the cursor to the previous small word.
e	Moves the cursor to the next end of a small word.
W	Moves the cursor to the next big word.
B	Moves the cursor to the previous big word.
E	Moves the cursor to the next end of a big word.

- Moving by line position

H	Moves the cursor to the top line on the screen.
L	Moves the cursor to the last line on the screen.
M	Moves the cursor to the middle line on the screen.
+	Moves the cursor to the next line at its first nonblank character.

- **-** Moves the cursor to the previous line at its first nonblank character.
- **Enter** Moves the cursor to the next line at its first nonblank character.

- Moving to sentences, paragraphs, or sections

  - **(** Places the cursor at the beginning of the previous sentence.
  - **)** Places the cursor at the beginning of the next sentence.
  - **{** Places the cursor at the beginning of the previous paragraph.
  - **}** Places the cursor at the beginning of the next paragraph, or at the next section if you are in C mode.
  - **]]** Places the cursor at the next section.
  - **[[** Places the cursor at the previous section.

15.1.4.2 Editing Text

The subcommands for editing enable you to perform the following tasks:

- Marking a specific location in a file and returning

  - **"** Moves the cursor to the previous location of the current line.
  - **"** Moves the cursor to the beginning of the line containing the previous location of the current line.
  - **mx** Marks the current position with the letter specified by the x parameter.
  - **‘x** Moves the cursor to the mark specified by the x parameter.
  - **’x** Moves the cursor to the beginning of the line containing the mark specified by the x parameter.

- Adding text to a file

  - **a*Text*** Inserts text specified by the *Text* parameter after the cursor. End text input mode by pressing the **Esc** key.
  - **A*Text*** Adds text specified by the *Text* parameter to the end of the line. End text input mode by pressing the **Esc** key.
  - **i*Text*** Inserts text specified by the *Text* parameter before the cursor. End text input mode by pressing the **Esc** key.
  - **I*Text*** Inserts text specified by the *Text* parameter before the first non-blank character in the line. End text input mode by pressing the **Esc** key.

o Adds an empty line below the current line. End text input mode by pressing the **Esc** key.

O Adds an empty line above the current line. End text input mode by pressing the **Esc** key.

- Changing text while in input mode

Ctrl-D Goes back to previous autoindent stop.

^ Ctrl-D Ends autoindent for this line only.

0Ctrl-D Moves cursor back to left margin.

Esc Ends insertion and returns to command state.

Ctrl-H Erases the last character.

Ctrl-Q Enters any character if xon is disabled.

Ctrl-V Enters any character.

Ctrl-W Erases the last small word.

\ Quotes the erase and kill characters.

Ctrl-? Interrupts and ends insert or the Ctrl-D key sequence.

- Changing text from command mode

C Changes the rest of the line (same as c$).

cc Changes a line.

cw Changes a word.

cw*Text* Changes a word to the text specified by the Text parameter.

D Deletes the rest of the line (same as d$).

dd Deletes a line.

dw Deletes a word.

J Joins lines.

rx Replaces the current character with the character specified by x.

R*Text* Overwrites characters with the text specified by the Text parameter.

s Substitutes characters (same as **cl**).

S Substitutes lines (same as **cc**).

u Undoes the previous change.

x Deletes a character at the cursor.

X Deletes a character before the cursor (same as **dh**).

<< Shifts one line to the left.

<L Shifts all lines from the cursor to the end of the screen to the left.

>> Shifts one line to the right.

>L Shifts all lines from the cursor to the end of the screen to the right.

~ Changes letter at the cursor to the opposite case.

- Copying and moving text

p Puts back text from the undo buffer after the cursor.

P Puts back text from the undo buffer before the cursor.

"xp Puts back text from the x buffer.

"xd Deletes text into the x buffer.

y Places the object that follows (for example, w for word) into the undo buffer.

"xy Places the object that follows into the x buffer, where x is any letter.

Y Places the line in the undo buffer.

- Restoring and repeating changes

u Undoes the last change.

> **Note**
>
> After an undo, the cursor moves to the first non-blank character on the updated current line.

U Restores the current line if the cursor has not left the line since the last change.

. Repeats the last change or increments the `"np` command.

Notes

1. This subcommand will repeat the last change, including an undo. Therefore, after an undo, repeat performs an undo rather than repeat the last change.
2. This subcommand is not meant for use with a macro. Enter `@@` (two at signs) to repeat a macro.

"*n*p Retrieves the nth last delete of a complete line or block of lines.

15.1.4.3 Manipulating Files

The subcommands for manipulating files allow you to do the tasks outlined in the following sections:

- Saving changes to a file

  :w Writes the edit buffer contents to the original file.

  :w *File* Writes the edit buffer contents to the file specified by the File parameter.

  :w! *File* Overwrites the file specified by the File parameter with the edit buffer contents.

- Editing a second file

  :e *File* Edits the specified file.

  :e! Re-edits the current file and discards all changes.

  :e + *File* Edits the specified file starting at the end.

  :e + *Number File* Edits the specified file starting at the specified line number.

  :e # Edits the alternate file. The alternate file is usually the previous file name before accessing another file with a `:e` command. However, if changes are pending on the current file when a new file is called, the new file becomes the alternate file. This subcommand is the same as the `Ctrl-A` subcommand.

  :r *File* Reads the file into the editing buffer by adding new lines below the current line.

  :r !*Command* Runs the specified AIX command and places its output into the file by adding new lines below the current cursor position.

:ta *Tag* Edits a file containing the Tag tag starting at the location of the tag. To use this subcommand, you must first create a database of function names and their locations using the `ctags` command.

Ctrl-A Edits the alternate file. The alternate file is usually the previous current file name. However, if changes are pending on the current file when a new file is called, the new file becomes the alternate file. This subcommand is the same as the `:e #` subcommand.

- Editing a list of files

  :n Edits the next file in the list entered on the command line.

  :n *Files* Specifies a new list of files to edit.

- Finding file information

  Ctrl-G Shows the current file name, current line number, number of lines in the file, and percentage of the way through the file where the cursor is located.

15.1.4.4 Other Actions

The vi editor provides the subcommands described in the following sections:

- Adjusting the screen

  Ctrl-L Clears and redraws the screen.

  Ctrl-R Redraws the screen and eliminates blank lines marked with @ (at sign).

  z*Number* Makes the window the specified number of lines long.

- Entering shell commands

  :sh Enters the shell to allow you to run more than one AIX command. You can return to the vi editor by pressing the **Ctrl-D** key sequence.

  :!*Command* Runs the specified AIX command and then returns to the vi editor.

Note

The **#** (alternate file), **%** (current file), and **!** (previous command) special characters are expanded when following a **:!** subcommand. To prevent any of these characters from being expanded, use the \ (backslash).

:!! Repeats the last **:!*Command*** subcommand.

Number*!!*Command Runs the specified AIX command and replaces the lines specified by Number with the output of the command. If a number is not specified, the default value is 1. If the command expects standard input, the specified lines are used as input.

!***Object Command*** Runs the specified AIX command and replaces the object specified by the Object parameter with the output of the command. If the command expects standard input, the specified object is used as input.

- Interrupting and ending the vi editor

Q Enters the ex editor in command mode

ZZ Exits the vi editor, saving changes.

:q Quits the vi editor. If you have changed the contents of the editing buffer, the vi editor displays a warning message and does not quit.

:q! Quits the vi editor, discarding the editing buffer.

Esc Ends text input or ends an incomplete subcommand.

Ctrl-? Interrupts a subcommand.

15.1.4.5 Other Actions

To set the vi editor up as your default editor, use the `EDITOR` command. The `EDITOR` variable can also be put into the user .profile or the /etc/profile file.

```
# EDITOR=vi
```

Note

The `EDITOR` command sets a variable and must not be confused with the `set -o vi` command that sets up command line editing.

15.2 Editing a File Using the vi Editor

In this section you will learn how to edit a file. You will learn how to replace multiple characters, replace one character, delete a character, delete a line, copy a line, find a word, insert characters, and insert a line.

In this example you have a file called *yourfile.* In this file you are running a few simple commands and sending the output for each to your screen.

The *yourfile* file looks like this:

```
#
# $HOME/yourfile
#
# This file contains some commands that are run by the user.
df
lsfs rootvg
lslv hdisk1
lsdev -Cc disk
```

15.2.1 Inserting Text Using the vi Editor

As you look at the file above you see that you want the `df` command to display the filesystem space in 1024 KB blocks, not 512. You also want the script to list what is in the current directory at the end of the script. To edit the file enter:

```
vi yourfile
```

Figure 124 is the display for the vi editor.

```
#
# $HOME/UserFile
#
# This file contains some commands that are run by the user.
df
lsfs rootvg
lspv hdisk1
lsdev -Cc disk
~
~
~
~
~
~
~
~
~
~
~
~
~
~
~
"yourfile" 8 lines, 124 characters
```

Figure 124. Image of yourfile after vi Command Was Run

You will note that the cursor is at the top left of the screen under the first character. Move your cursor down five lines to under the df using one of the following keys - **Down Arrow** or **j** or **Ctrl-J** or **Ctrl-N**. There are now two options for you to add the -k flag to the `df` command.

Option 1

Go to the end of the text using Shift-A, which appends to the end of the line. You will notice that your cursor is to the right of the `f`, press the **Space Bar** and insert the `-k`.

Option 2

Go to the end of the line using one of the following keys - **Right Arrow** or **l** or **$**. Your cursor will now be under the `f`, press the **a** key, your cursor will move one space to the right, press the Space key and then insert the `-k`.

Your line will look like this,

```
df -k
```

Press the **Esc** key twice; you will hear a single beep. You have now moved out of edit mode back into command mode. Your cursor will be under the `k`.

Now add the `ls -l` of the current directory at the end of the file. Using any one of the **Down Arrow** or **j** or **Ctrl-J** or **Ctrl-N** keys, go to the bottom of the file, the cursor will be under the `v` in the `lsdev` command, either use the **Left Arrow** or **h** or **Ctrl-H** or **0** keys to move to the beginning of the line. Your cursor should be under the `l` of the `lsdev` command. To insert a new line below the current line press **o**, you will see the cursor under the `l` of the `lsdev` command but one line down, type the following:

```
s -l
```

Press **Esc** twice to go back into command mode. You will notice that this command is incorrect. What you need to do is insert the `l` for the `ls -l` command, press **0** to take you to the beginning of the line, your cursor is under the `s`, press the **i** key then type:

```
l
```

Press **Esc** twice to go back to command line. Your line should look like this:

```
ls -l
```

To save the file there are two options to save and quit.

Option 1

Hold the **Shift** and **;** (**:**), the cursor will go to the bottom left of the screen next to a `:`. At the `:` you can type `wq!`, which overwrites the original file and then quits.

Option 2

Hold the **Shift** and press **z** twice (**ZZ**). This will save and quit, taking you back to your AIX command prompt.

To view the file type:

```
# cat yourfile
```

The output of the `cat` command is as follows:

```
#
# $HOME/yourfile
#
# This file contains some commands that are run by the user.
df -k
lsfs rootvg
lspv hdisk1
lsdev -Cc disk
ls -l
```

15.2.2 Changing Text Using the vi Editor

On closer inspection of the file *yourfile* you notice that there are a few mistakes, and you now want to correct them. To correct them type:

```
vi yourfile
```

You will see the cursor at the top right side of your monitor.

The first thing you want to do is fix the `lsfs` command, you do not want it to be `lsfs` because it should be the `lsvg` command. You also want to check the volume group `uservg` not `rootvg`.

Press any of the **Down Arrow**, **j**, **Ctrl-J**, or **Ctrl-N** keys until you are under the `l` of the `lsfs` command.

You can also use the find option. Press the / key, it will take you to the bottom right of the screen and you will see a / before the cursor, here you can type `lsfs` and it will take you to the beginning of the `lsfs` command.

Using the **Right Arrow** or **l** key move the cursor below the `f` of the `lsfs` command. Press the **Shift** key and **r** (**R**) simultaneously. The cursor will still be under the `f` of the `lsfs` command. Type `vg`; you will see that it has overwritten the `fs` with `vg`. Press **Esc** twice to go back into command mode. Your cursor is now under the `g` in the `lsvg` command.

Using the Right Arrow move the cursor to underneath the `r` of `rootvg`. Type `cw`, and you will see a `$` sign at the end of the word `rootvg`. Type `uservg`; you will notice that it has overwritten `rootvg`. Press **Esc** twice and your cursor will be under the `g` of `uservg`.

Issue the command `lspv` on both `hdisk1` and `hdisk0`. Press **Down Arrow** once to go down one line. You will notice that your cursor is under the `1` of `hdisk1`. Press your **y** key twice (**yy**), you have just yanked or copied the line. Press **p** key to place your yanked line and you will see that the line has been duplicated.Notice that your cursor is at the beginning of the new line. Your file should look like this:

```
lspv hdisk1
lspv hdisk1
```

Using the Right Arrow key move your cursor until it is under the `1` of the second `hdisk1`. Use your Up Arrow key to go up to the first `hdisk1`. Press the `r` key and then the `0`. You will notice that the `1` has changed to a `0`. You do not need to press the **Esc** key since this is a single character replacement. Your lines should now look like this:

```
lspv hdisk0
lspv hdisk1
```

Looking at the line with the `lsdev -Cc disk` command, you decide that you want this command to display all the devices, not just the disks. Using the Down Arrow go to the line with the `lsdev` command. Using the Right Arrow key put the cursor under the `c`, press the **x** and you will see the `c` disappear. Use the Right Arrow to go under the `d` of the word `disk`. Press the **d** key twice (**dd**), you will notice the whole line has disappeared. Press the **u** key once and you will notice that the line has come back. Now press the **d** key, then the **w** key. The word disk has now disappeared. Press **Esc** twice. Your line will now look like this:

```
lsdev -C
```

Press the **Shift zz** (**ZZ**) to save and exit.

Type the command:

```
cat yourfile
```

to display your file. It should appear like this:

```
#
# $HOME/yourfile
#
# This file contains some commands that are run by the user.
```

```
df -k
lsvg uservg
lspv hdisk1
lspv hdisk0
lsdev -C
ls -l
```

To replace multiple occurrences of text you can use the `s` subcommand. In the above example if you wanted to change the `lspv` commands to have the `-p` flag, edit the file using vi and then change the command using a subcommand as follows:

```
vi yourfile
```

The cursor will be at the top left hand side. Type `Shift` and ; (:), the cursor will go into the command line editor at the bottom left. To edit type:

```
%s/lspv/lspv -p
```

This will replace all `lspv` commands to `lspv -p`. Save the file and exit.

Type the command:

```
cat yourfile
```

to display your file. It should appear like this:

```
#
# $HOME/yourfile
#
# This file contains some commands that are run by the user.
df -k
lsvg uservg
lspv -p hdisk1
lspv -p hdisk0
lsdev -C
ls -l
```

15.3 Viewing Files and String Settings

The `cat` command is used to view an ASCII file and there are various commands available. The `cat` command concatenates or displays files. The `cat` command reads each file parameter in sequence and writes it to standard output. If you do not specify a file name, the `cat` command reads from standard input. You can also specify a file name of - (dash) for standard input.

Note

Do not redirect output to one of the input files using the redirection symbol, > (caret). If you do this, you lose the original data in the input file because the shell truncates the file before the `cat` command can read it.

The `cat` command syntax is as follows:

```
cat [ -q ] [ -r ] [ -s ] [ -S ] [ -u ] [ -n [ -b ] ] [ -v [ -e ] [ -t ] ] [
- | File ... ]
```

Table 24 provides the flags that can be used with the `cat` command.

Table 24. The cat Command Flags and Flag Descriptions

Flag	Flag Description
-b	Omits line numbers from blank lines, when specified with the -n flag.
-e	Displays a $ (dollar sign) at the end of each line, when specified with the -v flag.
-n	Displays output lines preceded by line numbers, numbered sequentially from 1.
-q	Does not display a message if the `cat` command cannot find an input file. This flag is identical to the -s flag.
-r	Replaces multiple consecutive empty lines with one empty line. This flag is identical to the -S flag.
-s	Does not display a message if the cat command cannot find an input file. This flag is identical to the -q flag.
-S	Replaces multiple consecutive empty lines with one empty line. This flag is identical to the -r flag.
-t	Displays tab characters as ^I if specified with the -v flag.
-u	Does not buffer output.
-v	Displays non-printing characters as visible characters.
-	Allows standard input to the `cat` command.

Examples using the `cat` command are listed in the following:

- To display a file at the workstation, enter:

  `cat /etc/hosts`

This command displays the data in the `/etc/hosts` file. If the file is more than one less than the number of available display lines, some of the file scrolls off the screen. To list a file one page at a time, use the `pg` command.

```
# @(#)47        1.1  src/bos/usr/sbin/netstart/hosts, cmdnet, bos430,
9737A_430
7/24/91 10:00:46
# IBM_PROLOG_BEGIN_TAG
.......... (Lines Removed)
#  /etc/hosts
#
# This file contains the hostnames and their address for hosts in the
# network.  This file is used to resolve a hostname into an Internet
# address.
#
# At minimum, this file must contain the name and address for each
# device defined for TCP in your /etc/net file. It may also contain
# entries for well-known (reserved) names such as timeserver
# and printserver as well as any other host name and address.
#
# The format of this file is:
# Internet Address      Hostname        # Comments
# Items are separated by any number of blanks and/or tabs. A '#'
# indicates the beginning of a comment; characters up to the end of the
# line are not interpreted by routines which search this file. Blank
# lines are allowed.

# Internet Address  Hostname          # Comments
# 192.9.200.1       net0sample        # ethernet name/address
# 128.100.0.1       token0sample      # token ring name/address
# 10.2.0.2          x25sample         # x.25 name/address
127.0.0.1     loopback localhost # loopback (lo0)
19.33.1.12       yourhost yourhost.hometown.com
#
```

- To concatenate several files, enter:

  ```
  cat /etc/passwd /etc/hosts > yourfile
  ```

  This command creates a file named `yourfile` that is a copy of `/etc/passwd` followed by `/etc/hosts`.

- To suppress error messages about files that do not exist, enter:

  ```
  cat -q /etc/password
  ```

  If you don't use the `-q` option you would get this error:

  ```
  cat: 0652-050 Cannot open /etc/password.
  ```

- To append one file to the end of another, enter:

  ```
  cat /etc/filesystems >> yourfile
  ```

  The >> (two carets) appends a copy of the file /etc/filesystems to the end of the file yourfile. If you want to replace the file, use the > (caret).

- To add text to the end of a file, enter:

  ```
  # cat >>yourfile
  Create new user bob.
  Ctrl-D
  ```

  This command adds Create new user bob to the end of the file called yourfile. The cat command does not prompt; it waits for you to enter text. Press the **Ctrl-D** key sequence to indicate you are finished.

- To concatenate several files with text entered from the keyboard, enter:

  ```
  # cat /etc/passwd - /etc/hosts >yourfile
  THIS IS THE SEPARATOR LINE
  Ctrl-D
  ```

  This command concatenates /etc/passwd, text from the keyboard - THIS IS THE SEPARATOR LINE (indicated by the minus sign), and /etc/hosts.

- To concatenate several files with output from another command, enter:

  ```
  ls | cat /etc/passwd - >yournewfile
  ```

  This command copies /etc/passwd, and then the output of the ls command to the file yournewfile.

15.3.1 Using the pg Command to View Files

Formats files to the display. The pg command reads a file name from the file parameter and writes the file to standard output one screen at a time. If you specify a - (dash) as the file parameter, or run the pg command without options, the pg command reads standard input. Each screen is followed by a prompt. If you press the Enter key, another page is displayed. Subcommands used with the pg command let you review or search in the file.

To determine workstation attributes, the pg command scans the file for the workstation type specified by the TERM environment variable. The default type is dumb.

The pg command syntax

```
pg [ -Number ] [ -c ] [ -e ] [ -f ] [ -n ] [ -p String ] [ -s ] [ +LineNumber
] [ +/Pattern/ ] [ File ... ]
```

Table 25 provides the flags that can be used with the `pg` command.

Table 25. The pg Command Flags and Flag Descriptions

Flag	Flag Description
-c	Moves the cursor to the home position and clears the screen before each page. This flag is ignored if the clear_screen field is not defined for your workstation type in the terminfo file.
-e	Does not pause at the end of each file.
-f	Does not split lines. Normally, the `pg` command splits lines longer than the screen width.
-n	Stops processing when a `pg` command letter is entered. Normally, commands must end with a new-line character.
-p *String*	Uses the specified string as the prompt. If the String contains a *%d* value, that value is replaced by the current page number in the prompt. The default prompt is : (colon). If the specified string contains spaces, you must enclose the string in quotation marks.
-s	Highlights all messages and prompts.
+*LineNumber*	Starts at the specified line number.
-*Number*	Specifies the number of lines in the window. On workstations that contain 24 lines, the default is 23.
+/*Pattern*/	Starts at the first line that contains the specified pattern.

When the `pg` command pauses and issues a prompt, you can issue a subcommand. Some of these subcommands change the display to a particular place in the file, some search for specific patterns in the text, and others change the environment in which the `pg` command works.

Table 26 provides a list of the subcommands for the `pg` command.

Table 26. pg Subcommands

Subcommand	Subcommand Description
The following subcommands display a selected place in the file:	
Page	Displays the page specified by the Page parameter.
+Number	Displays the page obtained by adding the Number value to the current page.
-Number	Displays the page as specified by the Number value before the current page.

Subcommand	Subcommand Description
The following subcommands display a selected place in the file:	
l	(Lowercase L) Scrolls the display one line forward.
Numberl	Displays at the top of the screen the line specified by the Number parameter.
+Numberl	Scrolls the display forward for the specified number of lines.
-Numberl	Scrolls the display backward for the specified number of lines.
d	Scrolls half a screen forward. Pressing the **Ctrl-D** key sequence functions the same as the **d** subcommand.
-d	Scrolls half a screen backward. Pressing the **-Ctrl-D** key sequence functions the same as the **-d** subcommand.
Ctrl-L	Displays the current page again. A single **.** (dot) functions the same as the **Ctrl-L** key sequence subcommand.
$	Displays the last page in the file. Do not use this when the input is from a pipeline.
The following subcommands search for text patterns in the text.	
[*Number*]*/Pattern/*	Searches for the occurrence of the *Pattern* value as specified by the *Number* variable. The search begins immediately after the current page and continues to the end of the current file, without wraparound. The default for the *Number* variable is 1.
Number?Pattern? *Number^Pattern^*	Searches backward for the occurrence of the *Pattern* value as specified by the *Number* variable. The searching begins immediately before the current page and continues to the beginning of the current file, without wraparound. The default for the *Number* variable is 1.
You can change the `pg` ***command environment with the following subcommands:***	
[*Number*]n	Begins examining the next file in the command line, as specified by the *Number* variable. The default for the *Number* variable is first.
[*Number*]p	Begins examining the previous file on the command line, as specified by the Number variable. The default for the ***Number*** variable is first.

Subcommand	Subcommand Description
The following subcommands display a selected place in the file:	
[*Number*]w	Displays another window of text. If the *Number* variable is specified, it sets the window size to the number of lines it specifies. This subcommand is the same as the [Number]z subcommand.
[*Number*]z	Displays another window of text. If the Number variable is specified, sets the window size to the number of lines it specifies. This subcommand is the same as the [Number]w subcommand.
s *File*	Saves the input in the specified file. Only the current file being examined is saved. This command must always end with a new-line character, even if you specify the -n flag.
h	Displays an abbreviated summary of available subcommands.
q or Q	Quits the `pg` command.
!*Command*	Sends the specified command to the shell named in the SHELL environment variable. If this is not available, the default shell is used. This command must always end with a new-line character, even if the -n flag is used.

Examples using the `pg` command are provided in the following:

- To look at the contents of a file one page at a time, enter:

```
# pg /etc/hosts
# @(#)47        1.1  src/bos/usr/sbin/netstart/hosts, cmdnet, bos430,
9737A_430
7/24/91 10:00:46
# IBM_PROLOG_BEGIN_TAG
.......... ( Lines Removed )
#  /etc/hosts
#
# This file contains the hostnames and their address for hosts in the
# indicates the beginning of a comment; characters up to the end of the
# line are not interpreted by routines which search this file. Blank
# lines are allowed.
.......... ( Lines Removed )
# Internet Address      Hostname        # Comments
# 192.9.200.1           net0sample      # ethernet name/address
# 128.100.0.1           token0sample    # token ring name/address
# 10.2.0.2              x25sample       # x.25 name/address
```

```
127.0.0.1                loopback localhost       # loopback (lo0)
name/address
(EOF):
```

This is the end of the file. Press **Enter** to go back to the command prompt.

- To view the contents of a file with all messages and prompts highlighted, enter:

  # pg -s /etc/hosts

  Figure 125 shows the output of the `pg -s` command. Notice the prompt (:) at the bottom of the screen has been highlighted.

```
# @(#)47        1.1  src/bos/usr/sbin/netstart/hosts, cmdnet, bos430, 9737A_430
7/24/91 10:00:46
# IBM_PROLOG_BEGIN_TAG
# This is an automatically generated prolog.
#
# bos430 src/bos/usr/sbin/netstart/hosts 1.1
#
# Licensed Materials - Property of IBM
#
# (C) COPYRIGHT International Business Machines Corp. 1985,1989
# All Rights Reserved
#
# US Government Users Restricted Rights - Use, duplication or
# disclosure restricted by GSA ADP Schedule Contract with IBM Corp.
#
# IBM_PROLOG_END_TAG
#
# COMPONENT_NAME: TCPIP hosts
#
# FUNCTIONS: loopback
#
# ORIGINS: 26  27
#
# (C) COPYRIGHT International Business Machines Corp. 1985, 1989
:
```

Figure 125. The pg -s Command with Highlighted Prompt

15.3.2 Using the view Command to View Files

The `view` command starts the vi full-screen editor in read-only mode. The read-only mode is only advisory to prevent accidental changes to the file.

The `view` command syntax is as follows:

```
view [ -cSubcommand ] [ -l ] [ -t Tag ] [ -wNumber ] [ -y ] [ -r [ File ] ]
[ + [ Subcommand ] ] [ File ... ]
```

Table 27 provides a list of the flags for the `view` command.

Table 27. Table of Flags for the view Command

Flag	Flag Description
-c*Subcommand*	Carries out the ex editor subcommand before viewing with vi begins. When a null operand is entered, as in -c '' , the editor places the cursor on the last line of the file.
-l	Enters a version of the vi editor with specialized features designed for writing programs in the LISP language. In this mode, the vi editor indents appropriately for LISP programming, and the (,), {, }, [[, and]] subcommands are modified to act appropriately for LISP.
-r [*File*]	Recovers a file after an editor or system crash. If you do not specify a File parameter, the editor displays a list of all saved files.
-t*Tag*	Edits the file containing the tag specified by the Tag parameter and positions the editor at its definition. To use this flag, you must first create a database of function names and their locations using the `ctags` command.
-w*Number*	Sets the default window size to the value specified by the Number parameter. This is useful when your terminal communicates with the system running the editor over a slow communications line.
-y	Overrides the maximum line setting of 1,048,560 with any value greater than 1024.
+[*Subcommand*]	Carries out the ex editor subcommand specified by the Subcommand parameter before viewing with vi begins. If you do not specify a subcommand, the cursor is placed on the last line of the file.

Check 15.1, "The vi File Editor" on page 311 to understand the vi editor.

15.3.3 Using the echo Command

The `echo` command writes character strings to standard output. *Strings* are separated by spaces, and a new-line character follows the last *String* parameter specified.

The `echo` command syntax is as follows:

```
echo [ String ... ]
```

The echo command recognizes the escape conventions as shown in Table 28:

Table 28. Escape Conventions Used with the echo Command

Escape Convention	Escape Convention Description
\a	Displays an alert character.
\b	Displays a backspace character.
\c	Suppresses the new-line character that otherwise follows the final argument in the output. All characters following the \c sequence are ignored.
\f	Displays a form-feed character.
\n	Displays a new-line character.
\r	Displays a carriage return character.
\t	Displays a tab character.
\v	Displays a vertical tab character.
\\	Displays a backslash character.
\0*Number*	Displays an 8-bit character whose ASCII value is a 0-, 1-, 2-, or 3-digit octal number.

Examples using the echo command are provided in the following:

- To write a message to standard output, enter:

```
# echo Please read your MAIL
Please read your MAIL
#
```

- To display a message containing special characters, enter:

```
echo "\n\n\nGone to lunch.\nWill be back at 2:00.
```

  This skips three lines and displays the message:

```
Gone to lunch.
Will be back at 2:00.
```

> **Note**
>
> You must put the message in " (quotation marks) if it contains escape sequences. Otherwise, the shell interprets the \ (backslash) as a metacharacter and treats the \ differently.

- To use the echo command with pattern-matching characters, enter:

```
echo The back-up files are: *.bak
```

This usage displays the message `The back-up files are:` followed by the file names in the current directory ending with `.bak`.

- To add a single line of text to a file, enter:

```
echo Remember to set the shell search path to $PATH. >>notes
```

This usage adds the message to the end of the file notes after the shell substitutes the value of the PATH shell variable.

- To write a message to the standard error output, enter:

```
echo Error: file already exists. >&2
```

This command redirects the error message to standard error. If the `>&2` is omitted, the message is written to standard output.

15.3.4 Using the file Command to Determine a File Type

The `file` command reads the files specified by the *File* parameter or the *FileList* variable, performs a series of tests on each file, and attempts to classify them by type. The command then writes the file types to standard output.

If a file appears to be in ASCII format, the `file` command examines the first 1024 bytes and determines the file type. If a file does not appear to be in ASCII format, the `file` command further attempts to distinguish a binary data file from a text file that contains extended characters.

If the *File* parameter specifies an executable or object module file and the version number is greater than 0, the `file` command displays the version stamp.

To classify the file type, use the following command syntax:

```
file [-m MagicFile] [-f FileList] [File...]
```

To check the magic file for Format Errors, use the following command syntax:

```
file-c [-m MagicFile]
```

Table 29 provides the flags that can be used by the `file` command.

Table 29. The file Command Flags and Flag Descriptions

Flag	Flag Description
-c	Checks the specified magic file (the /etc/magic file, by default) for format errors. This validation is not normally done. File typing is not done under this flag.

Flag	Flag Description
-f *FileList*	Reads the specified file list. The file must list one file per line and must not contain leading or trailing spaces.
-m *MagicFile*	Specifies the file name of the magic file (the /etc/magic file, by default).

Examples using the `file` command are provided in the following:

- To display the type of information a file contains, enter:

```
# file /etc/hosts
/etc/hosts:     commands text
```

  This displays the file type of myfile (such as directory, data, ASCII text, C-program source, and archive).

- Create a file called `filenames`, in this file put three entries, **/etc/hosts**, **/etc/wall** and **/usr/sbin/wall**. To display the type of each file named in a list of file names, enter:

```
# cat filenames
/etc/hosts
/etc/wall
/usr/sbin/wall
# file -f filenames
/etc/hosts:     commands text
/etc/wall:      symbolic link to /usr/sbin/wall.
/usr/sbin/wall: executable (RISC System/6000) or object module
```

  This displays the type of each file named in the `filenames` list. Each file name must appear alone on a line.

15.3.5 Using the strings Command in Object or Binary Files

The `strings` command looks for printable strings in an object or binary file. A string is any sequence of 4 or more printable characters that end with a new-line or a null character. The strings command is useful for identifying random object files.

The `strings` command syntax is as follows:

```
strings [ -a ] [ - ] [ -o ] [ -t Format ] [ -n Number ] [ -Number ] [ File
... ]
```

Table 30 provides the flags that can be used with the `strings` command.

Table 30. The strings Command Flags and Flag Descriptions

Flag	Flag Description
-a	Searches the entire file, not just the data section, for printable strings.
-	Searches the entire file, not just the data section, for printable strings.
-n *Number*	Specifies a minimum string length other than the default of 4 characters. The maximum value of a string length is 4096. This flag is identical to the *-Number* flag.
-o	Lists each string preceded by its octal offset in the file. This flag is identical to the `-to` flag.
-t *Format*	Lists each string preceded by its offset from the start of the file. The format is dependent on the character used as the Format variable. d - Writes the offset in decimal. o - Writes the offset in octal. x - Writes the offset in hexadecimal
-*Number*	Specifies a minimum string length other than the default of 4 characters. The maximum value of a string length is 4096. This flag is identical to the `-n` *`Number`* flag.
File	Binary or object file to be searched.

Note

When the `-o` and the `-t` format flags are defined more than once on a command line, the last flag specified controls the behavior of the `strings` command.

Examples using the `strings` command are as follows:

- To search a file, enter:

```
# strings wall
@(#)61
1.11  src/bos/usr/ccs/lib/libc/__threads_init.c, libcthrd, bos43K,
9823A_43K 6/12/98 12:37:06
wall.cat
/etc/utmp
libIN.cat
Cannot open "%s".
/etc/utmp
```

```
0123456789
/dev/
.......... ( Lines Removed )
libIN.cat
Error %d
libIN.cat
No system error
libc.cat
@(#)53
1.8  src/bos/usr/ccs/lib/libIN/ERsysmsg.c, libIN, bos430, 9737A_430
11/10/93 15:13:03
@(#)71
1.6  src/bos/usr/ccs/lib/libIN/CSlen.c, libIN, bos430, 9737A_430 6/10/91
10:14:51
@(#)88
1.6  src/bos/usr/ccs/lib/libIN/CSsname.c, libIN, bos430, 9737A_430
6/10/91 10:15:13
@(#)47
1.6  src/bos/usr/ccs/lib/libIN/CSskpa.c, libIN, bos430, 9737A_430
6/10/91 10:52:46
```

• To search for strings at least 12 characters long, enter:

```
# strings -12 wall
1.11  src/bos/usr/ccs/lib/libc/__threads_init.c, libcthrd, bos43K,
9823A_43K 6/12/98 12:37:06
Cannot open "%s".
Cannot open "%s".
wall: Cannot allocate enough memory.
Broadcast message from %s@%s (%s) at %s ...
Message too long (max %d chars).
wall: Cannot create another process at this time.
@(#)11 1.16.1.7  src/bos/usr/sbin/wall/wall.c, cmdcomm, bos430,
9737A_430 9/5/97 13:48:32
1.7  src/bos/usr/ccs/lib/libIN/ERcmderr.c, libIN, bos430, 9737A_430
6/10/91 10:15:39
No system error
1.8  src/bos/usr/ccs/lib/libIN/ERsysmsg.c, libIN, bos430, 9737A_430
11/10/93 15:13:03
1.6  src/bos/usr/ccs/lib/libIN/CSlen.c, libIN, bos430, 9737A_430 6/10/91
10:14:51
1.6  src/bos/usr/ccs/lib/libIN/CSsname.c, libIN, bos430, 9737A_430
6/10/91 10:15:13
1.6  src/bos/usr/ccs/lib/libIN/CSskpa.c, libIN, bos430, 9737A_430
6/10/91 10:52:46
```

• To search for strings at least 20 characters long and show the offset in hexadecimal, enter:

```
# strings -t x -n 20 wall
   1ac7 1.11  src/bos/usr/ccs/lib/libc/__threads_init.c, libcthrd,
bos43K, 9823A_43K 6/12/98 12:37:06

   1bc0 wall: Cannot allocate enough memory.
   1bec Broadcast message from %s@%s (%s) at %s ...
   1c1c Message too long (max %d chars).
   1c40 wall: Cannot create another process at this time.
   1c74 @(#)11 1.16.1.7  src/bos/usr/sbin/wall/wall.c, cmdcomm, bos430,
9737A_430 9/5/97 13:48:32
   1ce7 1.7  src/bos/usr/ccs/lib/libIN/ERcmderr.c, libIN, bos430,
9737A_430 6/10/91 10:15:39
   1d87 1.8  src/bos/usr/ccs/lib/libIN/ERsysmsg.c, libIN, bos430,
9737A_430 11/10/93 15:13:03
  1de7 1.6  src/bos/usr/ccs/lib/libIN/CSlen.c, libIN, bos430, 9737A_430
6/10/91 10:14:51
   1e4b 1.6  src/bos/usr/ccs/lib/libIN/CSsname.c, libIN, bos430,
9737A_430 6/10/91 10:15:13
   1ea7 1.6  src/bos/usr/ccs/lib/libIN/CSskpa.c, libIN, bos430,
9737A_430 6/10/91 10:52:46
```

In this section you learned how to edit a file using the vi editor. You also learned how to view a file with the pg and cat commands and the differences between the two. You can echo text to the screen or a file. The file characteristics can be found using the file command. You can also find strings within a file using the `strings` command. A lot of what you have learned in this section will be used in Chapter 16, “The Shell, and Shell Scripts” on page 341.

15.4 Quiz

1. Use the following file contents to answer the following question:

```
#!/usr/bin/ksh
tctl -f /dev/rmt0 rewind
mkszfile
mksysb -i /dev/rmt0
tctl -f /dev/rmt0 offline
```

In the above script the system administrator is editing a routine backup script using vi because the `mkszfile` command is unnecessary. What steps should the system administrator use to delete the line containing the `mkszfile` command?

A. Move to line 3, and press **dd**

B. Move to line 3, and press **xx**

C. Move to line 2 and press **o**

D. Move to line 3 and press **d**

2. Use the following directory listing to answer the following question:

```
-rwsr-xrw-   1 root     system     76528 Nov 24 16:21
/usr/local/bin/scan_it
```

A long listing of the file /usr/local/bin/scan_it is shown above. When the command is executed as a nonroot user, it fails to run as root. What would be the first action to take?

A. file /usr/local/bin/scan_it

B. chmod 4764 /usr/local/bin/scan_it

C. Run the command in the background

D.Copy /usr/local/bin/scan_it to the own home directory and execute it from there

15.4.1 Answers

1. A
2. A

15.5 Exercises

1. What is the difference between the `cat`, `echo`, `pg`, and `view` commands?
2. Use the `file` command to determine what type of file /etc/swapspaces is.
3. Set up your environment to use vi as your default system editor. Use the `env` command to check that it is set correctly.

Chapter 16. The Shell, and Shell Scripts

The primary interface to the operating system is called a *shell*. The shell is the outermost layer of the operating system. Shells incorporate a programming language to control processes and files, as well as to start and control other programs. The shell manages the interaction between you and the operating system by prompting you for input, interpreting that input for the operating system, and then handling any resulting output from the operating system.

Shells provide a way for you to communicate with the operating system. This communication is carried out either interactively (input from the keyboard is acted upon immediately) or as a shell script. A *shell script* is a sequence of shell and operating system commands that are stored in a file and may be reused.

In essence, a shell script is simply a combination of command line commands put into a single file. Variables and environments can also be set up in a shell script.

16.1 The Korn Shell or POSIX Shell

The Korn shell is an interactive command interpreter and command programming language. It conforms to the Portable Operating System Interface for Computer Environments (POSIX), an international standard for operating systems. POSIX is not an operating system, but is a standard aimed at portability of applications, at the source level, across many systems. POSIX features are built on top of the Korn shell. The Korn shell (also known as the POSIX shell) offers many of the same features as the Bourne and C shells, such as I/O redirection capabilities, variable substitution, and file name substitution.

16.2 Bourne Shell

The Bourne shell is an interactive command interpreter and command programming language. The `bsh` command runs the Bourne shell.

The Bourne shell can be run either as a login shell or as a subshell under the login shell. Only the `login` command can call the Bourne shell as a login shell. It does this by using a special form of the `bsh` command name: -bsh. When called with an initial `-` (hyphen), the shell first reads and runs commands found in the system /etc/profile file and your $HOME/.profile, if one exists.

The /etc/profile file sets variables needed by all users. Finally, the shell is ready to read commands from your standard input.

16.3 C Shell

The C shell is an interactive command interpreter and a command programming language. It uses syntax that is similar to the C programming language. The `csh` command starts the C shell.

When you log in, it first searches the systemwide setup file /etc/csh.cshrc. If it is there, the C shell executes the commands stored in that file. Next, the C shell executes the systemwide setup file /etc/csh.login if it is available. Then, it searches your home directory for the .cshrc and .login files. If they exist, they contain any customized user information pertinent to running the C shell. All variables set in the /etc/csh.cshrc and /etc/csh.login files may be overridden by your .cshrc and .login files in your $HOME directory. Only the root user can modify the /etc/csh.cshrc and /etc/csh.login files.

The /etc/csh.login and $HOME/.login files are executed only once at login time. They are generally used to hold environment variable definitions, commands that you want executed once at login, or commands that set up terminal characteristics.

The /etc/csh.cshrc and $HOME/.cshrc files are executed at login time, and every time the `csh` command or a C shell script is invoked. They are generally used to define C shell characteristics like aliases and C shell variables (for example, history, noclobber, or ignoreeof). It is recommended that you only use the C shell built-in commands in the /etc/csh.cshrc and $HOME/.cshrc files because using other commands increases the start-up time for shell scripts.

16.4 Restricted Shell

The restricted shell is used to set up login names and execution environments whose capabilities are more controlled than those of the regular Bourne shell. The `Rsh` or `bsh -r` command opens the restricted shell. The behavior of these commands is identical to those of the `bsh` command, except that the following actions are not allowed:

- Changing the directory (with the `cd` command)
- Setting the value of PATH or SHELL variables
- Specifying path or command names containing a / (slash)

- Redirecting output

If the restricted shell determines that a command to be run is a shell procedure, it uses the Bourne shell to run the command. In this way, it is possible to provide an end user with shell procedures that access the full power of the Bourne shell while imposing a limited menu of commands. This scheme assumes that the end user does not have write and execute permissions in the same directory.

16.5 Setting the Shell Environment

When you log in, the shell defines your user environment after reading the initialization files that you have set up. The characteristics of your user environment are defined by the values given to your environment variables. You maintain this environment until you log off the system.

The shell uses two types of profile files when you log in to the operating system. It evaluates the commands contained in the files and then executes the commands to set up your system environment. The files have similar functions except that the /etc/profile file controls profile variables for all users on a system whereas the .profile file allows you to customize your own environment.

The shell first evaluates the commands contained in the /etc/profile file and then runs the commands to set up your system environment in the /etc/environment file.

After these files are run, the system then checks to see if you have a .profile file in your home directory. If the .profile file exists, it runs this file. The .profile file will specify if there also exists an environment file. If an environment file exists, (usually called .env), the system then runs this file and sets up your environment variables.

The /etc/profile, /etc/environment, and the .profile files are run once at login time. The .env file, on the other hand, is run every time you open a new shell or a window.

16.5.1 The /etc/profile File

The first file that the operating system uses at login time is the /etc/profile file. This file controls systemwide default variables such as:

- Export variables
- File creation mask (umask)

- Terminal types
- Mail messages to indicate when new mail has arrived.

The system administrator configures the profile file for all users on the system. Only the system administrator can change this file.

An example of the /etc/profile file is shown in the following:

```
# @(#)27        1.20  src/bos/etc/profile/profile, cmdsh, bos430,
9737A_430 8/9/
94 12:01:38
# IBM_PROLOG_BEGIN_TAG
.......... ( Lines Removed )
# (C) COPYRIGHT International Business Machines Corp. 1989, 1994
# All Rights Reserved
# Licensed Materials - Property of IBM
#
# US Government Users Restricted Rights - Use, duplication or
# disclosure restricted by GSA ADP Schedule Contract with IBM Corp.
#
################################################################

# System wide profile. All variables set here may be overridden by
# a user's personal .profile file in their $HOME directory. However,
# all commands here will be executed at login regardless.

trap "" 1 2 3
readonly LOGNAME

# Automatic logout, include in export line if uncommented
# TMOUT=120

# The MAILMSG will be printed by the shell every MAILCHECK seconds
# (default 600) if there is mail in the MAIL system mailbox.
MAIL=/usr/spool/mail/$LOGNAME
MAILMSG="[YOU HAVE NEW MAIL]"

# If termdef command returns terminal type (i.e. a non NULL value),
# set TERM to the returned value, else set TERM to default lft.
TERM_DEFAULT=lft
TERM=`termdef`
TERM=${TERM:-$TERM_DEFAULT}

# If LC_MESSAGES is set to "C@lft" and TERM is not set to "lft",
# unset LC_MESSAGES.
if [ "$LC_MESSAGES" = "C@lft" -a "$TERM" != "lft" ]
then
```

```
        unset LC_MESSAGES
fi

export LOGNAME MAIL MAILMSG TERM

trap 1 2 3
```

16.5.2 The /etc/environment File

The second file that the operating system uses at login time is the /etc/environment file. The /etc/environment file contains variables specifying the basic environment for all processes. When a new process begins, the exec subroutine makes an array of strings available that have the form Name=Value. This array of strings is called the environment. Each name defined by one of the strings is called an environment variable or shell variable. The exec subroutine allows the entire environment to be set at one time.

When you log in, the system sets environment variables from the environment file before reading your login profile, .profile. The following variables make up the basic environment:

HOME The full path name of the user's login or HOME directory. The login program sets this to the name specified in the /etc/passwd file.

LANG The locale name currently in effect. The LANG variable is initially set in the /etc/profile file at installation time.

NLSPATH The full path name for message catalogs.

LOCPATH The full path name of the location of National Language Support tables.

PATH The sequence of directories that commands, such as `sh`, `time`, `nice` and `nohup`, search when looking for a command whose path name is incomplete.

TZ The time zone information. The TZ environment variable is initially set by the /etc/profile file, the system login profile.

An example of the /etc/environment file is shown in the following example:

```
# @(#)18        1.21  src/bos/etc/environment/environment, cmdsh, bos430,
9737A_
430 5/13/94 15:09:03
# IBM_PROLOG_BEGIN_TAG
.......... ( Lines Removed )
# US Government Users Restricted Rights - Use, duplication or
```

```
# disclosure restricted by GSA ADP Schedule Contract with IBM Corp.
#
##################################################################
# System wide environment file. This file should only contain
#      1. comment lines which have a # in the first column,
#      2. blank lines, and
#      3. Lines in the form name=value.
#
# WARNING: This file is only for establishing environment variables.
#          Execution of commands from this file or any lines other
#          than specified above may cause failure of the initialization
#          process.
#
# Searching the current directory last is usually a BIG time saver.
# If /usr/ucb is at the beginning of the PATH the BSD version of commands
will
# be found.
#
PATH=/usr/bin:/etc:/usr/sbin:/usr/ucb:/usr/bin/X11:/sbin
TZ=CST6CDT
LANG=en_US
LOCPATH=/usr/lib/nls/loc
NLSPATH=/usr/lib/nls/msg/%L/%N:/usr/lib/nls/msg/%L/%N.cat
LC__FASTMSG=true

# ODM routines use ODMDIR to determine which objects to operate on
# the default is /etc/objrepos - this is where the device objects
# reside, which are required for hardware configuration

ODMDIR=/etc/objrepos
```

16.5.3 The .profile File

The third file that the operating system uses at login time is the .profile file. The .profile file is present in your home ($HOME) directory and enables you to customize your individual working environment. Because the .profile file is hidden, use the `li -a` command to list it.

After the login program adds the LOGNAME (login name) and HOME (login directory) variables to the environment, the commands in the $HOME/.profile file are executed if the file is present. The .profile file contains your individual profile that overrides the variables set in the /etc/profile file. The .profile file is often used to set exported environment variables and terminal modes. You can tailor your environment as desired by modifying the .profile file. Use the .profile file to control the following defaults:

- Shells to open

- Prompt appearance
- Keyboard sound

You can also use the .profile file (or if it is not present, the /etc/profile file) to determine login shell variables. You can also customize other shell environments. For example, use the .cshrc file and .kshrc file to tailor a C shell and a Korn shell, respectively, when each type of shell is started.

An Example of a .profile file is shown in the following:

```
PATH=/usr/bin:/etc:/usr/sbin:/usr/ucb:$HOME/bin:/usr/bin/X11:/sbin:.

export PATH

if [ -s "$MAIL" ]               # This is at Shell startup. In normal
then echo "$MAILMSG"            # operation, the Shell checks
fi                              # periodically.
# pg .profile


PATH=/usr/bin:/etc:/usr/sbin:/usr/ucb:$HOME/bin:/usr/bin/X11:/sbin:.

export PATH

if [ -s "$MAIL" ]               # This is at Shell startup. In normal
then echo "$MAILMSG"            # operation, the Shell checks
fi                              # periodically.
```

16.5.4 The .env File

A fourth file that the operating system uses at login time is the .env file, if your .profile has the following line: `export ENV=$HOME/.env`

The .env file enables you to customize your individual working environment variables. Because the .env file is hidden, use the `li -a` command to list it. The .env file contains the individual user environment variables that override the variables set in the /etc/environment file. You can tailor your environment variables as desired by modifying your .env file.

An example of the .env file is as follows:

```
export  myid=`id | sed -n -e 's/).*$//' -e 's/^.*(//p'` \
        bold=`tput smso` \
        norm=`tput rmso`
#set prompt: login & system name (reverse video) & path (normal)
if [ $myid = root ]
        then    typeset -x PSCH='${bold}#:${norm}\${PWD}> '
```

```
                PS1="${bold}#:${norm}\${PWD}> "
        else    typeset -x PSCH='>'
                PS1="${bold}$LOGNAME@$UNAME:${norm}\${PWD}> "
                PS2=">"
                PS3="#?"
fi
export PS1 PS2 PS3
#setup my command aliases
alias   ls="/bin/ls -CF" \
        d="/bin/ls -Fal | pg" \
        rm="/bin/rm -i" \
        up="cd .."
```

Note

When modifying the .env file, ensure that newly created environment variables do not conflict with standard variables such as MAIL, PS1, PS2, and IFS.

16.5.5 Changing Your Environment from the Command Line

You can also change the environment variable from the command line. These variables will only be valid until you exit the shell.

To change the default **#** prompt in the command line to a `mysystem>` prompt enter:

```
# PS1=mysystem\ \>
mysystem> pwd
/etc
mysystem> ls -l host*
-rw-rw-r--   1 root     system      1864 Nov 20 10:44 hosts
-rw-r--r--   1 root     system      2060 Aug 25 09:41 hosts.equiv
-rw-rw-r--   1 root     system      1906 Aug 25 09:41 hosts.lpd
mysystem>
```

To set the language environment variable to `en_UK` for one session enter:

```
# LANG=en_UK
# export LANG
```

To check current environment variable enter:

```
# env
_=/usr/bin/env
LANG=en_US
LOGIN=root
NLSPATH=/usr/lib/nls/msg/%L/%N:/usr/lib/nls/msg/%L/%N.cat
```

```
inetd_dummy=xxx
PATH=/usr/bin:/etc:/usr/sbin:/usr/ucb:/usr/bin/X11:/sbin
LC__FASTMSG=true
WINDOWID=4194312
LOGNAME=root
LOCPATH=/usr/lib/nls/loc
USER=root
AUTHSTATE=compat
DISPLAY=sv1051b:0.0
SHELL=/bin/ksh
ODMDIR=/etc/objrepos
HOME=/
TERM=aixterm
PWD=/
TZ=CST6CDT
#
```

16.6 Creating and Running a Shell Script

Shell scripts provide an easy way to execute tedious commands, large or complicated sequences of commands, and routine tasks. A shell script is a file that contains one or more commands. When you type the name of a shell script file, the system executes the command sequence contained by the file.

16.6.1 General Script Remarks

You can create a shell script using a text editor. Your script can contain both operating system commands and shell built-in commands.

The following steps are general guidelines for writing shell scripts:

1. Use a text editor to create and save a file. You can include any combination of shell and operating system commands in the shell script file.

   By convention, shell scripts that are not set up for use by many users are stored in the $HOME/bin directory.

   > **Note**
   >
   > The operating system does not support the setuid or setgid subroutines within a shell script.

2. Use the `chmod` command to allow only the owner to run (or execute) the file. For example, if your file is named myscript, enter:

```
chmod u=rwx myscript
```

3. Enter the script name on the command line to run the shell script. To run the shell script, myscript, enter:

```
myscript
```

Note

You can run a shell script without making it executable if a shell command (`ksh`, `bsh`, or `csh`) precedes the shell script file name on the command line. For example, to run a nonexecutable file named `myscript` under the control of the Korn shell, type:

```
# ksh myscript
```

When you run an executable shell script in either the Korn (the POSIX Shell) or Bourne shell, the commands in the script are carried out under the control of the current shell (the shell from which the script is started) unless you specify a different shell. When you run an executable shell script in the C shell, the commands in the script are carried out under the control of the Bourne shell (/usr/bin/bsh) unless you specify a different shell.

You can cause a shell script to run in a specific shell by including the shell within the shell script. To run an executable shell script under a specific shell, enter *#!Path* on the first line of the shell script. The *#!* characters identify the file type. The Path variable specifies the path name of the shell from which to run the shell script. For example, if the first line in a shell script is *#!/usr/bin/bsh*, the script is run under control of the Bourne shell.

When you precede a shell script file name with a shell command, the shell specified on the command line overrides any shell specified within the script file itself. Therefore, entering `ksh myfile` runs the file named `myfile` under the control of the Korn shell, even if the first line of myfile is *#!/usr/bin/csh*.

16.6.2 Creating a Script

In this section, the Korn shell (ksh) will be the focus to create a script that will run a backup. The script will start with daily backups then move through to weekly and then finally a monthly backup. It will also need user input to continue or abort the operation.

The shell script should have the following format:

- The #!/usr/bin/ksh

- Script Comments
- Search Path
- Shell Variables or Arguments
- Standard Input, standard Output and standard Error
- Exit Status

16.6.2.1 The #!/usr/bin/ksh

The first line of the Korn shell script should begin with:

```
#!/usr/bin/ksh
```

in order for the shell to execute under the control of the Korn shell, irrespective of the shell that called it.

16.6.2.2 Script Comments

Script comments is a description of the script that begin with the pound (#) sign. It will have all comments about the script or explain actions of the script.

16.6.2.3 Search Path

The shell script should include a search path. A search path is used because if a user with a different search path tries to use the script, it may fail.

16.6.2.4 Shell Variables

Variables are used to hold information that will be passed onto the script for utilization.

In the backup example the variables will be used to give the day of the week and day of the month variables to the rest of the script to determine the type of backup to use. The bye variable is also used for the exit routine.

16.6.2.5 Standard I/O and Redirection in Scripts

There are three types of I/O in scripts namely *stdin*, *stdout*, and *stderr*. Standard input (*stdin*) normally comes from the keyboard. Standard Output (*stdout*) normally goes to the screen. Standard Error (*stderr*) normally goes to the screen. Each of these errors has a descriptor, for stdin it is 0, for stdout it is *1* and for stderr it is *2*. You can redirect these to or from a file if needed as described below:

<	redirect input
>	redirect output
>>	append output
2>	redirect stderr

1>&2 redirect stdout to stderr

2>&1 redirect stderr to stdout

16.6.2.6 Exit Status

A good shell script should have a single point of exit. The exit variable can be selected by a variable and used during the script.

16.6.2.7 The *if/then* statement

The *if/then* statement is the most basic conditional statement. What the if/then statement does is read a variable, and if the variable is true it executes a command. It executes between `if` and `fi`.

if/then Statement Format

```
if [ $variable = true ]
then
    command(s)
fi
```

16.6.2.8 The *if/else* Statement

The *if/else* statement is the next logical step to the if/then statement. What the if/else statement does is read the variable, if the variable is true then it executes a command `else`, which it executes another command. It executes between `if` and `fi`.

if/else Statement Format

```
if [ $variable = true ]
then
    command(s)
else
    command(s)
fi
```

16.6.2.9 The *if/elif/else* statement

The *if/elif/else* statement is again a progression on the *if/else* statement. What it does is read the variable if it is true then it executes a command, if another statement is true (elif) it performs that command until it reaches the `else` command, which tells the script that if none of the above are true execute the `else` command. It executes between `if` and `fi`.

if/elif/else Statement Format

```
if [ $variable = true ]
then
    command(s)
elif [ $variable = true ]
then
    command(s)
else
    command(s)
fi
```

16.6.2.10 The *while* loop

The *while* loop basically tells the script that while a statement is true it will execute the loop until the statement becomes false. It executes the commands between `do` and `done`.

***while* Loop Format**

```
while [ $statement = true ]
do
    command(s)
done
```

16.6.2.11 The *for* loop

The *for* loop is used to execute commands a set number of times. The number of times is determined by the list after the *for* command. It executes the commands between `do` and `done`.

***for* Loop Format**

```
for wordlist variables
do
    command(s)
done
```

16.6.2.12 The *case* Command

The `case` command is used as a substitute for the `if/elif` commands. What the `case` command does is read a variable, and then according to the response it will execute a command. It executes the commands between `case` and `esac`.

case Command format

```
case variable in
value 1)
    command(s) ;;
value 2)
    command(s) ;;
esac
```

Now that you have a basic idea of what is needed in a script, here is an example of a script called mybackup.

First line of script

```
#!/usr/bin/ksh
```

Script Comments

```
# Script Name: mybackup
# Author: I.T. Wasme
# This script will run a backup.
```

Script Variables

```
# Set variables here
DAILY='date +%a'
MONTHLY='date +%d'
BYE=stay
```

Script Start

```
# Start Script Here
```

Start of the while loop

```
while [ $BYE  = stay ]
do
```

Start of the for loop

```
for i in rootvg uservg tempvg
do
  # Interactive Prompting.
```

Standard I/O. First if/then statement

```
  if tty -s
  then
    echo "\n\n\n\n\n\n\n\n\n\nWould you like you like to backup" $i
```

```
echo "\n Type Y/y to CONTINUE or N/n to ABORT: \c"; read inp
```

Start of the case command. Reading stdin

```
case "$inp" in
        y*|Y*)
        echo  Backup will Run
        BYE=stay
        ;;
        n*|N*|*)
        echo    Backup will Not Run
```

Exit status

```
        BYE=go
```

End of case command

```
esac
```

End first if statement

```
fi
```

Start first if/else statement

```
if [ $BYE = stay ]
then
        # Backup Section Starts here
        echo "\nBackup procedure starting"
```

Start first if/elif/else statement

```
                if [ $MONTHLY = 25  ]
                then
                        echo This will run the MONTHLY BACKUP
                          savevg -f/dev/rmt0 $i
                elif [ $DAILY = Fri ]
                then
                          echo Will run a WEEKLY BACKUP
                          savevg -mf/dev/rmt0 $i
                else
                          echo Will run a DAILY BACKUP
                          savevg -ef/dev/rmt0 $i
```

End first if/elif/else statement

```
                fi
else
```

Exit status

```
BYE=go
```

End first if/else statement

```
        fi
```

End for loop

```
    done
```

Set exit point for multiple exit status points in script

```
    # Set single exit point
```

Start second if statement

```
    if [ $BYE = go ]
    then
        echo Backup procedure complete
```

Actual exit point

```
        exit
```

End second if statement

```
    fi
```

End while loop and shell exits

```
done
```

The preceding example is just a basic idea of what is needed to create a basic script and how you can utilize the various functions within the script to complete your tasks. Depending on your local IS organization, your shell scripts may need to conform to specific specifications, such as comments and programming style. Therefore, the preceding code may need further modification before is can be put into production.

16.7 Quiz

1. Use the following example for the questions in this topic.

```
#!/usr/bin/ksh
#
# If srcmstr is running, ensure that it is active before issuing the
# startsrc commands
#
if [ -n "$src_running"];then
echo "Checking for srcmstr active...\c"
i=10 # try ten times to contact it
while [ $i != 10 ] ; do
lssrc -s inetd >/dev/null 2>&1 && break # break out on success
sleep 1
echo ".\c"
```

```
i='expr $i -1'
done
if [ $i=0 ];then
echo "\n\n ERROR:srcmstr is not accepting connections.\n"
exit 1
fi
echo "complete"

else
src_running=""
fi
```

In the above section of code, what is the problem?

A. The while loop is never executed.

B. There are no break statements in the loop.

C. The variable i should be initialized to zero.

D. The while loop does not have the done statement.

2. A marketing manager would like her shell prompt to reflect the directory she is in so that she needs to remove a file, she will be sure to be in the proper directory. Which of the following environment variables can be set to accomplish this?

   A. PS1

   B. PATH

   C. DISPLAY

   D. LOCPATH

3. A client has changed their personal .profile to allow for a search of the /usr/local/bin filesystem. This was needed to test new software on the development machine. The client will be going production with the new software the next weekend, impacting about 500 users. Which of the following should be recommended to the client in order to avoid any potential problems?

   A. modify /etc/hosts to allow the production users to use the software

   B. modify /etc/profile to allow the production users to use the software

   C. modify /etc/hosts.equiv to allow the production users to use the software

   D. modify /etc/resolv.conf to allow the production users to use the software}

16.7.1 Answers

1. A
2. A
3. B

16.8 Exercises

1. Create a script with a while loop that will greet people as they log in, as long as you are logged in.
2. What should go into the .profile file and what should go into /etc/profile?

Appendix A. Special Notices

This publication is intended to help IBM business partners, technical professionals, and customers of IBM prepare for the AIX V4 Support exam as part of the IBM Certified Specialist program. The information in this publication is not intended as the specification of any programming interfaces that are provided by AIX Version 4.3. See the PUBLICATIONS section of the IBM Programming Announcement for AIX Version 4.3 for more information about what publications are considered to be product documentation.

References in this publication to IBM products, programs or services do not imply that IBM intends to make these available in all countries in which IBM operates. Any reference to an IBM product, program, or service is not intended to state or imply that only IBM's product, program, or service may be used. Any functionally equivalent program that does not infringe any of IBM's intellectual property rights may be used instead of the IBM product, program or service.

Information in this book was developed in conjunction with use of the equipment specified, and is limited in application to those specific hardware and software products and levels.

IBM may have patents or pending patent applications covering subject matter in this document. The furnishing of this document does not give you any license to these patents. You can send license inquiries, in writing, to the IBM Director of Licensing, IBM Corporation, 500 Columbus Avenue, Thornwood, NY 10594 USA.

Licensees of this program who wish to have information about it for the purpose of enabling: (i) the exchange of information between independently created programs and other programs (including this one) and (ii) the mutual use of the information which has been exchanged, should contact IBM Corporation, Dept. 600A, Mail Drop 1329, Somers, NY 10589 USA.

Such information may be available, subject to appropriate terms and conditions, including in some cases, payment of a fee.

The information contained in this document has not been submitted to any formal IBM test and is distributed AS IS. The information about non-IBM ("vendor") products in this manual has been supplied by the vendor and IBM assumes no responsibility for its accuracy or completeness. The use of this information or the implementation of any of these techniques is a customer responsibility and depends on the customer's ability to evaluate and integrate them into the customer's operational environment. While each item may have been reviewed by IBM for accuracy in a specific situation, there is no guarantee that the same or similar results will be obtained elsewhere. Customers attempting to adapt these techniques to their own environments do so at their own risk.

Any pointers in this publication to external Web sites are provided for convenience only and do not in any manner serve as an endorsement of these Web sites.

Any performance data contained in this document was determined in a controlled environment, and therefore, the results that may be obtained in other operating environments may vary significantly. Users of this document should verify the applicable data for their specific environment.

The following document contains examples of data and reports used in daily business operations. To illustrate them as completely as possible, the examples contain the names of individuals, companies, brands, and products. All of these names are fictitious and any similarity to the names and addresses used by an actual business enterprise is entirely coincidental.

Reference to PTF numbers that have not been released through the normal distribution process does not imply general availability. The purpose of including these reference numbers is to alert IBM customers to specific information relative to the implementation of the PTF when it becomes available to each customer according to the normal IBM PTF distribution process.

The following terms are trademarks of the International Business Machines Corporation in the United States and/or other countries:

AIX®
PowerPC 60
eNetwork
IBM ®
IBMLink
Magstar®
Micro Channel®
SP
TURBOWAYS®
PowerPC Architecture
POWER2 Architecture
POWER3 Architecture
RETAIN®
RISC System/6000®
RS/6000®
Service Director®
POWERparallel®
PowerPC®

The IBM Certified Specialist mark is a trademark of International Business Machines Corporation.

The following terms are trademarks of other companies:

C-bus is a trademark of Corollary, Inc. in the United States and/or other countries.

Java and all Java-based trademarks and logos are trademarks or registered trademarks of Sun Microsystems, Inc. in the United States and/or other countries.

Microsoft, Windows, Windows NT, and the Windows logo are trademarks of Microsoft Corporation in the United States and/or other countries.

PC Direct is a trademark of Ziff Communications Company in the United States and/or other countries and is used by IBM Corporation under license.

ActionMedia, LANDesk, MMX, Pentium and ProShare are trademarks of Intel Corporation in the United States and/or other countries. (For a complete list of Intel trademarks see www.intel.com/dradmarx.htm)

UNIX is a registered trademark in the United States and/or other countries licensed exclusively through X/Open Company Limited.

Other company, product, and service names may be trademarks or service marks of others.

Appendix B. Related Publications

The publications listed in this section are considered particularly suitable for a more detailed discussion of the topics covered in this redbook.

B.1 International Technical Support Organization Publications

For information on ordering these ITSO publications see "How to Get ITSO Redbooks" on page 365.

- *Communication Solutions Guide for RS/6000 and AIX V4*, SG24-4899
- *Understanding IBM RS/6000 Performance and Sizing*, SG24-4810
- *AIX Version 4.3 Differences Guide*, SG24-2014
- *AIX Version 4.3 Migration Guide*, SG24-5116
- *AIX Storage Management*, GG24-4484
- *The Basics of IP Network Design*, SG24-2580
- *A Technical Introduction to PCI-based RS/6000 Servers*, SG24-4690
- *Monitoring and Managing IBM SSA Disk Subsystems*, SG24-5251

B.2 Redbooks on CD-ROMs

Redbooks are also available on CD-ROMs. **Order a subscription** and receive updates 2-4 times a year at significant savings.

CD-ROM Title	Subscription Number	Collection Kit Number
System/390 Redbooks Collection	SBOF-7201	SK2T-2177
Networking and Systems Management Redbooks Collection	SBOF-7370	SK2T-6022
Transaction Processing and Data Management Redbook	SBOF-7240	SK2T-8038
Lotus Redbooks Collection	SBOF-6899	SK2T-8039
Tivoli Redbooks Collection	SBOF-6898	SK2T-8044
AS/400 Redbooks Collection	SBOF-7270	SK2T-2849
RS/6000 Redbooks Collection (HTML, BkMgr)	SBOF-7230	SK2T-8040
RS/6000 Redbooks Collection (PostScript)	SBOF-7205	SK2T-8041
RS/6000 Redbooks Collection (PDF Format)	SBOF-8700	SK2T-8043
Application Development Redbooks Collection	SBOF-7290	SK2T-8037

B.3 Other Publications

These publications are also relevant as further information sources:

- *AIX Version 4.3 Installation Guide*, SC23-4112
- *AIX Version 4.3 Commands Reference, Volume 1*, SC23-4115
- *AIX Version 4.3 Commands Reference, Volume 3*, SC23-4117
- *AIX Version 4.3 Commands Reference, Volume 4*, SC23-4118
- *AIX Version 4.3 System Management Guide: Operating System and Devices*, SC23-4126
- *AIX Versions 3.2 and 4 Asynchronous Communications Guide,* SC23-2488
- *AIX Version 4.3 Messages Guide and Reference*, SC23-4129
- *AIX Version Problem Solving Guide and Reference*, SC23-4123
- *AIX Version 4.3 Kernel Extensions and Device Support Programming Concepts*, SC23-4125
- *AIX Version 3.2 & 4 Performance Tuning Guide*, SC23-2365
- *AIX Version 4.3 Guide to Printers and Printing, SC23-4130*

B.3.1 Limited Internet Resources

- *URL:* `http://service.software.ibm.com/support`
- *URL:* `http://www.developer.ibm.com`
- *URL:* `http://service.software.ibm.com/rs6k/techdocs`
- *URL:* `http://tesch.aix.dfw.ibm.com/index.html`
- *URL:* `http://tesch.aix.dfw.ibm.com/ppptips/modems.html`

How to Get ITSO Redbooks

This section explains how both customers and IBM employees can find out about ITSO redbooks, CD-ROMs, workshops, and residencies. A form for ordering books and CD-ROMs is also provided.

This information was current at the time of publication, but is continually subject to change. The latest information may be found at http://www.redbooks.ibm.com/.

How IBM Employees Can Get ITSO Redbooks

Employees may request ITSO deliverables (redbooks, BookManager BOOKs, and CD-ROMs) and information about redbooks, workshops, and residencies in the following ways:

- **Redbooks Web Site on the World Wide Web**

  http://w3.itso.ibm.com/

- **PUBORDER** – to order hardcopies in the United States
- **Tools Disks**

  To get LIST3820s of redbooks, type one of the following commands:

  ```
  TOOLCAT REDPRINT
  TOOLS SENDTO EHONE4 TOOLS2 REDPRINT GET SG24xxxx PACKAGE
  TOOLS SENDTO CANVM2 TOOLS REDPRINT GET SG24xxxx PACKAGE (Canadian users only)
  ```

  To get BookManager BOOKs of redbooks, type the following command:

  ```
  TOOLCAT REDBOOKS
  ```

  To get lists of redbooks, type the following command:

  ```
  TOOLS SENDTO USDIST MKTTOOLS MKTTOOLS GET ITSOCAT TXT
  ```

  To register for information on workshops, residencies, and redbooks, type the following command:

  ```
  TOOLS SENDTO WTSCPOK TOOLS ZDISK GET ITSOREGI 1998
  ```

- **REDBOOKS Category on INEWS**
- **Online** – send orders to: USIB6FPL at IBMMAIL or DKIBMBSH at IBMMAIL

Redpieces

For information so current it is still in the process of being written, look at "Redpieces" on the Redbooks Web Site (http://www.redbooks.ibm.com/redpieces.html). Redpieces are redbooks in progress; not all redbooks become redpieces, and sometimes just a few chapters will be published this way. The intent is to get the information out much quicker than the formal publishing process allows.

How Customers Can Get ITSO Redbooks

Customers may request ITSO deliverables (redbooks, BookManager BOOKs, and CD-ROMs) and information about redbooks, workshops, and residencies in the following ways:

- **Online Orders** – send orders to:

	IBMMAIL	**Internet**
In United States	usib6fpl at ibmmail	usib6fpl@ibmmail.com
In Canada	caibmbkz at ibmmail	lmannix@vnet.ibm.com
Outside North America	dkibmbsh at ibmmail	bookshop@dk.ibm.com

- **Telephone Orders**

United States (toll free)	1-800-879-2755
Canada (toll free)	1-800-IBM-4YOU
Outside North America	(long distance charges apply)
(+45) 4810-1320 - Danish	(+45) 4810-1020 - German
(+45) 4810-1420 - Dutch	(+45) 4810-1620 - Italian
(+45) 4810-1540 - English	(+45) 4810-1270 - Norwegian
(+45) 4810-1670 - Finnish	(+45) 4810-1120 - Spanish
(+45) 4810-1220 - French	(+45) 4810-1170 - Swedish

- **Mail Orders** – send orders to:

IBM Publications	IBM Publications	IBM Direct Services
Publications Customer Support	144-4th Avenue, S.W.	Sortemosevej 21
P.O. Box 29570	Calgary, Alberta T2P 3N5	DK-3450 Allerød
Raleigh, NC 27626-0570	Canada	Denmark
USA		

- **Fax** – send orders to:

United States (toll free)	1-800-445-9269
Canada	1-800-267-4455
Outside North America	(+45) 48 14 2207 (long distance charge)

- **1-800-IBM-4FAX (United States)** or **(+1) 408 256 5422 (Outside USA)** – ask for:

  Index # 4421 Abstracts of new redbooks
  Index # 4422 IBM redbooks
  Index # 4420 Redbooks for last six months

- **On the World Wide Web**

Redbooks Web Site	http://www.redbooks.ibm.com
IBM Direct Publications Catalog	http://www.elink.ibmlink.ibm.com/pbl/pbl

Redpieces

For information so current it is still in the process of being written, look at "Redpieces" on the Redbooks Web Site (`http://www.redbooks.ibm.com/redpieces.html`). Redpieces are redbooks in progress; not all redbooks become redpieces, and sometimes just a few chapters will be published this way. The intent is to get the information out much quicker than the formal publishing process allows.

IBM Redbook Order Form

Please send me the following:

Title	**Order Number**	**Quantity**

First name   Last name

Company

Address

City   Postal code   Country

Telephone number   Telefax number   VAT number

☐ Invoice to customer number ______________________

☐ Credit card number ______________________

Credit card expiration date   Card issued to   Signature

We accept American Express, Diners, Eurocard, Master Card, and Visa. Payment by credit card not available in all countries. Signature mandatory for credit card payment.

List of Abbreviations

ABI	Application Binary Interface
AC	Alternating Current
AIX	Advanced Interactive Executive
ANSI	American National Standards Institute
APAR	Authorized Program Analysis Report
API	Application Programming Interface
ARP	Address Resolution Protocol
ASCII	American National Standards Code for Information Interchange
BFF	Backup File Format
BIST	Built-in Self-test
BOS	Base Operating System
CAE	Computer-aided Engineering
CD	Compact Disk
CDRFS	CD-ROM File System
CEC	Central Electronics Complex
CHRP	Common Hardware Reference Platform
CMOS	Complimentary Metal Oxide Semiconductor
CPU	Central Processing Unit
CRC	Cyclic Redundancy Check
CSU	Channel Servicing Unit
DC	Direct Current
DDC	Display Data Channel
DIMM	Dual Inline Memory Module
DMA	Direct Memory Access
DOS	Disk Operating System
DIP	Direct Insertion Probe
DMA	Direct Memory Access
DRAM	Dynamic Random Access Memory
DSU	Data Servicing Unit
EC	Engineering Change
ECC	Error Checking And Correction
EEPROM	Electrically Erasable Programmable Read Only Memory
EIA	Electronics Industry Association
EISA	Extended Industry Standard Architecture
ELA	Error Log Analysis
EPOW	Environmental And Power Warning
FCP	Fibre Channel Protocol
FDDI	Fiber Distributed Data Interface
FRU	Field Replaceable Unit
GB	Gigabytes
HTTP	Hypertext Transfer Protocol
Hz	Hertz
ICMP	Internet Control Message Protocol
ID	Identification
IDE	Integrated Device Electronics

IEEE Institute of Electrical and Electronics Engineers

I^2C Inter Integrated-circuit Communications

I/O Input/Output

IP Internetwork Protocol (OSI)

IPL Initial Program Load

IrDA Infrared Data Association (which sets standards for infrared support including protocols for data interchange)

IRQ Interrupt Request

ISA Industry Standard Architecture

ISDN Integrated-Services Digital Network

ISV Independent Software Vendor

ITSO International Technical Support Organization

JFS Journaled File System

LAN Local Area Network

LED Light Emitting Diode

LFT Low Function Terminal

LPP Licensed Program Product

LRU Least-Recently Used

LVM Logical Volume Manager

MAP Maintenance Analysis Procedure

MCA Micro Channel Architecture

MCAD Mechanical Computer-Aided Design

MP Multiprocessor

MTU Maximum Transmission Unit

NCP Network Control Point

NFS Network File System

NUMA Non-uniform Memory Access

NVRAM Non-volatile Random Access Memory

OCS Online Customer Support

ODM Object Data Model

PAP Privileged Access Password

PCI Peripheral Component Interconnect

PID Program Identification

POP Power-On Password

POSIX Portable Operating Interface for Computing Environments

POST Power-On Self-Test

POWER Performance Optimization With Enhanced RISC (architecture)

PPP Point-to-point Protocol

PREP PowerPC Reference Platform

P2SC Power2 Super Chip

PV Physical Volume

PVID Physical Volume Identifier

RAM Random Access Memory

RAN Remote Async. Node

RAS Reliability, Availability, And Serviceability

RAID Redundant Array Of Independent Disks

RIPL Remote Initial Program Load

ROLTP Relative Online Transaction Processing

RPA RS/6000 Platform Architecture

RTC Real-Time Clock

SCSI Small Computer System Interface

SDRAM Synchronous Dynamic Random Access Memory

SDLC Synchronous Data Link Control

SLIP Serial Line Internet Protocol

SMIT System Management Interface Tool

SMS System Management Services

SMP Symmetric Multiprocessing

SP Service Processor

SPEC Standard Performance Evaluation Corp.

SPOT Shared Product Object Tree

SRC System Resource Controller

SSC System Support Controller

SSA Serial Storage Architecture

STP Shielded Twisted Pair

TCP/IP Transmission Control Protocol/internet Protocol

TCQ tagged command queuing

UP uniprocessor

USB Universal Serial Bus

UUCP UNIX-toUNIX communication protocol

VESA Video Electronics Standards Association

VG Volume Group

VGDA Volume Group Descriptor Area

VMM Virtual Memory Manager

VPD Vital Product Data

VSM Visual Systems Management

Index

Symbols

Numerics

A

B

C

G

H

I

Q

R

S

T

U

ITSO Redbook Evaluation

IBM Certification Study Guide AIX V4.3 System Support
SG24-5139-00

Your feedback is very important to help us maintain the quality of ITSO redbooks. **Please complete this questionnaire and return it using one of the following methods:**

- Use the online evaluation form found at http://www.redbooks.ibm.com
- Fax this form to: USA International Access Code + 1 914 432 8264
- Send your comments in an Internet note to redbook@us.ibm.com

Which of the following best describes you?
_ **Customer** _ **Business Partner** _ **Solution Developer** _ **IBM employee**
_ **None of the above**

Please rate your overall satisfaction with this book using the scale:
(1 = very good, 2 = good, 3 = average, 4 = poor, 5 = very poor)

Overall Satisfaction __________

Please answer the following questions:

Was this redbook published in time for your needs? Yes___ No___

If no, please explain:

____

____

____

____

What other redbooks would you like to see published?

____

____

____

Comments/Suggestions: (THANK YOU FOR YOUR FEEDBACK!)

____

____

____

____